Charles Francis

Patents granted to Charles F. Brush relating to electric machinery and apparatus

Charles Francis

Patents granted to Charles F. Brush relating to electric machinery and apparatus

ISBN/EAN: 9783743322097

Manufactured in Europe, USA, Canada, Australia, Japa

Cover: Foto ©ninafisch / pixelio.de

Manufactured and distributed by brebook publishing software (www.brebook.com)

Charles Francis

Patents granted to Charles F. Brush relating to electric machinery and apparatus

The United States of America

TO ALL TO WHOM THESE PRESENTS SHALL COME:

Whereas _____

_____ has presented to the Commissioner of Patents a petition praying for the _____ of LETTERS PATENT for an alleged new and useful

_____

a description of which invention is contained in the Specification of which a copy is hereunto annexed and made a part thereof, and has complied with the various requirements of Law in such cases made and provided, and

Whereas upon due examination made the said Claimant is adjudged to be justly entitled to a Patent under the Law;

Now therefore these **LETTERS PATENT** are to grant unto the said _____ heirs or assigns for the term of _____ years from the _____ day of _____ one thousand eight hundred and _____ the exclusive right to make, use and vend the said invention throughout the United States and the Territories thereof.

In testimony whereof I have hereunto set my hand and caused the seal of the Patent Office to be affixed at the City of Washington this _____ day of _____ in the year of our Lord one thousand eight hundred and _____ and of the Independence of the United States of America the _____

A. Bell
Secretary of the Interior

Countersigned:
_____
Commissioner of Patents

86566

C. F. BRUSH.
Magneto-Electric Machine.

No. 203,412. Patented May 7, 1878.

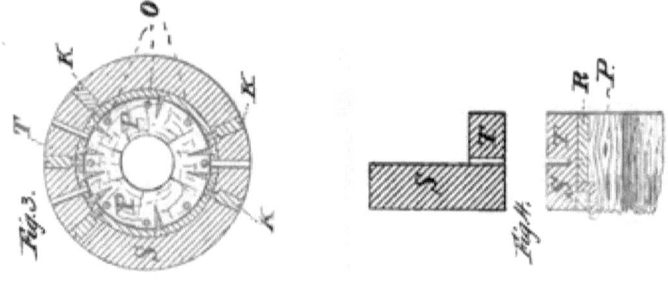

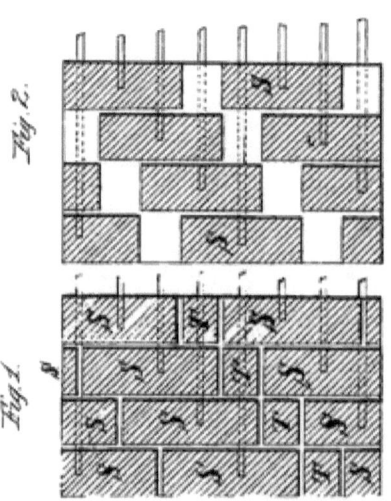

UNITED STATES PATENT OFFICE.

CHARLES F. BRUSH, OF CLEVELAND, OHIO.

IMPROVEMENT IN MAGNETO-ELECTRIC MACHINES.

Specification forming part of Letters Patent No. 203,412, dated May 7, 1878; application filed March 23, 1878.

To all whom it may concern:

Be it known that I, CHARLES F. BRUSH, of Cleveland, in the county of Cuyahoga and State of Ohio, have invented certain new and useful Improvements in Commutators for Electric Machines; and I do hereby declare the following to be a full, clear, and exact description of the invention, such as will enable others skilled in the art to which it pertains to make and use it, reference being had to the accompanying drawings, which form part of this specification.

My invention relates to dynamo-electric machines, or apparatus for the conversion of mechanical into electrical energy; and it consists of improvements in the construction of the commutator. In short, the commutator about to be specified is an improvement, in point of mechanical construction, simplicity, durability, and facility of repair, over the commutator shown in United States Patent No. 189,997, granted to me April 24, 1877; and inasmuch as the essential characteristics and principles of operation of my present invention and of the commutator specified in the above-named patent are the same, I shall refer, for a full understanding of my present device, to said patent, instead of here entering into any more specific description than is required to point out the mechanical differences between it and my formerly-patented device.

In the drawings, Figure 1 is a developed view of my present commutator. Fig. 2 is a copy, for purpose of convenient comparison with my present commutator, of Fig. 7 of the drawings of my said Patent No. 189,997, which shows a developed view of my said former commutator. Fig. 3 is a view, in cross-section, of the device shown developed in Fig. 1. Fig. 4 shows a detached portion of my present device as developed and in end elevation.

As in my said prior patent, so here, S S represent the conducting plates or segments of the commutator, that connect with the different bobbins on the armature, on the same plans as set forth in my said prior patent. T T are insulating-segments intervening between the ends of the conducting-segments S. R represents separate metallic plates or sub-segments, to which are attached the wearing-segments S T. P is a hub or cylinder, of wood or any suitable non-conducting material, which serves as a carrier and as means of attachment to the entire commutator, and is made of suitable length, style, and dimensions to suit this object. O O are the bobbin-wires, that connect between the armature and commutator-segments in the same manner as shown in my said former patent.

It will first be noticed that I have dispensed with one-half of my original number of insulating-segments T, (corresponding to the insulating-spaces in said prior patent,) for the sufficient reason that I have found them to be practically unnecessary, as it is obvious that when the brush or plate F (see said original patent) is insulated from a pair of segments, S, by a segment, T, the electric circuit through the corresponding bobbin or bobbins on the armature is just as effectually interrupted as if the other brush, F, was also insulated from the segments S.

In my present device the insulating-segments T are composed of the same metal (preferably copper, on account of its durability and good conducting quality) as the segments S; but, being insulated from the pair of segments between whose ends it is located, a segment, T, performs the function of an insulating material as far as its particular pair of segments is concerned.

I prefer to make the insulating-segments T of the same material as the segments S, both for the sake of facility of construction and to insure a uniformity of wear over the entire face of the commutator.

It will next be observed (in Fig. 4) that any insulating-segment T may, if desired, be united to the side and form a part of an adjoining segment, S. Such a union will obviously not interfere with the function of a segment, T, as an insulator, so far as concerns the pair of segments S between whose ends it is placed. Such a construction I prefer simply for the purpose of securing the segments S T more firmly in proper position.

Beneath the segments S T are the bases or sub-segments R, corresponding in fashion and location to the segments S T above them.

The sub-segments R are secured to the hub P by suitable screws, or the like, substantially as shown in Fig. 3 of the drawings; and to said sub-segments R are attached the bobbin-wires O, in any suitable manner to insure good electrical connections, as shown in Fig. 4.

The segments S are secured to the sub-segments R by peculiarly-shaped screws K, as shown in Fig. 3. It will be seen that the bearing portion of the heads of these screws is near the lower side of the segments S, while the heads above their bearing portion are cylindrically elongated until they reach the outer surface of the commutator, with whose face they are evenly dressed and finished.

By this peculiar construction of screws K, the segments S T may be worn nearly through and still be firmly held in position, while an even surface in the location of said screws will be presented.

By providing the sub-segments R and detachably affixing thereto the segments S T, it will readily appear that, when worn or damaged, the said segments S T may be easily renewed without any disturbance of the sub-segments and their wire connections with the armature of the machine.

I desire it to be understood that the insulators T need not of necessity be metallic. They may be of any other suitable non-conducting substance, or, if desirable, be mere spaces, exposing the hub P in case the segments S are thin.

It will be apparent that the space separating the ends of the segments S opposite to the insulators T is merely for the purpose of insulating the segments S from each other, and not from the brush or plate F, and is, therefore, not intended, in any manner, to perform the function of the insulators T.

What I claim is—

1. A commutator-cylinder consisting of an insulating hub or body, to which are attached sub-segments, placed in proper electrical connection with the general machine in which the commutator is employed, and wearing-segments detachably attached to said sub-segments, substantially as shown.

2. The combination of sub-segments R, wearing-segments S or T, and screws K, substantially as shown.

3. A commutator having metallic insulating-segments T, substantially as shown.

4. A commutator having metallic insulating-segments T attached to and forming part of the adjoining conducting-segments S, substantially as shown.

5. A commutator having two conducting-segments, S, two opposing ends of which said segments are separated by an intervening insulator, T, the other ends of said segments, while insulated from each other, being closely associated, and not provided with an insulator, T, or its equivalent, substantially as shown.

In testimony whereof I have signed my name to this specification in the presence of two subscribing witnesses.

CHARLES F. BRUSH.

Witnesses:
F. TOUMEY,
LEVERETT L. LEGGETT.

Assigned to Brush Electric Co. -- JAN 8 18**

203413

No 203,415

The United States of America

TO ALL TO WHOM THESE PRESENTS SHALL COME:

Whereas Charles F. Brush, of Cleveland, Ohio

has presented to the Commissioner of Patents a petition praying for the grant of LETTERS PATENT for an alleged new and useful Improvement in Regulators for Dynamo-Electric Machines

a description of which invention is contained in the Specification of which a copy is hereunto annexed and made a part hereof, and has complied with the various requirements of Law in such cases made and provided, and

Whereas upon due examination made the said Claimant is adjudged to be justly entitled to a Patent under the Law;

Now therefore these LETTERS PATENT are to grant unto the said Charles F. Brush his heirs or assigns for the term of seventeen years from the seventh day of May one thousand eight hundred and seventy-eight the exclusive right to make, use and vend the said invention throughout the United States and the Territories thereof.

In Testimony whereof I have hereunto set my hand and caused the seal of the Patent Office to be affixed at the City of Washington this seventh day of May in the year of our Lord one thousand eight hundred and seventy-eight and of the Independence of the United States of America the one hundred and second.

Countersigned
[signature]
Commissioner of Patents

[signature]
Secretary of the Interior

C. F. BRUSH.
Armature for Dynamo-Electric Machines.

No. 203,413. Patented May 7, 1878.

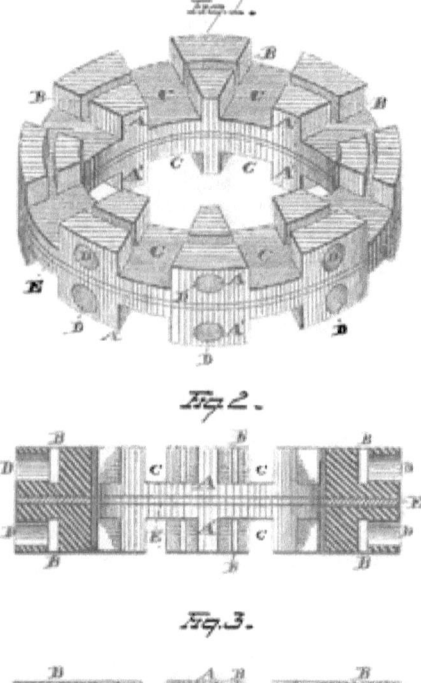

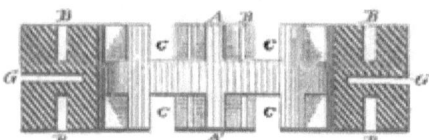

WITNESSES
INVENTOR
Chas. F. Brush,
By Leggett & Leggett,
ATTORNEYS

UNITED STATES PATENT OFFICE.

CHARLES F. BRUSH, OF CLEVELAND, OHIO.

IMPROVEMENT IN ARMATURES FOR DYNAMO-ELECTRIC MACHINES.

Specification forming part of Letters Patent No. 203,113, dated May 7, 1878; application filed January 23, 1878.

To all whom it may concern:

Be it known that I, CHARLES F. BRUSH, of Cleveland, in the county of Cuyahoga and State of Ohio, have invented certain new and useful Improvements in Armatures for Dynamo-Electric Machines; and I do hereby declare the following to be a full, clear, and exact description of the invention, such as will enable others skilled in the art to which it pertains to make and use it, reference being had to the accompanying drawings, which form part of this specification.

My invention relates to that class of dynamo-electric machines in which annular armatures are employed, and especially to the armature of such machines.

My said invention consists, first, in so splitting or dividing the armature and insulating its parts from each other as to practically or entirely prevent the induction of currents in the same when it is revolved in a magnetic field, thus eliminating the principal source of heat and waste of power in such armatures; second, (when the armature is of such pattern as to make it desirable,) in perforating portions of the same, both for the purpose of removing superfluous stock of metal, and to increase the heat-radiating surface, and thus favor the dissipation of the heat which is always generated in armatures when in service, and due to the rapidly-changing magnetism.

In the drawings, Figure 1 represents, in perspective, one form of annular armature constructed according to my invention; and Fig. 2 represents a cross-section of the same.

In both the above figures the armature is shown naked of its wire and disconnected from the other parts of the machine. I prefer to construct the armature from cast-iron, although in this respect I do not limit myself in any degree, as any suitable metal may be used.

The armature is constructed substantially as shown in the drawings; and consists primarily of two parts, A A', firmly secured together, with any suitable insulating material, E, interposed between them. B represents an annular groove formed upon one or both sides of the armature, and, for reasons which will appear, there may be more of these grooves than are shown, if desirable. C C are depressions in the armature, which, in the completed machine, are wound full of insulated wire. D D are holes piercing the armature from its periphery to the annular grooves B, and are provided for the purpose already specified.

When this armature is revolved (in its own plane) in a suitable magnetic field, electric currents will be induced in a direction at right angles to its circumferential length, and will traverse the wire wound in the depressions C. It will now be obvious that if such an armature is made of one solid piece of metal, the induced currents will also circulate in the armature itself, thereby wasting a large portion of the inductive effect of the magnetic field and rapidly heating the armature. The insulating material E prevents the passage of these currents around the entire cross-section of the armature, and confines them, in greatly-diminished force, to each half of the cross-section. These diminished currents are again checked by the grooves B, (which may properly be regarded as insulating air-spaces,) on the principle that if an electric circuit is broken in one point, the entire current is stopped. The passage of the current is thus confined to each quarter of the armature's cross-section, and thus becomes so reduced as to be insignificant.

It will now be obvious that the insulating material E may be replaced by a deep groove, G, as shown in Fig. 3 of the drawings, thus leaving the metal of the armature in a single piece, and still accomplishing the desired end.

Another modification would be to construct the body of the armature from separate concentric rings, insulated from each other, placed one within another, and thus secured.

I am aware that in previous devices armatures have been constructed of a bundle of wires formed into annular shape; but I have found this description of armature not to be practicable.

I am also aware that in Patent No. 189,997, granted to me April 24, 1877, I mention incidentally that an armature, instead of being made from one solid piece, may be formed from parallel disks or plates; but in this patent I did not specify, nor did I contemplate, any insulation between the component disks going to make up my armature; and it will more-

Assigned to Brush Electric Co. — JAN 8 18__   2/2183

THE UNITED STATES OF AMERICA

No. 212183

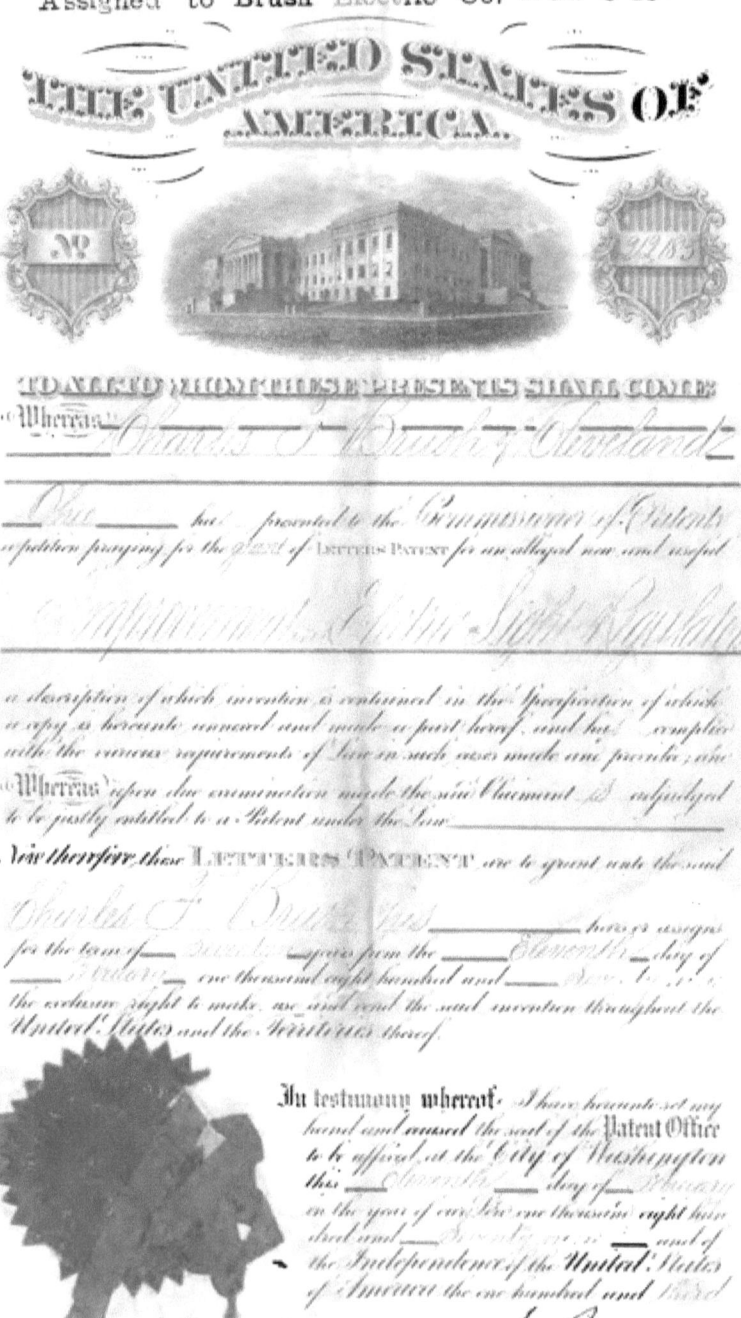

To all to whom these presents shall come:

Whereas Charles F. Brush of Cleveland, Ohio has presented to the Commissioner of Patents a petition praying for the grant of Letters Patent for an alleged new and useful Improvement in Electric Light Regulators, a description of which invention is contained in the Specification of which a copy is hereunto annexed and made a part hereof, and has complied with the various requirements of Law in such cases made and provided; and

Whereas upon due examination made the said Claimant is adjudged to be justly entitled to a Patent under the Law.

Now therefore these Letters Patent are to grant unto the said Charles F. Brush, his heirs or assigns for the term of seventeen years from the Eleventh day of February, one thousand eight hundred and seventy-nine, the exclusive right to make, use and vend the said invention throughout the United States and the Territories thereof.

In testimony whereof I have hereunto set my hand and caused the seal of the Patent Office to be affixed at the City of Washington this Eleventh day of February in the year of our Lord one thousand eight hundred and seventy-nine and of the Independence of the United States of America the one hundred and third.

Countersigned:
H. E. Paine
Commissioner of Patents

A. Bell
Acting Secretary of the Interior

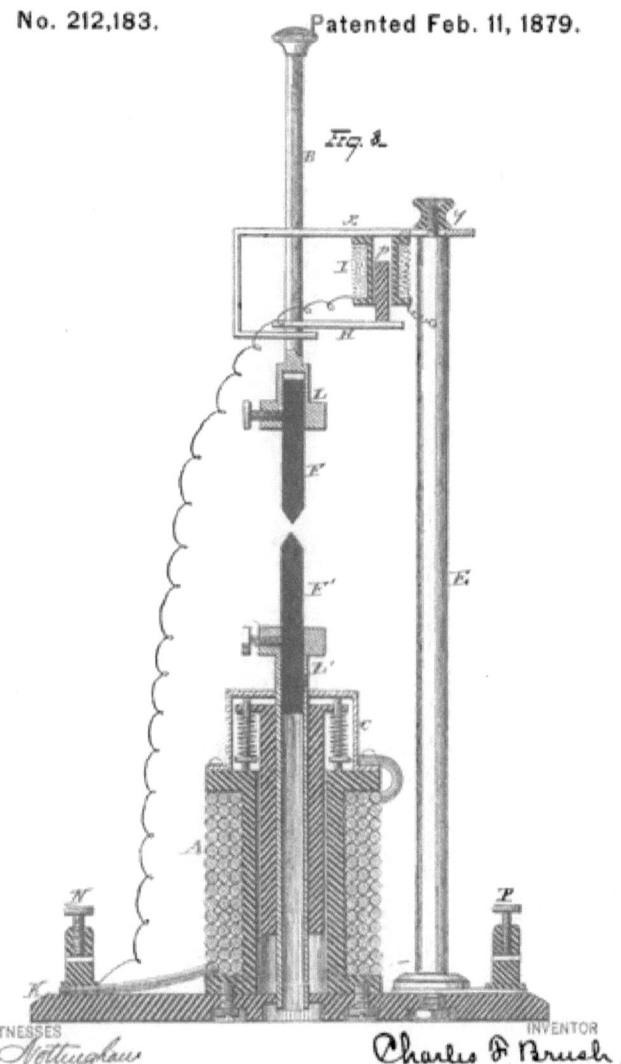

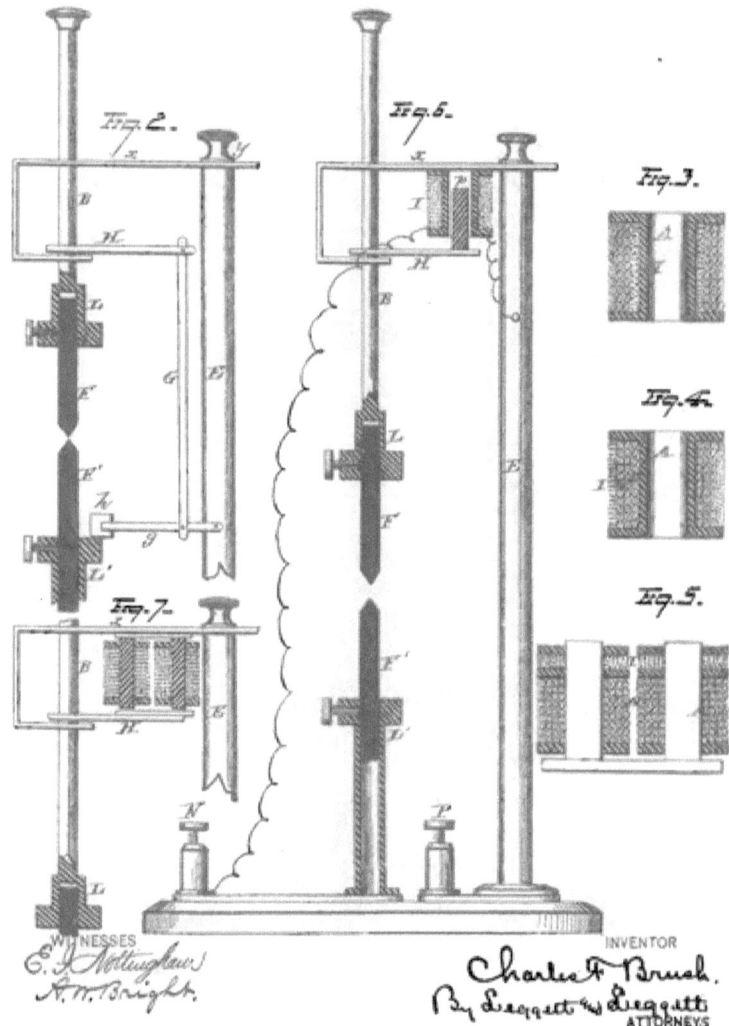

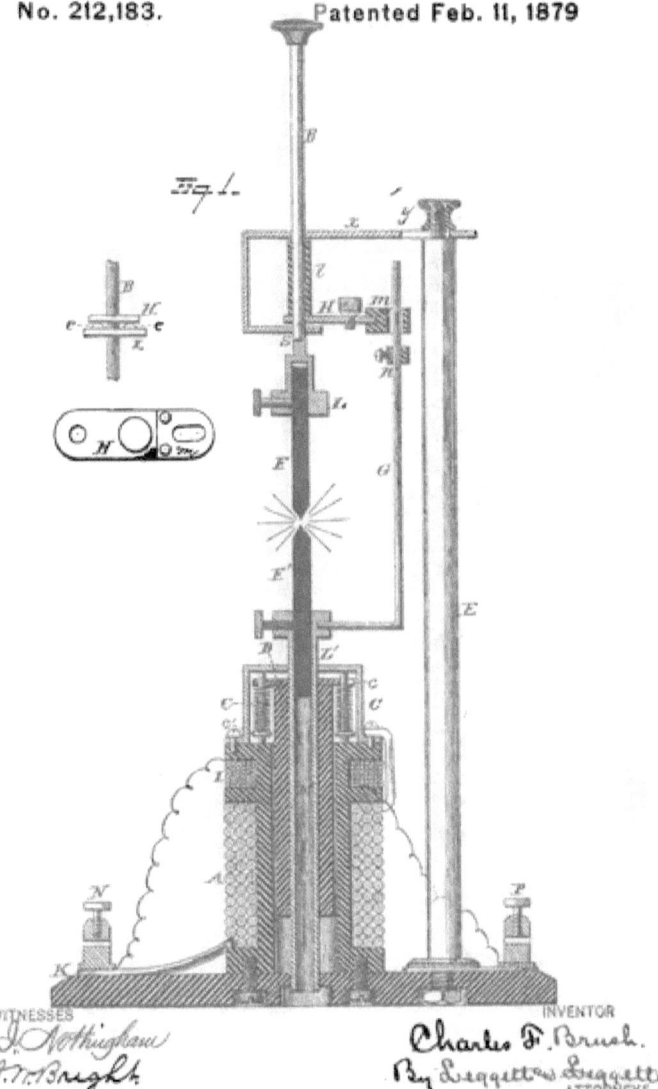

UNITED STATES PATENT OFFICE.

CHARLES F. BRUSH, OF CLEVELAND, OHIO.

IMPROVEMENT IN ELECTRIC-LIGHT REGULATORS.

Specification forming part of Letters Patent No. **212,183**, dated February 11, 1879; application filed May 7, 1878.

To all whom it may concern:

Be it known that I, CHARLES F. BRUSH, of Cleveland, in the county of Cuyahoga and State of Ohio, have invented certain new and useful Improvements in Electric-Light Regulators; and I do hereby declare the following to be a full, clear, and exact description of the invention, such as will enable others skilled in the art to which it pertains to make and use it, reference being had to the accompanying drawings, which form part of this specification.

My invention relates to improvements in electric-light regulators; and consists in the devices and appliances hereinafter set forth and claimed.

In the drawings, Figure 1 represents a vertical section of an electric-light regulator embodying my several improvements. Fig. 2 shows a modified arrangement of releasing mechanism and clutch G H. Fig. 3 shows a modified arrangement of principal helix A and adjusting-helix I. Fig. 4 shows another modification of the same. Fig. 5 shows one method of applying the adjusting-helix I to an ordinary magnet, such as is involved in many regulators in common use. Fig. 6 shows the adjusting-helix I as used without a principal helix. Fig. 7 shows a modification of the same. Fig. 8 shows the adjusting-helix and principal helix operating different cores or magnets.

In Fig. 1, K is a base, of suitable material, to which is attached a metallic post, E, supporting the arm X, which carries the rod B. This rod moves through holes in the arm X, and has at its lower end a carbon-holder, which clamps the carbon F firmly in position, so that it is carried up and down with the rod.

H is a ring-clamp surrounding the rod B, and prolonged and weighted at one side, as shown. This clamp is supported on projections e, attached to the arm X. l is a tube loosely surrounding the rod B, for the purpose of preventing the clamp H being carried up with the rod B when the latter is raised.

D is an iron core rigidly attached to the tube M, which, projecting above and below the core, passes through suitable bearings, as shown, and terminates above in the carbon-holder L', which clamps the carbon F', the latter extending down the tube M as far as may be desirable.

c are arms attached to the upper end of the core D, by means of which the spiral springs C support and force upward the core D, and with it the carbon F'. c' are adjusting-screws, for regulating the tension of the springs C.

G is an arm carried by the carbon-holder L', and its upper end passes loosely through a hole in the prolonged end of the clamp H. This clamp is provided at its end with an insulating material, m, so that the arm G cannot make electrical contact with it. The arm G is provided with an adjustable collar, n, so placed that when the core D is at the limit of its upward movement the end of the clamp H will be slightly raised.

The lower portion of the core D is surrounded by a helix of coarse wire, A, having one of its ends attached to the binding-post N, and the other, in connection with the carbon-holder L', through the tube M and its upper bearing, as shown. P is a binding-post, connecting with the post E.

When the regulator is not in operation, the springs C will force the core D upward, the collar n on the arm G will raise the end of the clamp H, the rod B will be released, and will fall until the carbons F F' are in contact. The arm X being provided with a slot through which the post E passes, the carbons F F' may be adjusted in proper apposition by loosening the nut J, which may then be tightened.

The operation of the device as far as described is as follows: The posts P N being attached to a suitable source of electricity, the current passes through the post E, arm X, and rod B to the carbon F; thence through the carbon F', tube M, and helix A to the other binding-post, N. Under these conditions the core D is drawn down by the axial magnetism of the helix A, carrying with it the carbon F' and arm G. The weighted end of the clamp H being thus allowed to fall at the beginning of the downward movement, the sides of the hole in the clamp through which the rod B passes impinges against the latter, and prevents its downward movement of carbon F.

The core D, continuing to move downward, separates the carbons F F', and the voltaic arc is developed between them, thus producing the electric light. The tension of the spring C is so adjusted that the downward movement of the core D will be arrested when the carbons F F' are sufficiently separated, the magnetism of the helix A being much reduced by the weakening of the electric current, due to the resistance of the arc between the carbons.

Now, as the carbons gradually burn away, their distance from each other is increased, the electric current is weakened, owing to the increased resistance, and the magnetism of the helix A is reduced so as to be overcome by the spring C. This allows the carbon F' to move upward until sufficiently near its neighbor, when it is stopped by the increased electric current acting on the core D. When the carbons have burned to such an extent that the core D approaches near to the limit of its upward movement, the clamp H is raised, and the rod B, being liberated, falls downward, carrying with it the carbon F, until the downward movement of the core D, caused by the shortening of the voltaic arc, allows the clamp H to again fasten the rod B.

By means of this simple device an electric light may be uniformly maintained for many hours, the only limit to the time being the length of carbon rods employed.

The releasing-arm G, Fig. 1, may be replaced by the arrangement shown in Fig. 2, consisting of a lever, g, pivoted at one end to the post E, and connected by a link, G, with the clutch or clamp H. One end of the lever g projects over the carbon-holder L', from which it is insulated by suitable material h, as shown. The lever g and link G are so arranged that when the carbon-holder L' is at its upper limit the lever will be raised by it, thus raising the clamp H and liberating the rod B.

Obviously, many forms of clamps H and releasing mechanism G may be employed, the essential element being such as will release the rod B when the core D approaches near to its upward limit, and clamp it when the core moves in the opposite direction. In case it becomes desirable to operate this regulator in other positions than the vertical one shown, it will only be necessary to so arrange matters that gravity or suitable springs, or both, may produce the same movements of the several parts which gravity and the springs C produce in the vertical position described.

We have now to consider the second important element of my invention, which consists in the introduction of the second helix, I, used alone or in combination with the principal helix A. I have styled this second helix the "adjusting-helix," and will so refer to it in my description. It is employed for the purpose of governing the automatic adjustments of the regulator, its value for this purpose being more apparent when two or more are used in a single electric circuit.

It is well known that when an attempt is made to use two or more regulators of ordinary forms in a single electric circuit they work very irregularly, some allowing their carbons to come and remain in contact, while others have their carbons widely separated. The cause of this irregularity may be explained as follows: Supposing two regulators are being used, at the commencement of the operation the regulators may start evenly, especially if a limit is fixed to the separation of their carbons. When, however, the carbons burn away, so that the weakened current allows them to move toward each other, this movement will commence in one regulator before it does in the other, as it is impossible to adjust the regulators so nicely that their automatic adjustments will take place simultaneously; but as soon as one pair of carbons approach each other, the electric current is strengthened, and the other pair of carbons, which were about to move forward, will be retained in their old position. When another adjustment becomes necessary, the same regulator which proved the more sensitive in the first instance may again advance its carbon first. These operations are liable to continue until the more sensitive regulator has its carbons in contact and ceases to afford light, while the other monopolized the whole voltaic arc, which was at first divided between the two. Hence it appears that no more than one regulator of the ordinary form can be successfully operated by a single current. If, however, a device can be applied to the regulators above considered which shall automatically tend to force the carbons together with a constantly increasing pressure as their distance increases, then the two regulators, or as many more as the current is capable of operating, will work uniformly, each maintaining its due portion of the voltaic arc. This important result I attain by means of the adjusting-helix I. This helix consists of wire very much finer than that of the helix A, and consequently the wire is much longer and makes more convolutions than the latter. The ends of the fine wire are connected with the binding-posts P and N, but in such a manner that the electric current shall pass through it in a direction opposite to that in the helix A.

It will now be seen that the electric current has two passages provided for it—one of high resistance through the adjusting-helix I, and the other of comparatively low resistance through the helix A, carbons F F', and the voltaic arc between them.

It is well known that when an electric current has two channels for its passage it will divide itself between them, the relative amounts passing through them being inversely as their resistance. Hence, any increase in the resistance of one conductor produces a corresponding increase of current in the other. It follows, from the difference in direction of the current in the two helices, that the helix I will constantly tend to neutralize the magnetism produced by the helix A in the core D, and thus diminish the force which draws the latter downward. The number of convolutions of the helix I and its resistance are so proportioned to the number of convolutions in the helix A and its resistance, together with that of the normal voltaic are, that the magnetizing power of the latter helix shall be much greater than that of the former. The magnetizing power of the former is, however, very considerable, notwithstanding the small amount of current which passes through it, owing to its great number of convolutions.

Suppose, now, that two or more regulators, provided with adjusting-helices, are introduced into a single suitable electric circuit. The preponderant magnetism of the helices A will operate to separate the carbons in the several regulators, as before explained, and the neutralizing effect of the adjusting-helices I will be equal in all, thus performing no function as long as the regulators work uniformly; but when any irregularity of action commences by which one pair of carbons are separated more than their normal distance, then, owing to the increased resistance of the main circuit in this particular regulator, the current in its adjusting-helix is increased, thus further neutralizing the effect of the principal helix, and allowing the springs C to push the carbons back to their normal position.

If the carbons in any instance approach too near together, the diminished resistance of the main circuit in this instance weakens the current through the adjusting-helix, allowing the principal helix to separate the carbons to their normal distance. Thus it may be seen that the use of this simple device obviates all the difficulties hitherto experienced in multiplying electric lights from a single source of electricity.

The adjusting-helix I may occupy various positions in relation to the principal helix A without interfering with its peculiar function. Thus, for instance, it may be placed within the principal helix instead of at either end, or it may be placed outside of the latter. These modifications are shown, respectively, in Figs. 3 and 4.

The adjusting-helix is equally applicable to those regulators in which an ordinary electro-magnet is employed, having its helix or helices rigidly attached to its core or cores. One method of so applying it is shown in Fig. 5. Or it may be applied to those regulators having two principal helices, like the well-known "Browning" and similar regulators. It is, of course, equally applicable to single principal-helix regulators other than that represented in Fig. 1—such, for example, as that described in a former application of my own.

When a single regulator is used in an electric circuit the adjusting-helix acts as a valuable governor, preventing sudden changes of position in the carbons, and insuring great uniformity of working.

We have yet to consider the application of the adjusting-helix to those regulators in which it may replace the principal helix entirely, while still performing its peculiar function. Such a regulator is shown in Fig. 6, in which the carbon F is stationary, being connected directly with the binding-post N. The adjusting-helix I here acts on an iron core, p, attached to the outer end of the clamp H, and taking the place of the weight similarly placed in Fig. 1. One end of the adjusting-helix is attached to the binding-post B through the post E, while the other is attached to the binding-post N.

The operation of the device is as follows: The electric current being supplied to the binding-posts P N, the carbons are properly separated by raising the rod B. The electric current then divides itself between the main circuit of the regulator, including the carbons F F', and that of the adjusting-helix, as before explained. When, now, the carbons burn away so that their separation becomes too great, the increased resistance of the main circuit strengthens the current in the adjusting-helix, so as to enable it to lift the core p, and with it the clamp H, thus allowing the rod B to move downward until the decreasing resistance of the main circuit again allows the core p to fall and clamp the rod B.

Fig. 7 shows a modified application of the adjusting-helix as applied to the regulator just described. Here the helix I and the core p, Fig. 6, are replaced by an ordinary electro-magnet wound with the adjusting helix or helices, and acting on an armature of iron attached to the clamp H, as shown.

Fig. 8 shows a modification or development of the regulator represented in Fig. 6. In this case the lower carbon, F', is operated by a principal helix, A, in the manner described in connection with Fig. 1, while the mechanism for releasing the rod B is operated by the adjusting-helix I, as described in connection with Fig. 6.

We have here the principal helix A and the adjusting-helix I performing their several characteristic functions, although separated from each other and operating upon different cores or magnets.

What I claim is—

1. The combination, in a single circuit, of two or more electric lights, each of which is provided with an upper carbon point, having mechanism connected therewith for releasing the carbon-holder and allowing it to be fed by gravity, and a lower carbon, the position of which is regulated by the resultant force of axial magnetism caused by the passage of electricity through a helix on the main circuit and a helix on a shunt circuit, substantially as set forth.

2. In an electric-light regulator, the combination, with a carbon-holder, of a magnet surrounded by two helices, one helix located in the main circuit, and the other in a shunt circuit, the main and subsidiary currents passing through said helices in opposite directions, substantially as set forth.

3. In an electric light, the combination, with

a movable core supporting a carbon point and upheld by suitable springs, of a helix surrounding the core and connected with the main circuit, and a superposed subsidiary helix, also surrounding the movable core and connected with a shunt-circuit, substantially as set forth.

4. In an electric light, the combination, with a movable core supporting one of the carbon points, and a main and subsidiary helix surrounding said core, and respectively connected with main and shunt circuits, of the upper carbon point and suitable intervening mechanism, whereby the upper carbon point is fed downward by the action of the lower carbon point, substantially as set forth.

5. In an electric light, the combination, with the upper and lower carbon points thereof, of a helix in the main circuit and a helix in a shunt-circuit, both of said helices surrounding a movable core, with which one of the carbon points is connected, and clamping mechanism connected with the upper and lower carbon points, substantially as set forth.

In testimony whereof I have signed my name to this specification in the presence of two subscribing witnesses.

CHARLES F. BRUSH.

Witnesses:
F. TOUMEY,
F. M. FABER.

Assigned to Brush Electric Co. — Jan 8 18__

THE UNITED STATES OF AMERICA

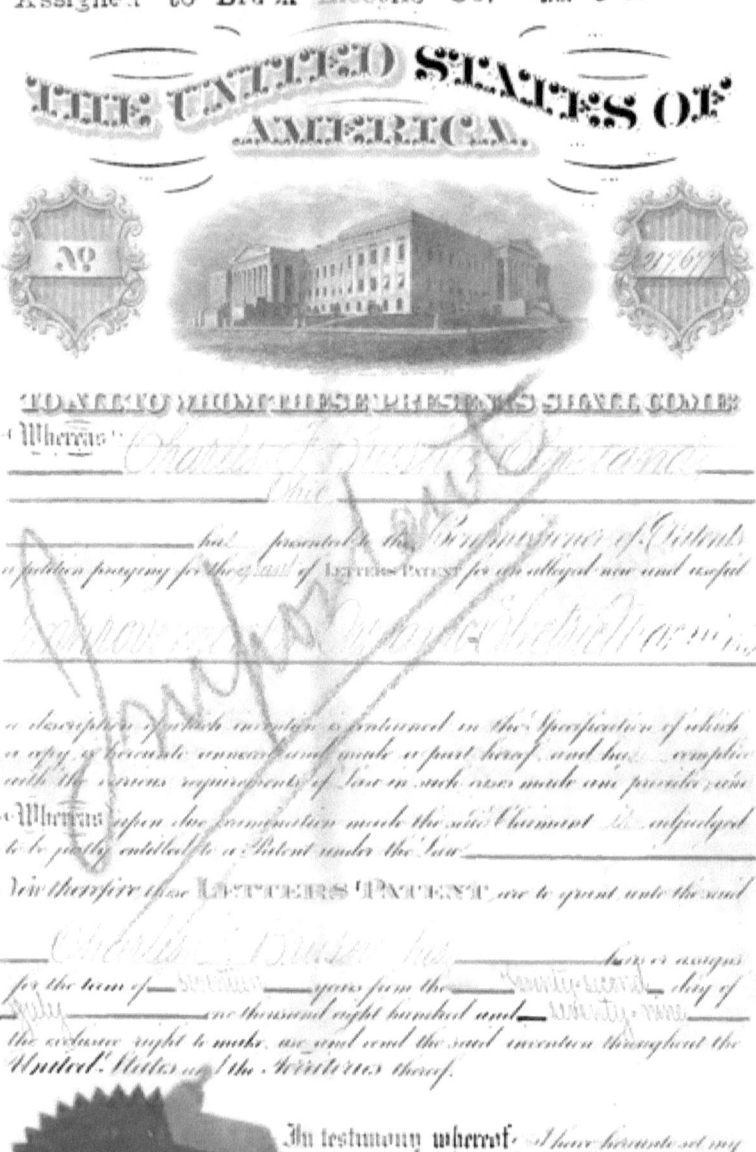

TO ALL TO WHOM THESE PRESENTS SHALL COME:

Whereas Charles F. Brush of Cleveland Ohio _____ has presented to the Commissioner of Patents a petition praying for the grant of LETTERS PATENT for an alleged new and useful Improvement in Dynamo Electric Machines _____ a description of which invention is contained in the Specification of which a copy is hereunto annexed and made a part thereof, and has complied with the various requirements of law in such cases made and provided, and

Whereas upon due examination made the said Claimant is adjudged to be justly entitled to a Patent under the Law.

Now therefore these LETTERS PATENT are to grant unto the said _____ Charles F. Brush his _____ heirs or assigns for the term of _____ seventeen _____ years from the _____ twenty-second _____ day of July _____ one thousand eight hundred and _____ seventy-two _____ the exclusive right to make, use and vend the said invention throughout the United States and the Territories thereof.

In testimony whereof I have hereunto set my hand and caused the seal of the Patent Office to be affixed at the City of Washington this _____ twenty-second _____ day of July _____ in the year of our Lord one thousand eight hundred and _____ seventy-two _____ and of the Independence of the United States of America the one hundred and _____ fourth.

Countersigned
H. E. Paine
Commissioner of Patents

A. Bell
Acting Secretary of the Interior.

2 Sheets—Sheet 2.

C. F. BRUSH.
Dynamo-Electric Machine.

No. 217,677.   Patented July 22, 1879.

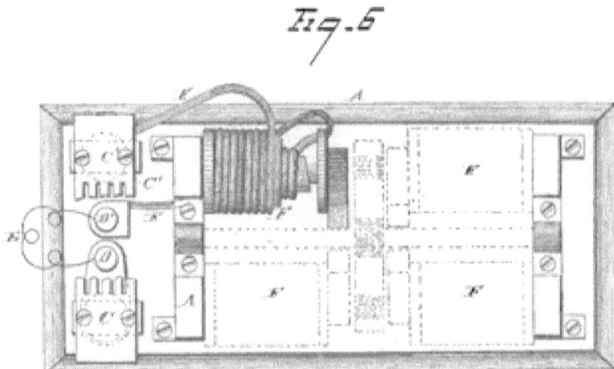

Fig. 6

WITNESSES
Ed. F. Attlinghaus
A. W. Bright.

INVENTOR
Chas F. Brush.
By Leggett & Leggett,
ATTORNEYS.

2 Sheets—Sheet 1.

C. F. BRUSH.
Dynamo-Electric Machine.

No. 217,677.   Patented July 22, 1879.

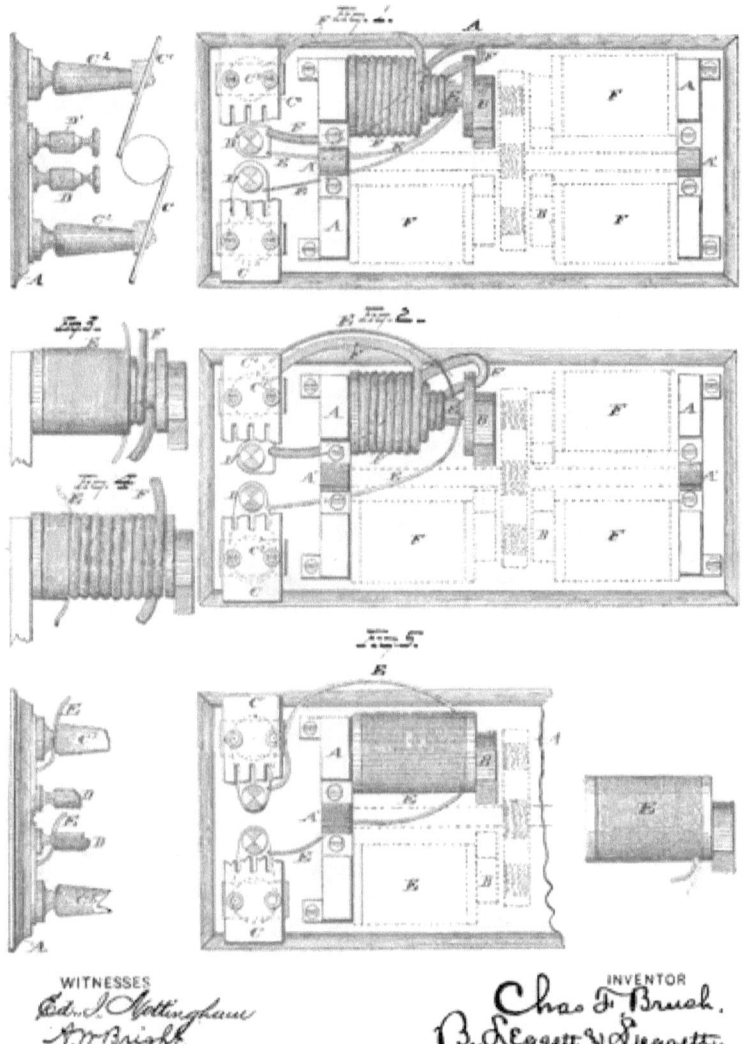

WITNESSES
Ed. J. Nottingham
A. W. Bright

INVENTOR
Chas F. Brush.
By Leggett & Leggett
ATTORNEYS

UNITED STATES PATENT OFFICE.

CHARLES F. BRUSH, OF CLEVELAND, OHIO.

IMPROVEMENT IN DYNAMO-ELECTRIC MACHINES.

Specification forming part of Letters Patent No. **217,677**, dated July 22, 1879; application filed March 11, 1878.

To all whom it may concern:

Be it known that I, CHARLES F. BRUSH, of Cleveland, in the county of Cuyahoga and State of Ohio, have invented certain new and useful Improvements in Dynamo-Electric Machines; and I do hereby declare the following to be a full, clear, and exact description of the invention, such as will enable others skilled in the art to which it pertains to make and use it, reference being had to the accompanying drawings, which form part of this specification.

My invention relates to dynamo-electric machines; and has for its object the maintenance in such machines of a "magnetic field" while the machine is running, whether the external circuit is closed or open.

In dynamo-electric machines as ordinarily constructed, no magnetic field is maintained when the external circuit is open, except that due to residual magnetism; hence the electromotive force developed by the machine in this condition is very feeble.

It is only when the external circuit is closed through a resistance not too large that powerful currents are developed, owing to the strong magnetic field produced by the circulation of the currents themselves around the field-magnets.

Such machines are not well adapted to certain kinds of work, notably that of electroplating. For this purpose a machine arranged to do a large quantity of work at one operation may fail entirely to do a small quantity, because of the comparatively high external resistance involved in the latter case and the low electro-motive force of the machine at the start. Again, it is well known that during the process of electroplating, a very considerable electro-motive force is developed in the plating-bath in a direction opposed to the current from the dynamo-electric machine. If, now, the current from the machine is momentarily weakened, by accident or otherwise, its magnetic field, and consequently its electro-motive force, are correspondingly reduced. If the latter falls below the opposing electro-motive force of the bath, it will be overcome by it, and the machine will have the direction of its current reversed. This accident often happens with plating-machines, and is a source of much annoyance.

It will now be obvious that if even a moderately-strong magnetic field be constantly maintained within the machine, both of the above-described difficulties will be eliminated. Other useful applications of a "permanent-field" machine will readily suggest themselves.

I attain my object by diverting from external work a portion of the current of the machine, and using it, either alone or in connection with the rest of the current, for working the field-magnets. I prefer the latter plan of the two just above mentioned, especially for electroplating-machines.

If, now, the external circuit be broken entirely, the magnetic field will, in the former plan just mentioned, remain unimpaired, and in the latter plan will remain sufficiently strong to effect the desired end.

In applying my invention to dynamo-electric machines, I wind the cores of the field-magnets with a suitable quantity of comparatively fine wire having a high resistance in comparison with that of the external circuit and the rest of the wire on the machine. The ends of this wire are so connected with other parts of the machine that when the latter is running a current of electricity constantly circulates in said wire, whether the external circuit be closed or not. The high resistance of this wire prevents the passage through it of more than a small proportion of the whole current capable of being evolved by the machine; therefore the available external current is not materially lessened.

When this device, which I have called a "teaser," is used in connection with field-magnets, also wound with coarse wire, as shown in Figure 1 of the drawings, for the purpose of still further increasing the magnetic field by employing the main current for this purpose, in the usual manner, then the "teaser" may be so arranged that the current which passes through it will also circulate in the coarse wire, thus increasing the efficiency of the device. This arrangement, illustrating one of the most common applications of my invention, is shown in Fig. 1 of the drawings.

Instead of the teaser and helix F being con-

Compound winding

structed from wire of different gages, the size of wire may be alike in both, or the teaser-wire may be coarser than the principal magnet-wire; but in these cases the waste of current through the teaser would be excessive, leaving comparatively little for use in the external circuit.

Instead of the magnet being surrounded with both teaser and ordinary helix F, the latter may be omitted, and the teaser increased in gage and length (thus still maintaining its high resistance) until it will of itself maintain sufficient magnetic field. This modified form of machine is shown in Fig. 5 of the drawings.

I will now proceed to describe the construction of one or more forms of device embodying my invention.

In the drawings, Fig. 1 represents in plan view a portion of a dynamo-electric machine, showing one of its magnetic helices partially wound and so arranged as to exhibit the teaser and helix F, also to show one form of arranging the currents of the teaser and main wire. Fig. 2 is the same, showing, however, a modified arrangement of the currents of teaser and main wire. Fig. 3 shows a modified method of applying the teaser by wrapping it upon the outside of the main helix instead of within it, as shown in Fig. 1. Fig. 4 shows another modified form of teaser, where it may be wrapped around the magnet alongside and independent of the main helix. Fig. 5 shows another modified form of my device, in which the main helix F is omitted, and the magnet clothed only with the teaser. Fig. 6 shows still another modification of my invention, wherein the teaser does not surround the magnet-cores at all.

A A represent the base and standards of a dynamo-electric machine. A′ A′ are the bearings in which revolves the shaft that carries the armature and commutator-cylinder.

B is one arm of a field-magnet, of which said magnets there are two in such a machine as here shown—one upon either side of the revolving armature.

C C′ are metallic brushes for collecting the current from the commutator-cylinder, and conducting the same down through their supports C′′ to suitable connections, where it is disposed of according to the arrangement of the circuits.

D D′ are binding-posts, representing the positive and negative poles of the machine, from which proceed the wires or other conductors for conveying said current to the place of its application.

E represents the teaser, already sufficiently described, so far as the principles of its application and operation are concerned.

It therefore only remains to explain a few of various modifications in the manner of applying said teaser and the arrangement of the currents.

As shown in Fig. 1 of the drawings, the teaser E is first wrapped, say, in two courses around the core of the magnet B, and the main helix-wire F is wound outside and independent of the teaser. One end of the teaser-wire is connected with the binding-post D and brush C, and the other with the post D′. The main helix-wire F passes from the post D′, to which it is connected, to the magnet-core, around which it forms a helix, and, finally, connects with the brush C′.

Thus arranged, the current will be as follows while the external circuit is closed: Tracing it from brush C, it divides itself between the external circuit and the teaser inversely as their respective resistances, and again uniting into an undivided current at the post D′, it passes on through the helix F to the brush C′.

If, now, the external circuit be opened, the reduced current consequently evolved by the machine will take the following course, by which it will be clearly perceived how in such case a permanent magnetic field is maintained. (The same conditions would obtain if the machine were to be originally started on an open external circuit.) Tracing, now, the current from the brush C, it passes through the teaser E, around its helical portion, down to binding-post D′, where it meets the wire F of the main helix, through which it passes again around the magnet, and finally to the brush C′.

This arrangement of circuits, as shown in Fig. 1, while for many purposes preferable, on account of the increased amount of current convolutions passed around the magnets, is not the only one that will prove effective in carrying out and embodying my said invention. Such an arrangement of currents as shown in Fig. 2 will serve an operative purpose. In this form the teaser E, instead of connecting with the wire F at the binding-post D′, as hereinbefore specified, takes the following course: Commencing, say, at its connection with the brush C and post D, it proceeds to describe a helix around the magnet, and then terminates in its connection with the brush C′.

It is not at all essential that the teaser be wrapped around the magnet underneath the wire F. A variety of methods would be equally as operative as the above, among which may be mentioned that illustrated in Fig. 3 of the drawings, where the teaser is wrapped outside of the helix F; also, that shown in Fig. 4, where the teaser is wrapped alongside the helix F, forming a separate and independent section or helix.

Fig. 5 of the drawings is designed to show the arrangement of the current when the wire F is omitted, as hereinbefore described, in which case the magnets are wound only with the teaser.

Fig. 6 of the drawings is designed to show the arrangement of parts and direction of current when the teaser-wire E does not surround a magnet-core, but merely serves to join, through a high resistance, the positive and negative poles D D′ of the machine. In this case the teaser-wire need not necessarily form

a helix, but may be disposed of in any convenient manner, either within the machine or exterior to it.

The direction of the current through the several parts of the apparatus is the same as described in connection with Fig. 1 of the drawings, and the effect produced is the same, but less in degree, since the magnetizing power of the helix F only is brought into action, instead of that of both helices, F and E, as in the former case.

It should be distinctly understood that I do not limit my invention to the form adaptable to any particular dynamo-electric machine, inasmuch as it is susceptible of a variety of modifications, whereby it may be applied to devices of various constructions without any material departure from its spirit and intent, or the essential principles of its construction and operation. The forms in which I have here chosen to demonstrate it are those best applicable to such a dynamo-electric machine as shown in United States Patent No. 189,997, granted to me April 24, 1877.

What I claim is—

1. In a dynamo-electric machine, the wire or helix E, having a comparatively high resistance and kept constantly in closed circuit while the machine is running, in combination with the magnet-wire or helix F, as commonly employed.

2. In a dynamo-electric machine in which the coils around the field-of-force electro-magnets are included in the main or operative circuits, the combination of such main circuit with a constantly-closed differential circuit of prescribed resistance, for the purpose of maintaining the flow of the current through the coils surrounding the electro-magnets in the machine when the main or operative (external) circuit is broken, substantially as shown.

In testimony whereof I have signed my name to this specification in the presence of two subscribing witnesses.

CHARLES F. BRUSH.

Witnesses:
LEVERETT L. LEGGETT,
JNO. CROWELL, Jr.

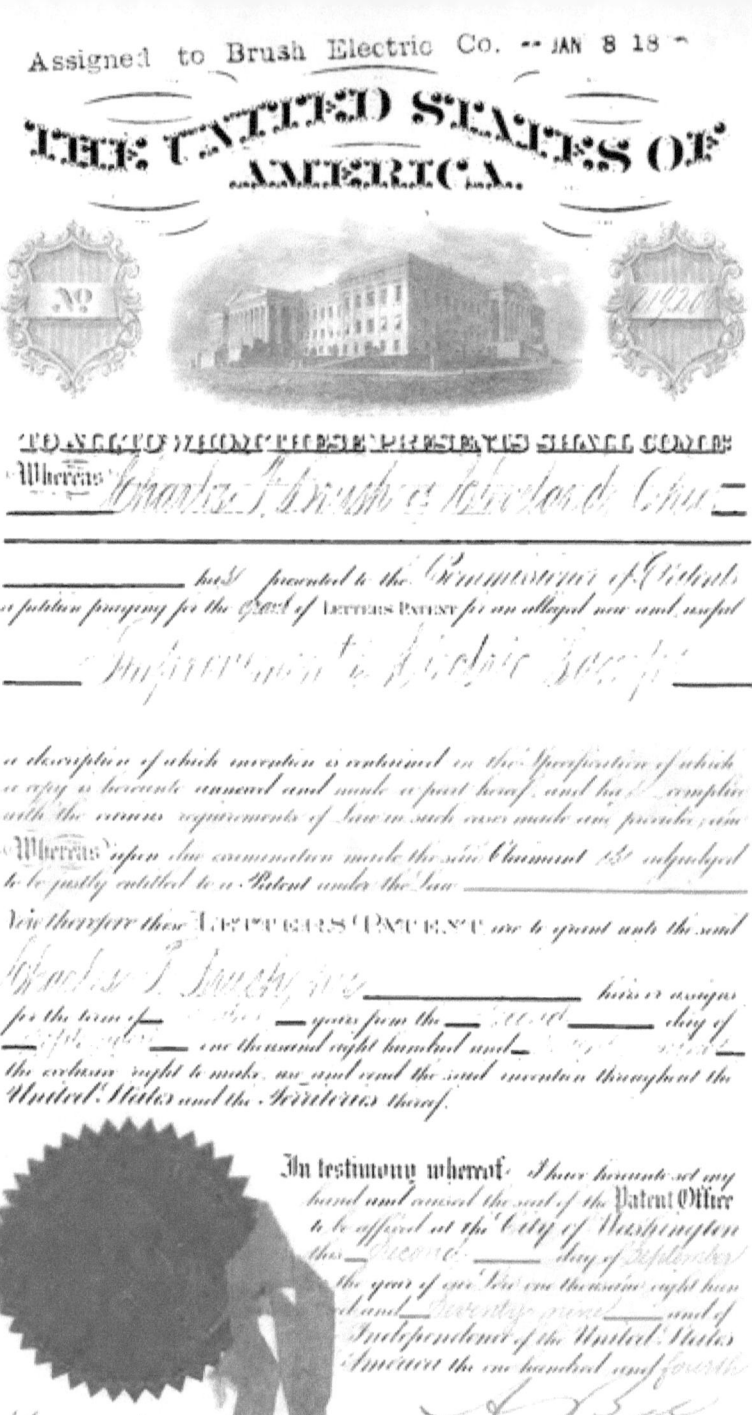

C. F. BRUSH.
Electric-Lamp.

No. 219,208. Patented Sept. 2, 1879.

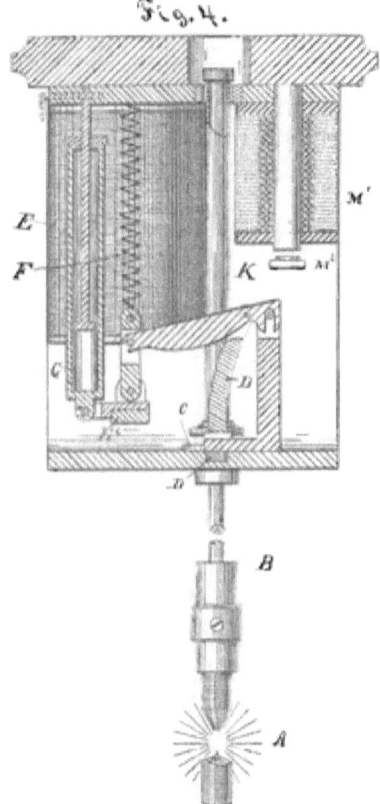

C. F. BRUSH.
Electric-Lamp.

No. 219,208.   Patented Sept. 2, 1879.

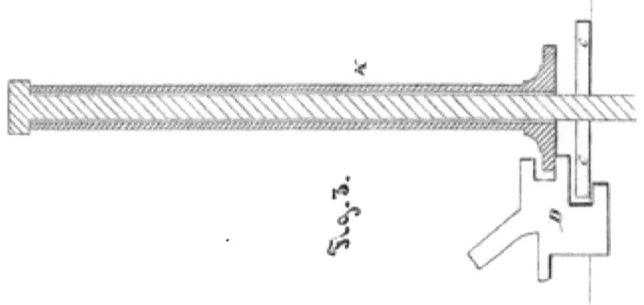

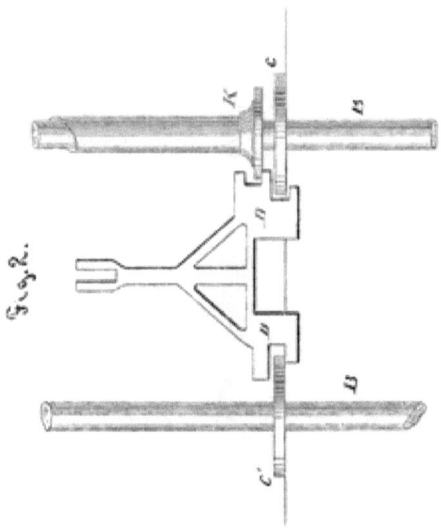

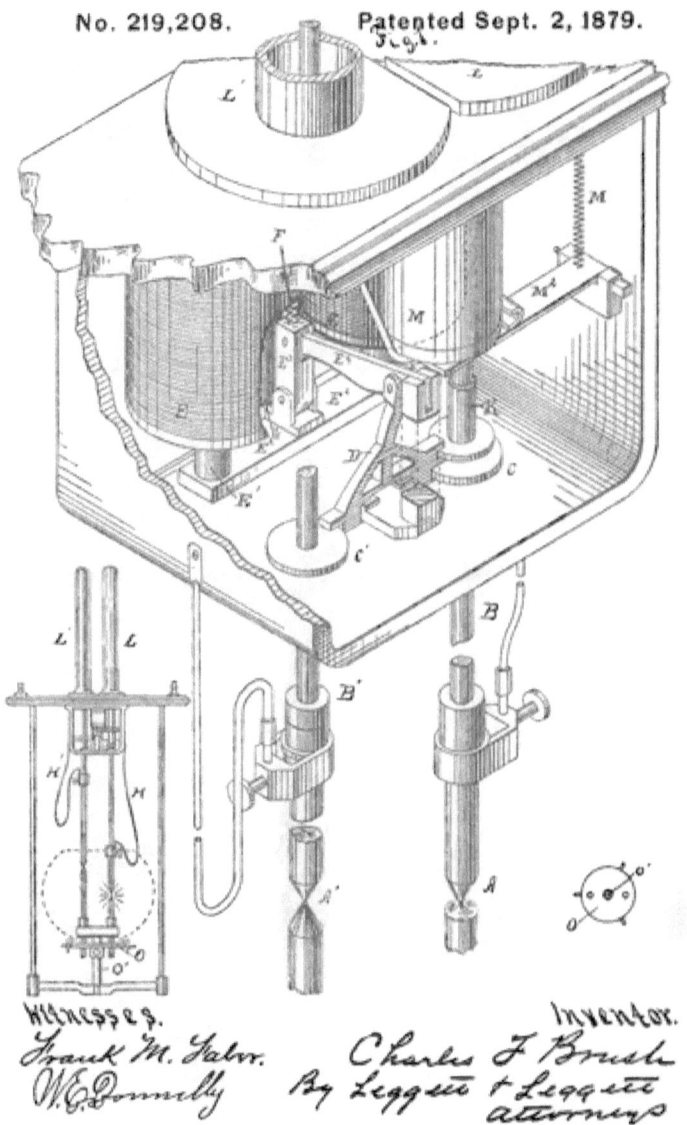

United States Patent Office.

CHARLES F. BRUSH, OF CLEVELAND, OHIO.

IMPROVEMENT IN ELECTRIC LAMPS.

Specification forming part of Letters Patent No. 219,208, dated September 2, 1879; application filed May 15, 1879.

To all whom it may concern:

Be it known that I, CHARLES F. BRUSH, of Cleveland, in the county of Cuyahoga and State of Ohio, have invented certain new and useful Improvements in Electric Lamps; and I do hereby declare the following to be a full, clear, and exact description of the invention, such as will enable others skilled in the art to which it pertains to make and use it, reference being had to the accompanying drawings, which form part of this specification.

My invention relates to electric lamps or light-regulators; and it consists, first, in a lamp having two or more sets of carbons adapted, by any suitable means, to burn successively—that is, one set after another; second, in a lamp having two or more sets of carbons, each set adapted to move independently in burning and feeding; third, in a lamp having two or more sets of carbons adapted each to have independent movements, and each operated and influenced by the same electric current; fourth, in a lamp having two or more sets of carbons, said carbons, by any suitable means, being adapted to be separated dissimultaneously, whereby the voltaic arc between but a single set of carbons is produced; fifth, in the combination, with one of the carbons or carbon-holders of a lamp employing two or more sets of carbons, as above mentioned, of a suitable collar, tube, or extended support, within or upon which the carbon or carbon-holder to which it is applied shall rest and be supported.

In the drawings, Figure 1 is an isometrical view of a lamp embodying my invention, the said lamp operating two sets of carbons. Accompanying Fig. 1 is a diminished view of the lamp, showing its general appearance and proportions. In this figure of drawings appears mechanism (marked M M¹ M²) representing a device for automatically shunting or cutting the lamp from circuit when, from any cause, said lamp shall offer an abnormally great resistance to the current operating it; but I do not here lay any claim to this or any other device or method for accomplishing the function just referred to, as I have made that the subject of another application. Fig. 2 is a detached view of the parts operating to lift the carbon-rods, and thus to dissimultaneously separate the carbons of the two sets there shown. Fig. 3 is a detached view, showing a supporting device (here appearing as a tube surrounding a carbon-holder) between the carbon lifting or separating apparatus and one of the lifted carbons; and Fig. 4, a section view of the device shown in Fig. 1.

I desire to state at the outstart that my invention is not limited in its application to any specific form of lamp. It may be used in any form of voltaic-arc light-regulator, and would need but a mere modification in mechanical form to be adaptable to an indefinite variety of the present known forms of electric lamps.

My invention comprehends, broadly, any lamp or light-regulator where more than one set of carbons are employed, wherein—say in a lamp having two sets of carbons—one set of carbons will separate before the other.

For the purpose merely of showing and explaining the principles of operation and use of my invention, I shall describe it, in the form shown in the drawings, as applied to an electric lamp of the general type shown in United States Letters Patent No. 203,411 granted to me May 7, 1878, reissued May 20, 1879, and numbered 8,718. The leading feature of this type of regulator is that the carbon-holder has a rod or tube which slides through or past a friction-clutch, which clutch is operated upon to grasp and move said carbon rod or holder, and thus to separate the carbons and produce the voltaic arc light; and I shall refer to such a lamp in my following description.

A represents one set of carbons; A′, another set, each carbon having an independent holder, B B′.

The carbon-holders B B′ may either be in the form of a rod or tube, and each of them is made to pass through a clamping and lifting device, C C′, respectively. These clamps and lifters C C′ are shown in the present instance in the shape of rings surrounding their respective carbon-holders B B′. This form, while I have found it for general purposes the best, is not necessarily the only form of clamp that may be used in carrying out my present invention.

Each ring-clamp C C′ is adapted to be lifted from a single point, thus tilting it and causing it to grasp and lift its inclosed carbon-

holder. This tilting and lifting movement is imparted to the clamps C C' by any suitable lifter, D, and this lifter may have its movement imparted either by magnetic attraction due to the current operating the lamp, or by the expansive action of heat upon any suitable apparatus connected with the lamp, said heat generated by the electric current operating the lamp.

I do not in any degree limit myself to any specific method or mechanism for lifting, moving, or separating the carbon points or their holders, so long as the peculiar functions and results hereinafter to be specified shall be accomplished.

The lifter D, in the present instance, is so formed that when it is raised it shall not operate upon the clamps C C' simultaneously, but shall lift first one and then the other, (preferably the clamp C first and C' second, for reasons which will hereinafter appear.) This function of dissimultaneous action upon the carbons or their holders, whereby one set of carbons shall be separated in advance of the other, constitutes the principal and most important feature of my present invention.

In the lamp shown in the drawings the lifter D is actuated and controlled through the agency of magnetic attraction due to the influence of the current operating the lamp, and this is accomplished as follows: One, two, or more spools or hollow helices, E, of insulated wire, are placed in the circuit, within whose cavities freely move cores E^1. The electric current, passing through the helices E, operate to strongly draw up within their cavities their respective cores E^1 in the same manner as specified in my former patent above referred to.

The cores E^1 are rigidly attached to a common bar, E^2, and the upward and downward movement of this bar, due to the varying attraction of the helices E, is imparted by a suitable link-and-lever connection, E^3 E^4, to the lifter D. By this connection the lifter will have an up-and-down movement in exact concert with the cores E^1; and it is apparent that this connection between magnet and lifter may be indefinitely varied without any departure from my invention; and therefore, while preferring for many purposes the construction just specified, I do not propose to limit myself to its use.

The lifter D may be so constructed and applied as to separate the carbons A and A' successively or dissimultaneously by being so balanced that any difference, however slight, between the weights of the carbons A A' or their holders B B' shall result in one being lifted and separated before the other.

In order properly to balance the attractive force of the magnets, a coil-spring, F, or its equivalent, may be employed, substantially as shown; and to insure a steady motion to the magnets and to the carbon points A A', a dash-pot, G, or its equivalent, should be employed, as this prevents any too sudden, abrupt, or excessive movement of parts.

H H' are metallic cables, through which the current is conducted from above the clamps C C' to the carbons A A'. By this provision is not only insured a good connection between the upper carbon points and the mechanism above it, but another important advantage is obtained, and that is the prevention of sparks due to any interruption of the current between the carbon-holder B B' and its clamp or bearings. This spark, if occurring too frequently, is liable to burn and roughen the rods B B', or their bearings or clamps, and thereby render their operation uncertain, because it is important that a free movement to any degree, however minute, may be allowed the carbon-holder. These cables H H', while operating as just specified, are sufficiently flexible and yielding not to interfere with any movement of their respective carbons or carbon-holders.

The operation of my device, as thus far specified, is as follows: When the current is not passing through the lamp the positive and negative carbons of each set A A' are in actual contact. When, now, a current is passed through the lamp, the magnetic attraction of the helices E will operate to raise the lifter D. This lifter, operating upon the clamps C and C', tilts them and causes them to clamp and lift the carbon holders B B', and thus separate the carbons and produce the voltaic-arc light; but it will be especially noticed that the lifting and separation of these carbons is not simultaneous. One pair is separated before the other, it matters not how little nor how short a time before. This separation breaks the circuit at that point, and the entire current is now passing through the unseparated pair of carbons A'; and now when the lifter, continuing to rise, separates these points, the voltaic arc will be established between them and the light thus produced.

It will be apparent by the foregoing that it is impossible that both pairs of carbons A A' should burn at once, for any inequality of weight or balance between them would result in one pair being separated before the other, and the voltaic arc would appear between the last-separated pair. This function, so far as I am aware, has never been accomplished by any previous invention; and by thus being able to burn independently and one at a time two or more carbons in a single lamp, it is evident that a light may be constantly maintained for a prolonged period without replacing the carbons or other manual interference.

In the form of lamp shown I can, with twelve-inch carbons, maintain a steady and reliable light without any manual interference whatever for a period varying from fourteen to twenty hours.

It is for some reasons desirable that one set of carbons—say the set A—should be consumed before the other set commences to burn, al-

though it is not essential, in carrying out my invention, that the carbons should be consumed in this manner, inasmuch as, if desirable, they may be arranged to burn alternately instead of successively.

It is apparent, however, if one set of carbons can be made to entirely consume before another set begins to burn, that there will be less interruption of the light than if the different pairs were allowed to consume in frequent alternation. I have therefore shown in the present invention one method of securing a consumption of one set of carbons before another shall begin to burn. This I accomplish through any suitable support K, and in such a construction of the lifter D that it shall be positive in its function of separating one set of carbons before the other; or, in case where more than two sets of carbons are employed, to separate said sets successively.

In the lamp as shown in the drawings the support K is in the form of a tube surrounding the carbon-holder B, and this support K is made of such a length that when the carbons A′ shall have been sufficiently consumed a head upon the carbon-holder B will rest upon the top of the support K, whereby the weight of the carbon-holder B and its support K shall at all times and under any circumstance be supported by the lifter D.

Besides the carbon-holder B, with its carbon, and the support K, the lifter D (when the lamp is in operation) should also be made to carry the carbon-holder B′ and its carbon.

The lamp is primarily adjusted so that the magnets through the lifter D shall always carry a definite load, to wit, (in the lamp shown,) the carbon-holders B and B′ and support K.

The desirability of this construction and arrangement may be explained as follows: Supposing, as is designed in the present instance, the carbons A are first consumed. During that time, of course, the magnets are lifting both carbon-holders B B′. Now, when the carbons A are consumed, if no provision was made to the contrary, the carbon-holder B would not be lifted during the consumption of the carbons A′, and this diminishment of the weight carried by the magnets would be liable to materially disturb the adjustment of the lamp and impair its operation accordingly.

To obviate this difficulty I have provided the support K, by which provision the magnets shall always be made to carry both carbon-holders B B′ and the support K.

The difference in weight, owing to the consumption of the carbons, is a practically unimportant matter, and does not materially interfere with the operation of the lamp.

In the case of a lamp where the carbon-holders B B′ are very light, and where the weight of one might be relieved from the magnet (or other moving agent) without material disturbance, the support K might be dispensed with. Said support K might also be omitted, if desired, in a lamp where the lifter is actuated through the agency of the expansion of a metal wire or bar by the action of heat generated by the current operating the lamp, inasmuch as, the force due to said expansion being practically irresistible it would not be so necessary to obtain a balance between various parts as is the case with a lamp as shown in the drawings.

I have incidentally mentioned in the foregoing specification a lamp wherein the voltaic arc is produced by a separation of the carbons due to the expansive action of heat, however generated, upon a metal wire or bar. It is my intention to apply for a patent upon a lamp involving this principle, and I therefore do not waive, by anything contained in this specification, any right of application for patent upon such a type of regulator.

Thus far I have mentioned but two ways of imparting dissimultaneous motion to the carbons of an electric lamp—viz., through magnetic attraction and through the expansive action of heat. This function of my device may be accomplished by clock-work or equivalent mechanical contrivance; and in this respect, as before stated, I do not limit my invention.

L L′ are metallic hoods or protectors for inclosing and shielding the upper projecting ends of the carbon-holders B B′.

In the form of lamp shown in the drawings I obtain very satisfactory results by constructing the helices E according to Letters Patent No. 212,183, granted to me February 11, 1879. In each helix E two independent wires surround the lifting magnets E′, one of fine and one of coarse wire, and each placed in the general circuit operating the lamp. These two wires (the fine and the coarse) are constructed and connected in such a manner as to carry current in opposite directions around the inclosed core, thus exerting a neutralizing influence upon each other, whereby a governing function is secured, for a better description and understanding of which reference is made to said Patent No. 212,183.

The poles of the lamp shown in the drawings are constructed in the form of suspending hooks or loops, from which the lamp is suspended, and the corresponding hooks or loops, with which they engage in the ceiling, (or other locality where the lamps are used,) are the positive and negative poles of the current-generating apparatus. Thus by the simple act of suspension the lamp is placed in circuit.

I will now specify a construction whereby the protecting-globe surrounding the light can be raised and lowered for convenience in renewing carbons and handling the lamp. This I accomplish by making the platform or gallery O, upon which the globe rests, vertically adjustable upon a rod, O′, attached to the lamp-frame in any convenient manner. A set-screw should be provided, whereby the globe can be adjusted to any desired position. By this arrangement the work of renewing carbons and the reliable adjustment of the

globe in relation to the voltaic arc are materially assisted.

In order to accommodate long sticks of carbon, the platform or gallery O should be perforated to allow passage down through it of said carbon sticks. I prefer making the platform or gallery O of metal, and of such shape as that globules of molten copper from the coverings of the carbons, in dropping away, shall not escape to do damage.

It will be particularly observed that in the form of dash-pot employed the cylinder is the movable and the piston or plunger the stationary element. This construction implies more than a mere reversal of the usual make and operation of the dash-pot, for by making the cylinder the movable element the general construction of a lamp can very often be materially simplified, as in the present instance. This form of dash-pot is designed to be employed in connection with any of the moving parts of the mechanism of an electric lamp where it is desired to retard a downward movement.

What I claim is—

1. In an electric lamp, two or more pairs or sets of carbons, in combination with mechanism constructed to separate said pairs dissimultaneously or successively, substantially as and for the purpose specified.

2. In an electric lamp, two or more pairs or sets of carbons, in combination with mechanism constructed to separate said pairs dissimultaneously or successively and establish the electric light between the members of but one pair, (to wit, the pair last separated,) while the members of the remaining pair or pairs are maintained in a separated relation, substantially as shown.

3. In an electric lamp having more than one pair or set of carbons, the combination, with said carbon sets or pairs, of mechanism constructed to impart to them independent and dissimultaneous separating and feeding movements, whereby the electric light will be established between the members of but one of said pairs or sets at a time, while the members of the remaining pair or pairs are maintained in a separated relation, substantially as shown.

4. In a single electric lamp, two or more pairs or sets of carbons, all placed in circuit, so that when their members are in contact the current may pass freely through all said pairs alike, in combination with mechanism constructed to separate said pairs dissimultaneously or successively, substantially as and for the purpose shown.

5. In an electric lamp wherein more than one set or pair of carbons are employed, the lifter D or its equivalent, moved by any suitable means, and constructed to act upon said carbons or carbon-holders dissimultaneously or successively, substantially as and for the purpose shown.

6. In an electric lamp wherein more than one pair or set of carbons are employed, a clamp, C, or its equivalent, for each said pair or set, said clamps C adapted to grasp and move said carbons or carbon-holders dissimultaneously or successively, substantially as and for the purpose shown.

7. In an electric lamp, the combination, with a carbon holder and the mechanism moving said carbon-holder, of a lifter or support, K, or its equivalent, constructed to operate in compelling the said moving mechanism to sustain the weight of the carbon-holder after its carbon is sufficiently consumed or removed, substantially as and for the purpose described.

In testimony whereof I have signed my name to this specification in the presence of two subscribing witnesses.

CHARLES F. BRUSH.

Witnesses:
LEVERETT L. LEGGETT,
JNO. CROWELL, Jr.

Assigned to Brush Electric Co. " Jan 8 13

THE UNITED STATES OF AMERICA

TO ALL TO WHOM THESE PRESENTS SHALL COME

Whereas Charles F. Brush & Cleveland Ohio

___ has presented to the Commissioner of Patents a petition praying for the ___ of LETTERS PATENT for an alleged new and useful ___

a description of which invention is contained in the Specification of which a copy is hereunto annexed and made a part hereof, and has complied with the various requirements of Law in such cases made and provided, and *Whereas* upon due examination made the said Claimant is adjudged to be justly entitled to a Patent under the Law ___

Now therefore these LETTERS PATENT are to grant unto the said ___ heirs or assigns for the term of ___ years from the ___ day of ___ one thousand eight hundred and ___ the exclusive right to make, use and vend the said invention throughout the United States and the Territories thereof.

In testimony whereof I have hereunto set my hand and caused the seal of the Patent Office to be affixed at the City of Washington this ___ day of ___ in the year of our Lord one thousand eight hundred and ___ and of the Independence of the United States of America the one hundred and ___

Countersigned
Acting
Commissioner of Patents

Acting
Secretary of the Interior

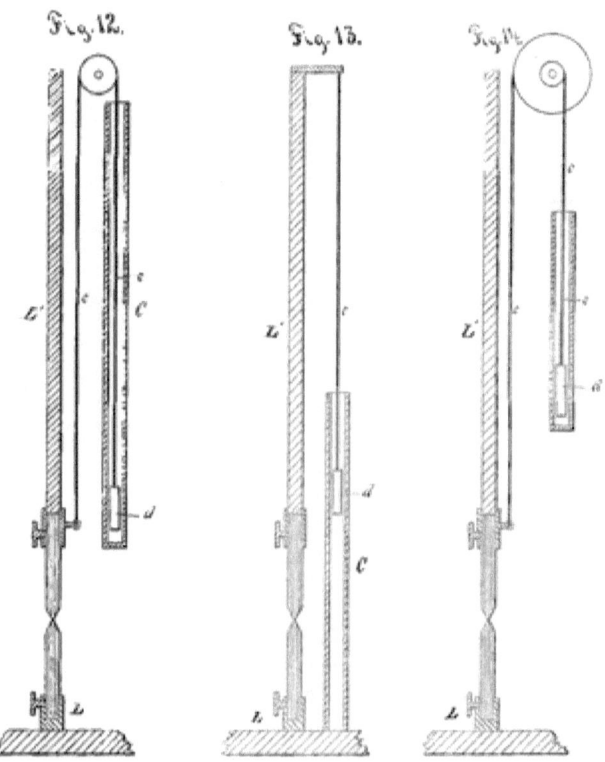

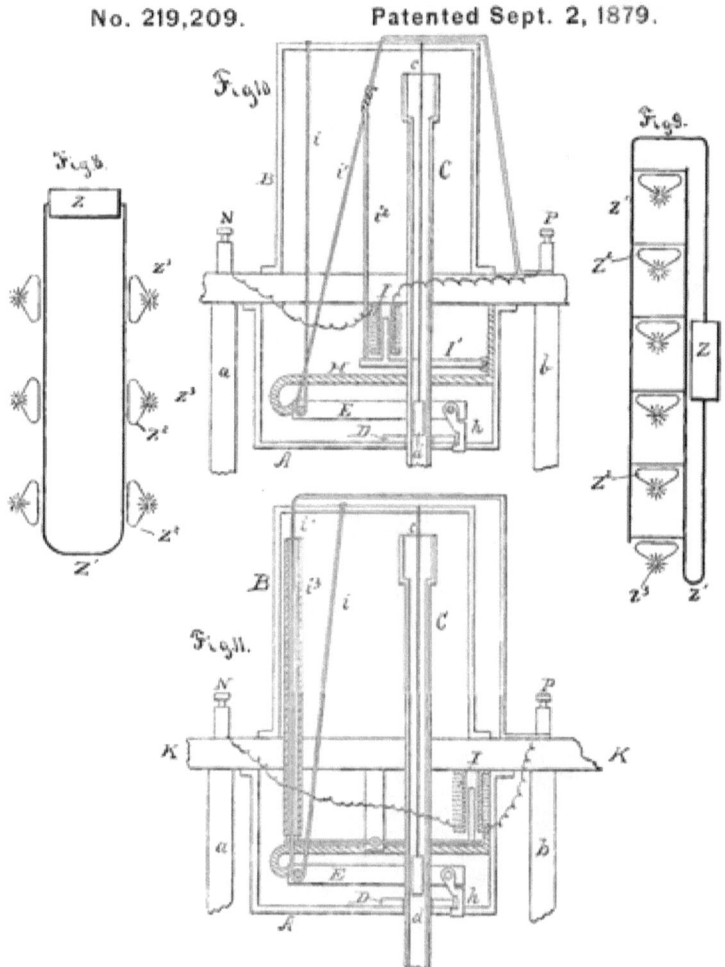

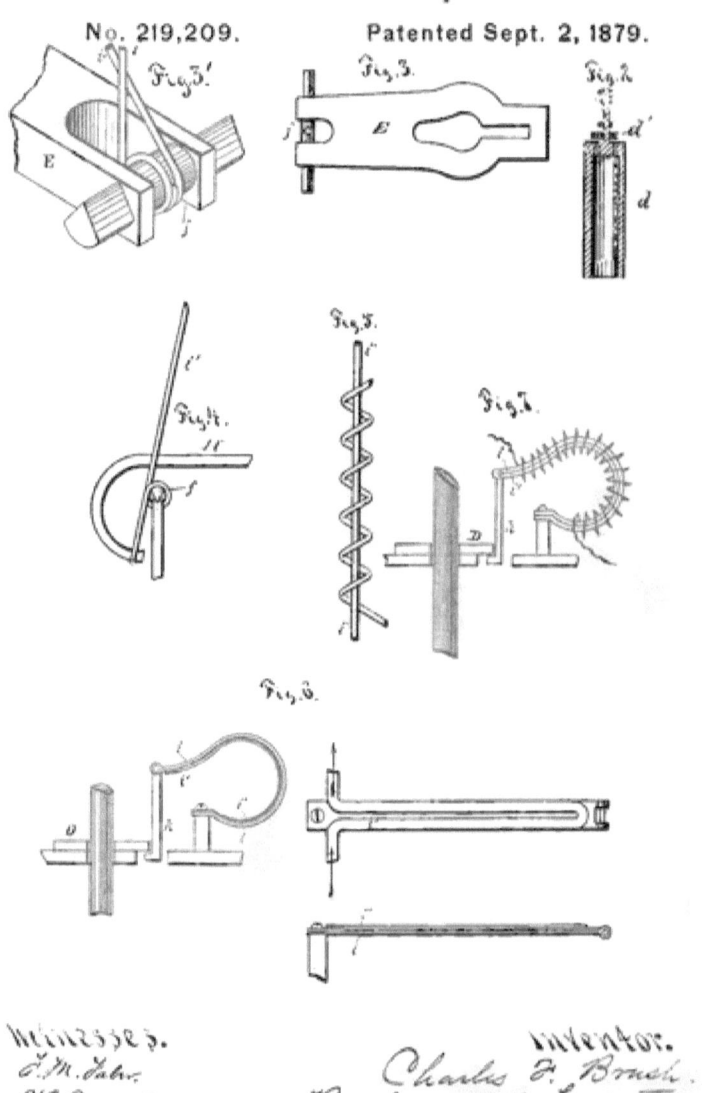

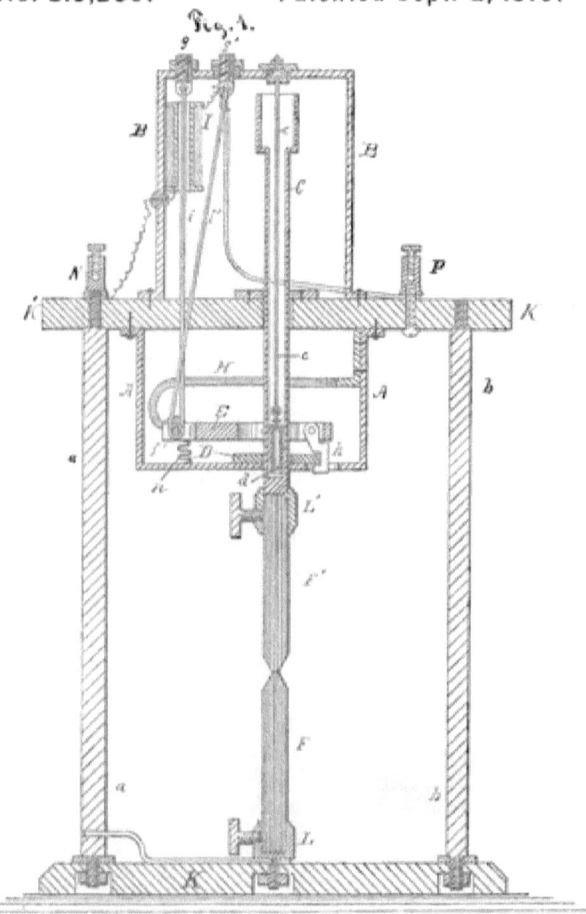

United States Patent Office.

CHARLES F. BRUSH, OF CLEVELAND, OHIO.

IMPROVEMENT IN ELECTRIC LAMPS.

Specification forming part of Letters Patent No. **219,209**, dated September 2, 1879; application filed May 16, 1879.

To all whom it may concern:

Be it known that I, CHARLES F. BRUSH, of Cleveland, in the county of Cuyahoga and State of Ohio, have invented certain new and useful Improvements in Electric Lamps; and I do hereby declare the following to be a full, clear, and exact description of the invention, such as will enable others skilled in the art to which it pertains to make and use it, reference being had to the accompanying drawings, which form part of this specification.

My invention relates to improvements in electric-light regulators; and it consists in the devices and appliances hereinafter set forth and claimed.

In the drawings, Figure 1 represents one form of my device as embodied in a lamp adapted for a to-and-fro current. Fig. 2 is a detached view, showing, in detail, my elongated plunger for use in the dash-pot, also showing its valvular construction. Fig. 3 is a detached plan view of the arm or lever E. Fig. 3' is a perspective view of the same device. Fig. 4 shows a modified arrangement of the heating wire or bar i^2. Fig. 5 shows the wire i^2 surrounded by the heating-spiral. Fig. 6 represents, in three views—viz., side elevation and two developed views—a modified arrangement of the elements $i\ i'$, in which my compensating principle is preserved. Fig. 7 shows a modification similar to Fig. 6, excepting that the compensating principle is not introduced. Figs. 8 and 9 are diagramatic representations, showing a system of several regulators having an induction apparatus and operated by a single current. Figs. 10 and 11 represent a lamp according to my invention adapted for use with a continuous current.

In Fig. 1, K is a base, of suitable material, to which are attached two metallic rods, $a\ b$, supporting a cross-piece of wood, K'. A carbon-holder, L, is attached to the base K, and carries the carbon F. This carbon-holder is electrically connected with the rod a, which latter carries a binding-post, N, at its upper end.

A B are metallic frames for supporting and containing the mechanism of the regulator, and are attached to the cross-piece K'. C is a tube of metal, closed at its lower end, and provided with a carbon-holder, L', in which is placed the carbon F'. The upper end of the tube C is enlarged, as shown. The tube C moves up and down freely through two bearings, one in the frame A, and the other attached to the cross-piece K', as shown. d is a piston, fitting freely in the tube C, and attached to the frame B by means of the rod or link e.

Fig. 2 shows the piston d enlarged. It is quite long, as compared with its diameter, is hollow the greater part of its length, and is provided at its upper end with several small openings, which are closed by a ring or washer fitting loosely on the rod which carries the piston. Thus the piston is provided with a valve opening upward.

In operation, the tube C, Fig. 1, is partly filled with glycerine or other suitable liquid, and then, with the piston d, forms a combined carbon-holder rod and dash-pot.

Owing to the valve d' in the piston d, the tube C may be pushed upward freely; but by the closing of this valve when a downward movement is commenced, the motion is greatly retarded, the rate of movement being determined by the rapidity of leakage of the glycerine past the piston d. This piston being made long, as before explained, renders the leakage very gradual, even when the piston does not fit very closely in the tube. Thus the descent of the tube C is very gradual, while its upward movement is free.

The valve d' in the piston d may be dispensed with, thus retarding both upward and downward movement of the tube C; but this is inconvenient when putting new carbons in the holder L', and is otherwise objectionable.

If the rod C is forcibly drawn down for any reason, a vacuum will be formed under the piston d, and the glycerine above the piston might overflow the tube, were it not for the enlargement of the latter at its upper end. This enlargement affords a reservoir for holding the glycerine in the case, as above described.

E, Fig. 1, is an arm or lever, of metal, provided at one end with a cylindrical cross-piece, of steel or other suitable material, f, as shown in plan in Fig. 3. The projecting ends of this cross-piece are formed into blunt knife-edges, as shown.

A wire, $i\ i^2$, of suitable size, and preferably of soft steel, is passed through a small hole in

the central part of the cross-piece or fulcrum f, and each half of the wire is then passed once or twice around the cylindrical portion of the cross-piece in opposite directions. The ends of this wire are then carried up and attached to the studs g g', as shown in Fig. 1. These studs are threaded, and provided with nuts above the frame B, as shown. The stud g' is insulated from the frame B by means of a suitable bushing in the hole through which it passes, but is electrically connected with the binding-post P.

H is a very stiff spring, of steel or other metal, attached to the frame A, and split at its free end, so as to engage with and form a support for the knife-edges at the extremities of the fulcrum f. The wires i i^2, being sufficiently strained by means of the screw-studs g g', hold the lever E firmly against the spring H, and in the position shown in the figure.

D is a ring-clamp or washer surrounding the tube C, and adapted to clamp and lift the latter when one side of the clamp is raised. h is a lifting-finger pivoted to the lever E, and adapted to lift the washer D when the free end of the lever E is raised. n is a flexible metallic connection between the lever E and frame A.

When the binding-posts P N are connected with a suitable source of electric current the path followed by said current will be as follows: From post P to stud g', thence through wire i^2 to lever E, then through n or H, or both, to frame A, tube C, carbons F' F, and rod a, to post N.

Under these conditions the wire i^2 will become more or less heated by the passage of the current through it, and will expand accordingly, while the wire i remains as before. The cylindrical portion of the fulcrum f, being partially relieved of its support on one side, will be carried downward by the powerful spring H, the free end of the lever E will be raised, and with it the lifting-finger h, clamp D, tube C, and carbon F', thus establishing the electric light between the carbons.

The amount of separation between the carbons may be adjusted by varying the relative tension of the wires i i^2 by means of the screw-studs g g'.

As the carbons burn away the current will diminish, owing to the increased resistance of the voltaic arc; the wire i^2 will become less hot, and will accordingly contract. The free end of the lever E will descend, and the carbon F' will move downward until the increased current caused thereby expands the wire i^2 and checks the movement. When the clamp D reaches the frame A under it, it will allow the tube C to slide through it until the increased current, due to the approach of the carbons, causes the washer D to again clamp and retain the tube C.

It will now be seen why the dash-pot arrangement of the tube C is provided; for if this provision were not made the tube C, being once released by the clamp D, would force the carbons entirely together before the clamping device could have time to act. The slow downward movement of the tube C prevents this accident.

A notable feature of my invention, as above described, is the use of two wires, i i^2, of the same metal. This feature I style my "compensating device." It insures the normal working of the apparatus at all temperatures, since it is the difference in temperature between the wires i i^2, and not the actual temperature of i^2, which determines the working of the apparatus.

In practice, the wires i i^2 are from fifteen to twenty inches long, and a difference in temperature between them of 200° Fahrenheit is ordinarily sufficient to operate the device. In ordinary working the temperature of the whole apparatus gradually rises considerably, and, of course, the absolute temperature of the wire i^2 augments accordingly, and were it not for my compensating device the operation of the regulator would be seriously affected.

Fig. 4 shows one of several forms of device in which but one wire, i^2, is employed. This device will obviously perform all the functions described in connection with Fig. 1, except compensation for changes of general temperature.

The wires i i^2 may be replaced by thin ribbons of metal, and this is even desirable, so far as that portion which passes around the fulcrum f is concerned, on account of greater flexibility; or this part may be ribbon and the rest wire.

The wire i^2 may be surrounded by a long helix, through which the current passes, while being itself insulated from the current, and thus be heated indirectly by the latter. Fig. 5 shows such a modification.

Instead of employing wires i i^2, as in Fig. 1, I may use narrow sheets of metal connected rigidly together, side by side, and insulated from each other both thermally and electrically.

The pair may be used straight, curved, or coiled, as in Fig. 6, which shows this form of my invention. Here the expansion of the inner strip of metal, i^2, by the heat due to the passage of current through it, while the outer strip, i, remains unheated, operates to raise the lifting-finger h. This arrangement of parts evidently embodies my compensating device, and is a mere modified form thereof.

Fig. 7 shows a device similar to Fig. 6; but the strips of metal i i^2 are of different metals, expanding unequally on the application of heat. They are riveted or soldered together, the metal i^2 being the more expansible of the two, and are both heated either by the passage of current through them, or by the passage of current through a helix surrounding them, as shown in the figure.

The operation of the device is evident, but it lacks the compensating feature, which was retained in the device shown in Fig. 6.

My invention, so far as described, is equally useful with rapidly intermittent, alternating,

it it is especially
nts where magnet-

tors, such as I have
single circuit, con-
nt, they will work
her regulators of
uous current. The
of action is fully
No. 212,183, grant-

rrect this irregu-
of the adjusting-
nate effect of this
s the same as that
scribed in the Let-
to; but its opera-

posed of many con-
ends of which are
 the binding-post
d its connections,
hus the helix forms
between the bind-
es are thus afforded
regulator—one of
e through the car-
omparatively high
: I—the amount of
ch channel being
ance; but the act-
is much greater for
s than for continu-
nductive action of
rrent on its neigh-
his disturbing ele-
hen calculating the

n insulating-spool,
s the wire i, which,
or steel.
 is operated by a
current, magnet-
olarity will be in-
will thus become

ous of the helix I
e so arranged that
lternating magnet-
s than the heat de-
be passage of the
hen the voltaic arc
mal length. Here,
in temperature be-
es the operation of

arbons burn away
eir normal distance
be materially less-
ors are in circuit,
in its temperature,
art; but, owing to
he voltaic are, more
rough the helix I,
of the wire i will be
y its temperature.
uction of tempera-

ture in the wire i^1, and the carbon F' is allowed to move downward. On the other hand,
if the carbons approach too near together less
current will pass through the helix, the wire i
will become cooler, which is equivalent to an
increase of temperature in the wire i^1, and the
carbon will be separated. Thus, by means of
the adjusting heating-helix I, any number of
these regulators may be operated uniformly on
a single suitable alternating current.

When a large number of regulators of any
kind are operated directly by a single electric
current, the danger of extinguishing all by
breaking the circuit in any one is considerable;
and in view of this fact I shall briefly, and in
a general way, refer to a method for correcting
this objectionable feature. It is my purpose,
however, soon to apply for separate Letters
Patent upon the system, or what may be termed
the "inductive method," which I shall pres-
ently refer to, and therefore I do not waive, on
account of what I shall now describe, any right
to a subsequent application for patent upon
such device or method. By combining my "ex-
pansion-regulator" (as I have styled the one
above described) with a suitable form of dy-
namic induction apparatus, and using a rap-
idly-alternating current, I avoid this danger,
since in this case the main circuit through which
the current passes is unbroken under all circumstances.

Figs. 8 and 9 of the drawings show in a diagramatic manner a battery, or preferably a
dynamo-electric machine, Z, designed to maintain a current through the circuit Z^1. It is
commonly the practice to cut the circuit Z^1
and introduce into it one or more electric
lamps, in such a manner that the current
through said circuit Z^1 shall pass through and
directly operate them. Instead of so doing,
however, I propose, if desired, to operate the
lamps by an induced current due to and generated by the current of the circuit Z^1.

I shall not here specify any particular elec-
tro-induction apparatus, reserving such a description for a proposed subsequent application, as above stated.

It is well known that when an electric current is started in one of two parallel and adjacent conductors an inverse current is induced
in the other conductor, lasting only until the
inducing-current has obtained its maximum
strength; and that when the inducing-current
is stopped or diminished a direct current is induced in the neighboring conductor. I propose to utilize these facts in the construction
of my induction apparatus alluded to, whereby
a current through the circuit Z^1 will set up an
induced current in each circuit Z^2 of an electric lamp, Z^3, as diagramatically illustrated in
Figs. 8 and 9. By such an arrangement and
system as just intimated, and as suggested in
Figs. 8 and 9 of the drawings, several lights
might be operated upon a single circuit, and
the removal or extinguishing of any one or
more from any cause whatever would not materially affect the operation of any other lamp

that might be operated by the current through the circuit Z'.

Having now, for the purposes of the present specification, sufficiently alluded to the induction system suggested in Figs. 8 and 9 of the drawings, and having hereinbefore alluded to the fact that my invention is equally applicable to lamps employing a to-and-fro, pulsating, or a constant current, I shall now briefly explain how my invention may be embodied in a lamp suitable for a continuous current operating more than one lamp; and for this purpose I have shown two forms of device in Figs. 10 and 11 of the drawings.

In Fig. 10 the wire i^3 is placed in the general circuit, and is made of sufficiently high resistance to be heated by the current operating the lamp, and the difference in temperature between the wires i and i^3 and the consequent difference in expansion and length of said wires, as before pointed out, is the direct means whereby the lifter D is moved.

In the form of lamp shown in Fig. 10, I is an adjusting-helix, which is always in closed circuit, and the amount of current passing through it is always regulated by the resistance of the voltaic arc—that is, if the voltaic arc becomes too long, and thereby offers an abnormally great resistance, the current is increased through the helix I, and vice versa, as already explained in Fig. 1. This helix is made to attract an armature, I', which is pivoted to the lamp and electrically connected with the general circuit.

i^3 is a branch wire from the wire i^2, and it is made to terminate just above the armature I' as it rests in its open-circuit position.

The operation of the device, as just described and shown in Fig. 10, will be as follows: The difference in tension between the wires i and i^3, due to the heating of the wire i^3 by the current operating the lamp, will act to raise the lifter D, as already specified, in the to-and-fro-current type of lamp. So long as the voltaic arc does not offer any abnormally great resistance, the parts will be substantially in the relative positions shown in the drawings, Fig. 10; but when, for any reason, it is necessary that the lamp should feed, or that the lifter D should descend, or the wire i^3 made cooler, such a necessity will result in a condition of things that will cause an increased current through the helix, sufficient to draw up the armature I' until it comes into electrical contact with the branch wire i^3. This will greatly diminish the current passing through the wire i^3, and its heat will be consequently and correspondingly decreased, and this will result in a re-establishment of normal relation between the carbons and other parts to put the lamp again in proper operation. And now, the current having a sufficiently free passage through the carbons, the magnetism of the helix I will be so weakened that the armature I' will be released, and break the circuit through the branch i^3, and now the current passing through the wire i^3 will again heat it. This operation is manifestly equivalent to cooling the wire i, as it is the relative temperatures of the wires i and i^3 that determine their relative tension, and, consequently, their lifting action upon the carbon-separating apparatus.

I have, in Fig. 10, shown how the wire i^3 may be cooled by automatically shunting its heating current from it as necessary. This function or equivalent is susceptible of being performed in a variety of ways—as, for instance, by any arrangement such as the interposition between the armature I' and branch wires i^3 of a variable resistance, governed by the condition of the voltaic arc and the resulting magnetism of the helix I; or the heat of the wire i^3 may be governed by purely mechanical contrivance, and one such arrangement is shown in Fig. 11, where the wire i^3 is surrounded by a tube.

The relative positions of the wires i i^3, Fig. 11, are modified as shown merely for convenience in locating and applying the tube i^2. This tube i^2, in the form shown in the drawings, is held stationary in the frame of the lamp, and is closed at its bottom by any suitable valve arrangement operated by a magnet-lever, which is moved by the attractive force of the helix I. Now, as the wire i^3 needs cooling for purposes before pointed out, the current through the helix I will be sufficient to draw up the magnet and open the valve at the bottom of the tube i^2, thus admitting air into said tube, and allowing the inclosed wire i^3 to cool, for when the tube i^2 is closed the loss of heat from the wire i^3 is greatly impeded, and a given amount of current will more rapidly and intensely heat it than though it were freely exposed to the air. Thus, by governing the circulation of air around the wire i^3 in any manner, its temperature may be controlled so as to insure a proper operation of the lifter D according to the varying conditions of the voltaic arc.

When the character of the current operating the lamp is such that the wire i^3, in order to be sufficiently heated, is too small to be of sufficient strength, one or more similar wires may be added to it, so connected with other parts of the apparatus that the current shall pass through them successively. Thus the strength of as many wires as may be necessary will be secured.

As respects the heating of the wires i or i^3, or their equivalent, I do not limit myself, as my invention consists in any appropriate method of accomplishing this heating, which might be accomplished by a shunt-current, either constant, pulsating, or alternating, or by the adjusting-helix, as shown, or by a variety of other methods; nor do I limit myself to any specific method of controlling the movement of the carbon rod or holder C by a dash-pot or equivalent contrivance. This may be effected by making the carbon-holder itself the cylinder of the dash-pot, as shown in Fig. 1 of the drawings; or, as shown in Figs. 12, 13, and 14, the carbon-holder may have a suf-

ficiently slow and steady movement by any suitable connection with a dash-pot placed adjacent to it.

Fig. 12 of the drawings illustrates one method where a carbon or carbon-holder, L', is connected with a dash-pot, C d, by a belt-and-pulley arrangement. Fig. 13 illustrates the same arrangement, where a pulley might be dispensed with; and Fig. 14 represents a belt-and-pulley connection between dash-pot and carbon, wherein a dash-pot of a shorter length than in the forms shown in Figs. 12 and 13 might be used.

What I claim is—

1. In combination with the wires i i', or their equivalent, an adjusting-helix, I, or its equivalent, through the influence of which the wires i i' are maintained at suitably different temperatures, substantially as and for the purposes described.

2. In an electric lamp wherein the carbon-moving apparatus is actuated by the expansive action of heat upon some portion of said apparatus, the wires i and i', or their equivalents, adapted, as required for the varying conditions for maintaining a continuous and steady light, to be differently heated, said difference of heating automatically caused and controlled substantially as and for the purposes described.

3. An electric lamp wherein the separation and government of the carbons are effected by reason of the difference in temperature between the wires i i', or their equivalent, substantially as and for the purposes described.

4. In an electric lamp, the combination, with a moving carbon or its holder, of a clamp constructed to grasp and move said carbon or carbon-holder, and, in connection with said clamp, suitable mechanism adapted to be set in motion or controlled by the expansive effect of heat generated by the electric current operating the lamp, substantially as shown.

5. In an electric lamp, the combination, with a moving carbon-holder, of a tube, C, said tube constituting the body or cylinder and a moving element of the dash-pot, substantially as shown.

In testimony whereof I have signed my name to this specification in the presence of two subscribing witnesses.

CHARLES F. BRUSH.

Witnesses:
LEVERETT L. LEGGETT,
JNO. CROWELL, Jr.

Assigned to Brush Electric Co. -- JAN 8 1...

THE UNITED STATES OF AMERICA

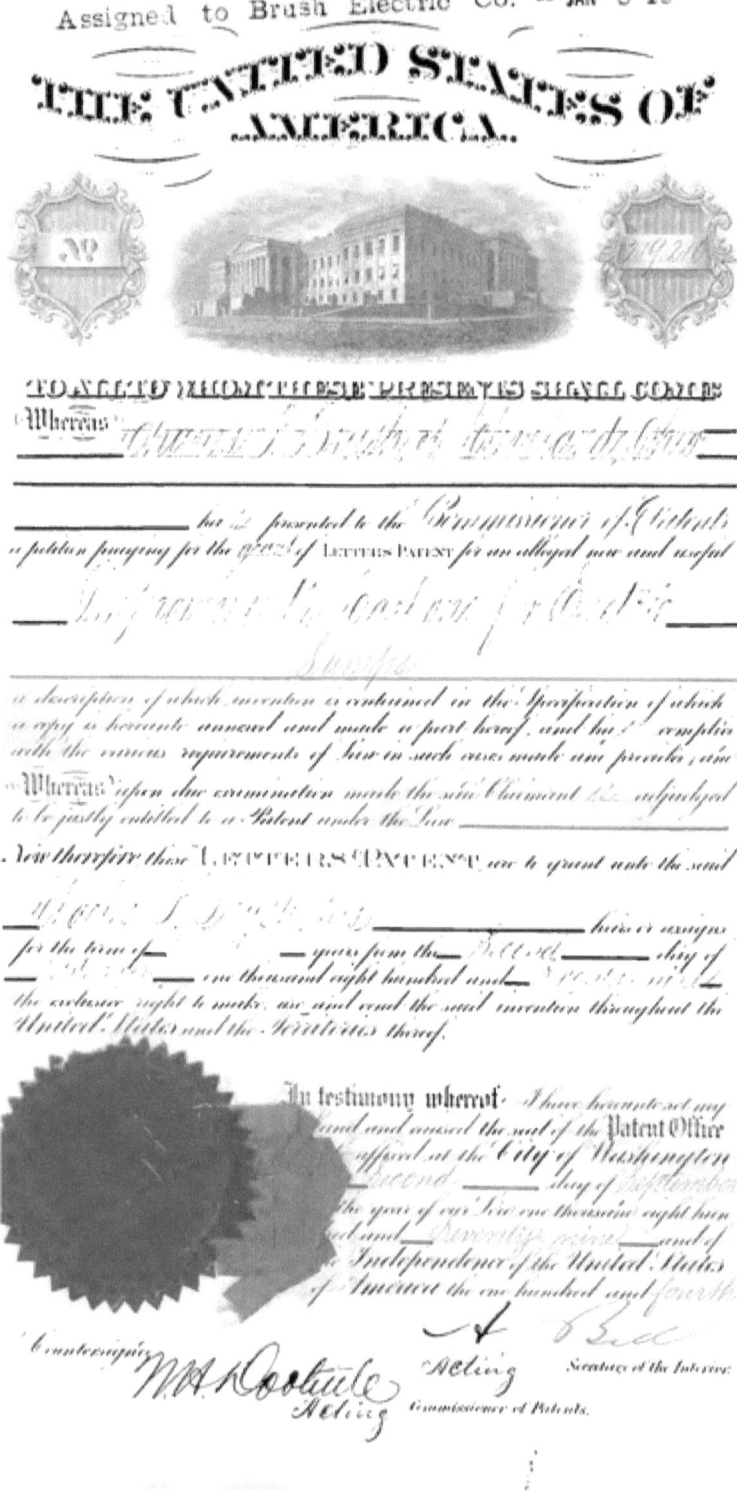

TO ALL TO WHOM THESE PRESENTS SHALL COME

Whereas _____

_____ has presented to the Commissioner of Patents a petition praying for the grant of LETTERS PATENT for an alleged new and useful

_____ Improvement in Carbons for Electric Lamps _____

a description of which invention is contained in the Specification of which a copy is hereunto annexed and made a part hereof, and has complied with the various requirements of law in such cases made and provided, and

Whereas upon due examination made the said Claimant is adjudged to be justly entitled to a Patent under the Law _____

Now therefore these LETTERS PATENT are to grant unto the said

_____ his or assigns

for the term of _____ years from the _____ day of _____ one thousand eight hundred and _____ the exclusive right to make, use and vend the said invention throughout the United States and the Territories thereof.

In testimony whereof I have hereunto set my hand and caused the seal of the Patent Office to be affixed at the City of Washington this _____ day of September in the year of our Lord one thousand eight hundred and Seventy-nine and of the Independence of the United States of America the one hundred and fourth.

Countersigned
W. H. Doolittle
Acting Commissioner of Patents

Acting Secretary of the Interior

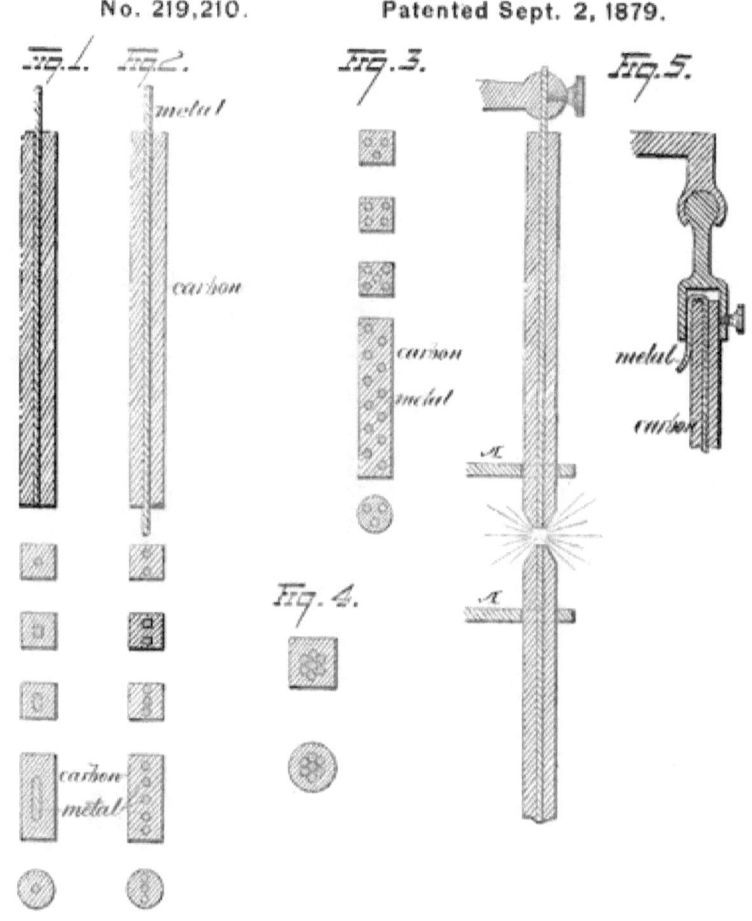

C. F. BRUSH.
Carbons for Electric-Lamps.

No. 219,210. Patented Sept. 2, 1879.

UNITED STATES PATENT OFFICE.

CHARLES F. BRUSH, OF CLEVELAND, OHIO.

IMPROVEMENT IN CARBONS FOR ELECTRIC LAMPS.

Specification forming part of Letters Patent No. **219,210**, dated September 2, 1879; application filed November 8, 1878.

To all whom it may concern:

Be it known that I, CHARLES F. BRUSH, of Cleveland, in the county of Cuyahoga and State of Ohio, have invented certain new and useful Improvements in Electric-Lamp Carbons and mode of attaching same; and do hereby declare the following to be a full, clear, and exact description of the invention, such as will enable others skilled in the art to which it pertains to make and use it, reference being had to the accompanying drawings, which form part of this specification.

My invention relates to electric-lighting apparatus, and especially to the carbons or illuminating-points of such apparatus; and my said invention consists in means for attaching these carbons to a lamp or regulator; also, in the combination, with either one or both carbons of any electric lamp, of a suitable supporting or guiding device, whereby a proper apposition of the carbons is insured, and whereby liability to a material lateral displacement of the carbons on account of jolting or other cause is prevented.

My invention, furthermore, consists in a carbon containing or inclosing a rod, cable, wire, or ribbon of copper, or equivalent electro-conducting substance, said electro-conductor extending throughout the length of the carbon, and projecting from one end of said carbon to afford, when attached to a lamp, a flexible and automatically-adjusting and yielding joint or connection between the carbon and lamp mechanism.

In the drawings, Figure 1 shows various forms of carbons inclosing a single metallic conductor of various forms of cross-section. Fig. 2 shows said carbons inclosing two or more of said metallic conductors. In both of these figures the conductors are shown, according to my invention, projecting from one or both ends of the carbons. Fig. 3 shows several of many ways of arranging several conductors within various forms of carbons. Fig. 4 shows a cable of several conductors inclosed within carbons; and Fig. 5 illustrates a method of utilizing the projecting ends of the conductors to afford a flexible and automatically-adjusting and yielding connection between the carbon and the lamp. Fig. 5 also shows one of an indefinite variety of forms of my support or guide, which operates to insure a proper presentation of the carbons to each other, and to prevent the liability of their material lateral displacement; and this guiding and supporting device I consider to be a very important feature of my invention, and I do not propose to be limited to the specific form shown in the drawings, inasmuch as this element of my device and invention is susceptible of an indefinite degree and variety of modification.

In the use of the electric light in places where the mechanism or carbons are subjected to jolting, (as, for instance, in a locomotive headlight,) any form of lamp of which I am aware would be inoperative, as its illuminating-points, not having any guides or supports, could not be maintained in that proper line or apposition with each other which is an essential requisite in maintaining a satisfactory light.

In Fig. 5 of the drawings, A represents the guide or support referred to, and this guiding or supporting device may partially or completely surround the carbon, or it may impinge against it in any manner so long as it shall operate to guide its carbon to a proper apposition with its fellow of opposite polarity, and also operate to maintain the illuminating-points of said carbons against material lateral displacement. This guiding and supporting device may be made adjustable in its position, so that its proper application to the carbon under all circumstances can be made. It is equally suitable to the carbons of any lamp, whether said carbons are attached to the lamp by a rigid or by a flexible or yielding connection.

I have found when experimenting with powerful electric currents that it is impracticable to employ sufficiently thin carbon sticks to produce the best illuminating effect on account of their high resistance and consequent rapid consumption, due to the action of the air on the highly-heated carbon. A great amount of heat is generated in small carbons in consequence of their resistance, aside from the heat produced at the ends by the voltaic arc. The resistance of the carbons is detrimental, not only for the reasons given above, but on account of the loss or waste of current occasioned thereby.

I have sought to provide a remedy for these

evils, and have fully accomplished my purpose by inclosing within the carbon rod, stick, disk, or plate one or more wires, rods, ribbons, or cables of copper or any good electro-conducting material. The main objects of this construction are to decrease the resistance of the carbons and to provide a ready means of electrically connecting the carbon to its holder in a thorough manner. This last important object is attained by allowing the copper or other conductors to project beyond the end of the carbons proper, thus allowing them to be connected with the source of electricity easily and thoroughly. This construction also allows the projecting conductor, when made of suitable pliable material, to perform the functions of a universal joint for centering the carbons in the regulator when the other ends of the carbons are provided with a support or guide, A, Fig. 5, through which the carbons slide as they are consumed. This method of using carbons is of great value when the regulator is subjected to much jolting or other violent motion, as in the case of electric locomotive head-lights, &c.

Although many other forms of universal joint, such as the ball-and-socket, &c., may be employed in combination with the carbon-supports, as above, using carbons either with or without the inclosed conductors, I find the use of the projecting conductor the most simple and effective device for this purpose.

I do not in any degree limit myself to any manner or method of inclosing said conductors in said carbons. I prefer to inclose a single copper wire of suitable size in each carbon during the process of its manufacture, and while the carbon (or mixture of carbon and other material for increasing its illuminating power, such as lime, alumina, magnesia, gypsum, &c.) is in a pulverized or plastic condition; but, instead of this, the carbons may be formed with suitable cavities, in which the metallic or other conductor is afterward inserted or cast in a melted state.

In operation, the intense heat generated by the voltaic arc melts and disperses the inclosed conductors at the opposing points of the carbons and for a proper distance beyond, while as fast as the carbons are consumed just so fast will the inclosed conductor be removed.

In Letters Patent numbered 196,425, granted to me October 23, 1877, I described carbons coated with a suitable metallic substance, thus securing some of the advantages of my present invention. The principal objection to my former device arises from the fact that the voltaic arc, seeking the path of least resistance, frequently leaves the center of the carbon rods—its normal position—and plays from side to side around the outer portion of the carbons, attracted by the vapor of the volatilized copper or other metal, or by the metal itself. This produces a disagreeable flickering of the light. Further, a deposit of metallic oxide, silicate, &c., often collects about the lower carbon at its edges, thus obstructing much of the light.

My present invention obviates these grave difficulties, while securing most of the advantages of my former one.

What I claim, broadly, is—

1. In an electric lamp, a carbon having a jointed or flexible connection with said lamp, and one or more guides partially or completely surrounding said carbon, for the purpose of directing it to a proper apposition with its fellow or opposite carbon, substantially as specified.

2. In an electric lamp, a carbon provided with the described inclosed conductor, made of pliable material, and projecting beyond the end of the carbon, said conductor being adapted to serve as a universal joint for centering the carbon in the regulator, substantially as set forth.

3. The combination of one or more guides, A, adapted to impinge against or to surround a carbon of an electric lamp, with a flexible or jointed connecting or attaching device between said carbon and electric lamp, substantially as and for the purpose shown.

In testimony whereof I have signed my name to this specification in the presence of two subscribing witnesses.

CHARLES F. BRUSH.

Witnesses:
WILLARD FRACKER,
W. E. DONNELLY.

Assigned to Brush Electric Co. -- JAN 8 18

THE UNITED STATES OF AMERICA.

TO ALL TO WHOM THESE PRESENTS SHALL COME

C. F. BRUSH.
Electric-Lighting Device.

No. 219,211. Patented Sept. 2, 1879.

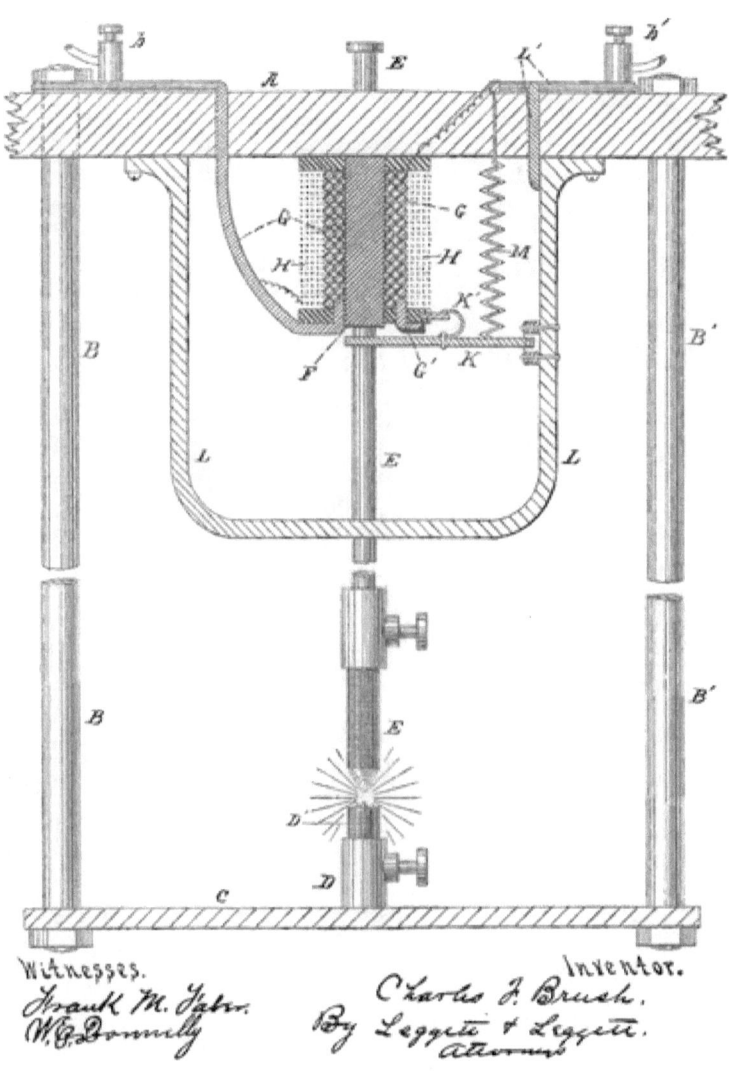

UNITED STATES PATENT OFFICE.

CHARLES F. BRUSH, OF CLEVELAND, OHIO.

IMPROVEMENT IN ELECTRIC LIGHTING DEVICES.

Specification forming part of Letters Patent No. **219,211**, dated September 2, 1879; application filed July 3, 1879.

To all whom it may concern:

Be it known that I, CHARLES F. BRUSH, of Cleveland, in the county of Cuyahoga and State of Ohio, have invented certain new and useful Improvements in Electric Lighting Devices; and I do hereby declare the following to be a full, clear, and exact description of the invention, such as will enable others skilled in the art to which it pertains to make and use it, reference being had to the accompanying drawing, which forms part of this specification.

My invention relates to electric lamps or light-regulators; and it consists in the combination, with the mechanism operating the carbons of the arc type of said lamps, of an automatic shunt or cut-off and a resistance, so constructed, combined, and electrically connected that if for any reason the said shunt or cut-off shall have operated to extinguish the lamp when it was in a normally operative condition the light shall be automatically re-established upon a reunion of the electrodes—as, for instance, if carbon a stick should break, and thus destroy the arc. In such a case, the resistance in the lamp being infinite, the cut-off would operate to shunt said lamp out of the circuit by establishing a path of low resistance for the current outside of the electrodes and the mechanism operating them. But whenever for any such accidental cause the cut-off mechanism is called into action it is not desirable that the lamp should be permanently extinguished, for the reason that the lamp proper is not at fault, and is still in a perfectly operative condition.

My design therefore is that upon a reunion of the electrodes the cut-off or shunting mechanism shall cease to operate, and that the current shall be properly re-established in the lamp and its light continued.

I will now describe a form of device by which the functions above alluded to may be automatically performed.

In the drawing is represented, in longitudinal vertical section, one form of device according to my invention.

A is a bar or slab, of wood or any suitable electro-non-conducting substance. B is an iron rod attached at its upper end to the slab A and at its lower end to an iron cross-piece, C. B' is another rod, of any material, mechanically connecting the parts A C. D is a holder for a carbon, D'. The parts B C D D' are electrically connected with each other.

E is a vertically-sliding rod or tube of brass or other suitable electro-conducting material, ending below in a holder for retaining a carbon, E'.

The separation of the electrodes D' E' is accomplished by moving the rod E. Instead of here specifying how movement is imparted to this rod, I will refer to United States Letters Patent No. 203,411, granted to me May 7, 1878, and reissued May 20, 1879, No. 8,718. In these will be found fully described a very effective form of mechanism for the purpose of moving the rod E.

But I desire it to be distinctly understood that in my present invention I do not in any degree limit myself either to the carbon-separating mechanism shown in the patents above named or to any other definite means for separating the electrodes or governing them in their relations to each other.

My invention is equally applicable to all forms of arc-lamps—*i. e.*, lamps wherein light is obtained by the passage of the electric current through separated electrodes.

F is an electro-magnet core of soft iron. It is surrounded by two helices, G H, and is attached to the slab A. The helix G is of coarse wire and of correspondingly low resistance. The helix H is of fine wire, and it offers a high resistance to the current. This helix H is always in closed circuit with the current operating the lamp, so that said current divides itself between the helix H and the lamp's electrodes in proportion to the relative resistances offered in these two paths in manner and effect hereinafter more fully to appear.

The coarse-wire helix G connects with the pole b at one end, and, after describing a sufficient number of convolutions about the core F, terminates blindly, as shown at G', thus forming no part of a closed circuit, while the armature K is separated from it, as shown in the drawing.

The armature K, while being insulated from the lamp-frame L, is pivotally attached thereto. Its drop and consequent distance in separation from the core F is determined by any suitable adjustable stop K'. As the armature K is held closer to or farther from the core F a

proportionately weaker or stronger current through the fine-wire helix H will be required to lift said armature into contact with the end G' of the coarse-wire helix G.

M is a resistance electrically connecting the armature K and the pole b' of the lamp.

The lamp-casing L is electrically connected with the rod E, and also, through the wire L', with the pole b'.

Having now specified one of a variety of means for carrying out my invention, I will describe the operation of the same.

While the lamp is in normal operation the various parts are in substantially the relation shown in the drawing, and the current is, say, from the pole b', through the wire L', frame L, and rod E, to the carbon E'; thence, through the carbon D', its holder D, the cross-piece C, and rod B, to the opposite pole, b. Here is the path for the major portion of the current; but, as already said, there are two paths between which the current divides itself, according to their respective and relative resistances. One is that already traced out. The other is, say, from the pole b', through the wire L', fine-wire helix H, coarse wire G, to the opposite pole b. Now, when the resistance in the lamp proper is normal the armature K is in its open-circuit position—i. e., dropped down and separated from the end G' of the coarse-wire helix G; but if, for any reason, the resistance in the lamp (say, at the electric arc) is abnormally great, then the current will be greatly increased through the fine-wire helix H until the core becomes sufficiently magnetic to draw up its armature K into contact with the end G' of the coarse-wire helix. As soon as this connection is made the electrodes are practically cut out of the circuit, for now the path of the current is from pole b', through the wire L', resistance M, armature K, and helix G, to the opposite pole b.

So long as the current takes this course the coarse-wire helix G forms a part of a closed circuit and strongly magnetizes the core F.

We now find the electrodes D' E' and the mechanism separating them released from the control of the operating current. Therefore the carbons, by force of gravity, will fall into contact with one another to the position of closed circuit.

At this time, if the lamp is in a normally operative condition, it is desirable that the cut-off or shunting mechanism cease its operation, and that the current be again established through the electrodes, so as to produce the arc-light; and this will be accomplished, for, now, the carbons being united, they will offer a passage to the current having a resistance so much lower than offered by the resistance M that the current through the coarse-wire helix G will be so weakened that the core F will not be sufficiently magnetic to sustain its armature K, which will drop, and thus break the circuit at that point and re-establish the normal flow through the electrodes; but if the lamp is in such inoperative condition as to continue its abnormal resistance to the passage of the current, then the armature K will not be released, but will be maintained in its closed-circuit position, and the lamp will be permanently extinguished.

It will thus be seen that any accidental or immaterial cause, while it may call into action for a time the shunting mechanism, will not result in the continued extinguishment of the lamp.

The great utility of this automatic shunt will easily be recognized when it is employed with lamps several of which are burning in a single circuit, for in such a case the putting out of one lamp would extinguish all the rest, unless the current be provided a passage, as it were, around and outside of the faulty lamp.

I have found by repeated experiment and practical use in a system according to my invention, where a number of lights are burning in a single circuit, that the extinguishment and relighting of any lamp, as heretofore specified, is certainly effected, and without any interruption of the remaining lights on the circuit, the only influence being an augmentation of the arc proportionate to the small increase of current passing through said remaining lamps.

I do not limit myself to any definite number, arrangement, or construction of parts in any device for carrying out my invention. The form shown in the drawing is merely given to exhibit one embodiment of said invention and to assist in explaining the same.

Any form or construction of mechanism may be adopted which shall operate, first, to automatically shunt the current from a lamp when for any cause it shall offer an abnormally great resistance to the passage of the current; and, second, to continue to afford a free passage to the current independent of said lamp so long as said abnormal resistance in the lamp shall exist; and, third, to re-establish the normal operation of the extinguished lamp upon a reunion of its electrodes.

I do not here claim a device performing merely as pointed out in the first and second features just above specified, as such an invention is shown and broadly claimed by me in a prior application. It is the third function above-named that particularly constitutes the essence of my present invention.

What I claim is—

1. The resistance M, or its equivalent, in combination with any contrivance adapted to shunt the current from an electric lamp when for any reason said lamp shall offer an abnormally great resistance to the passage of the current operating it, substantially as and for the purpose shown.

2. The combination, with the electrodes D' E' of an electric lamp and the mechanism separating and governing said electrodes, of a suitable shunt or cut-off and a resistance, M, or its equivalent, said shunt or cut-off adapted automatically to afford a sufficiently free pas-

sage for the current independent of the lamp when from any cause said lamp shall offer an abnormally great resistance to the passage of said current, and said resistance adapted, on the union of said electrodes, to weaken or break the circuit through said shunt, and thus to re-establish the normal flow of current through the electrodes and reproduce the electric light, substantially as shown.

3. In combination with the carbons of an electric lamp and the mechanism operating them, an automatic shunt or cut-off device constructed to offer a resistance greater than the resistance offered by the said carbons when in contact, said shunt or cut-off constructed, first, to be called into operation to extinguish said lamp whenever from any cause it (the said lamp) shall offer an abnormally great resistance to the passage of the electric current, and, second, to be automatically relieved from said operation upon a reunion of the extinguished electrodes by reason of said electrodes offering a path to the current of a lower resistance than the resistance offered by said shunt or cut-off device, substantially as and for the purposes shown.

In testimony whereof I have signed my name to this specification in the presence of two subscribing witnesses.

CHARLES F. BRUSH.

Witnesses:
LEVERETT L. LEGGETT,
JNO. CROWELL, Jr.

Assigned to Brush Electric Co. -- JAN 8 18

THE UNITED STATES OF AMERICA

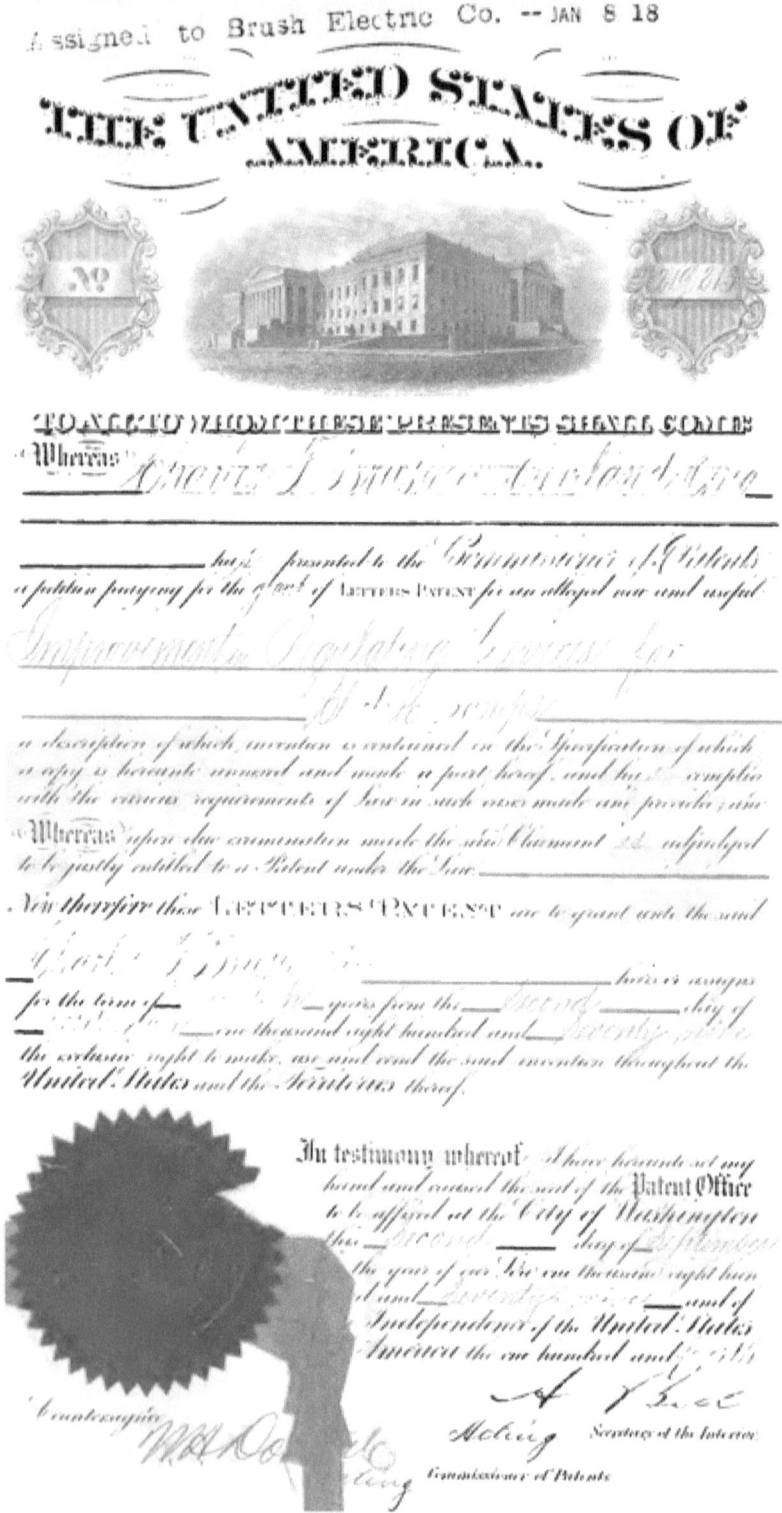

TO ALL TO WHOM THESE PRESENTS SHALL COME

Whereas _____

_____ has presented to the Commissioner of Patents a petition praying for the grant of LETTERS PATENT for an alleged new and useful Improvement in _____

_____

a description of which invention is contained in the Specification of which a copy is hereunto annexed and made a part hereof, and has complied with the various requirements of law in such cases made and provided, and

Whereas upon due examination made the said Claimant is adjudged to be justly entitled to a Patent under the law _____

Now therefore these LETTERS PATENT are to grant unto the said _____ his heirs or assigns for the term of _____ years from the _____ day of _____ one thousand eight hundred and _____ the exclusive right to make, use and vend the said invention throughout the United States and the Territories thereof.

In testimony whereof I have hereunto set my hand and caused the seal of the Patent Office to be affixed at the City of Washington this _____ day of September in the year of our Lord one thousand eight hundred and Seventy _____ and of the Independence of the United States of America the one hundred and _____.

Secretary of the Interior.

Countersigned
_____
Commissioner of Patents.

C. F. BRUSH.
Regulating Device for Electric-Lamps.

No. 219,213. Patented Sept. 2, 1879.

Fig. 5.

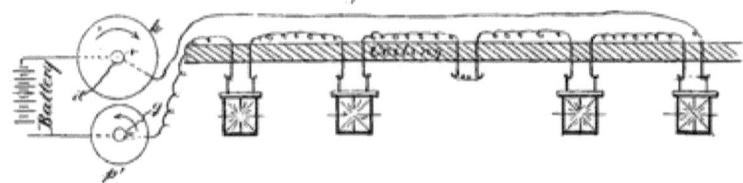

Fig. 6.

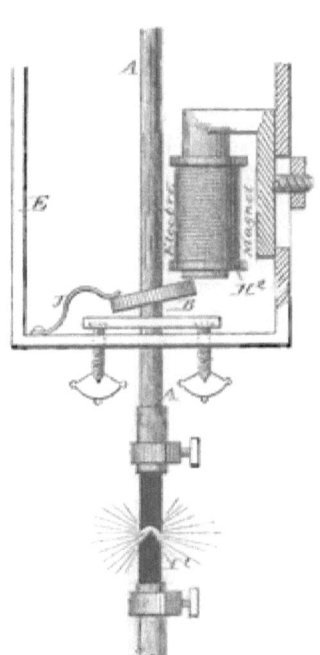

WITNESSES
E. F. Nottingham
Geo. D. Seymour

INVENTOR
Chas. F. Brush.
By Leggett & Leggett,
ATTORNEYS

C. F. BRUSH.
Regulating Device for Electric-Lamps.

No. 219,213. Patented Sept. 2, 1879.

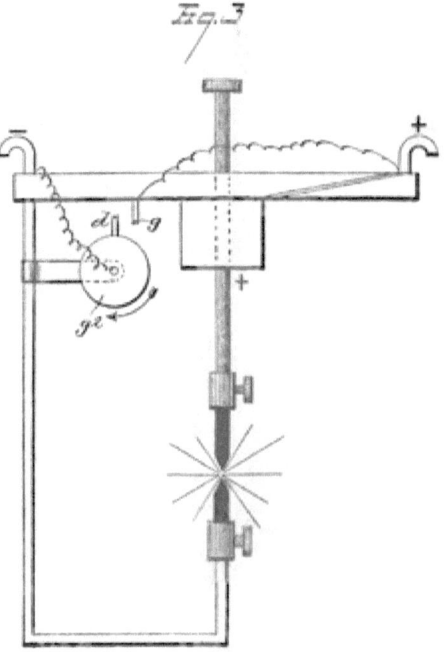

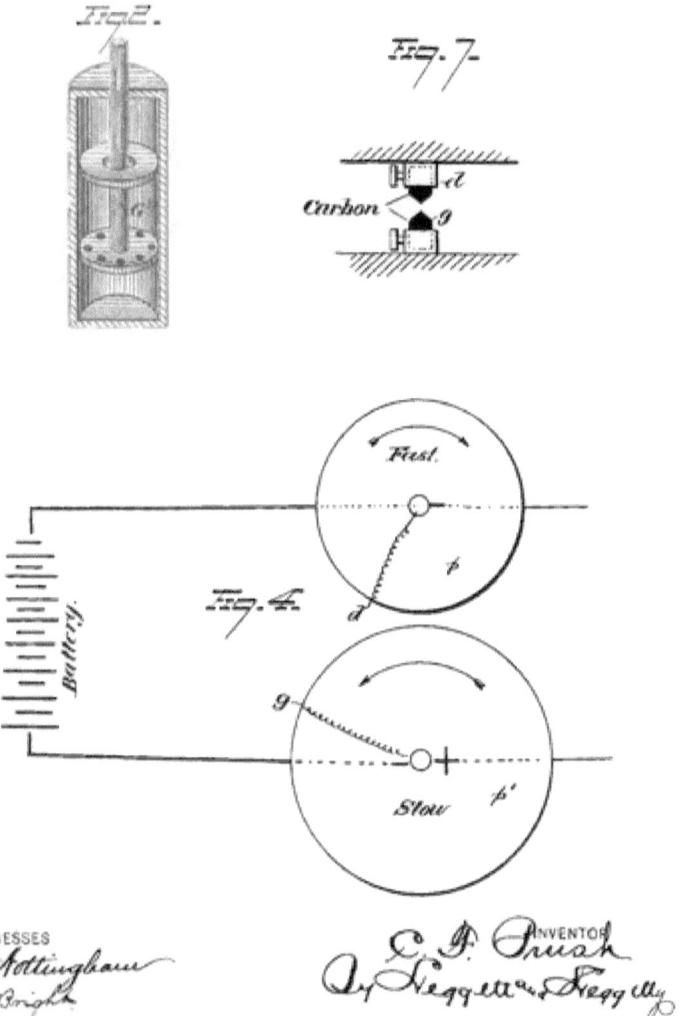

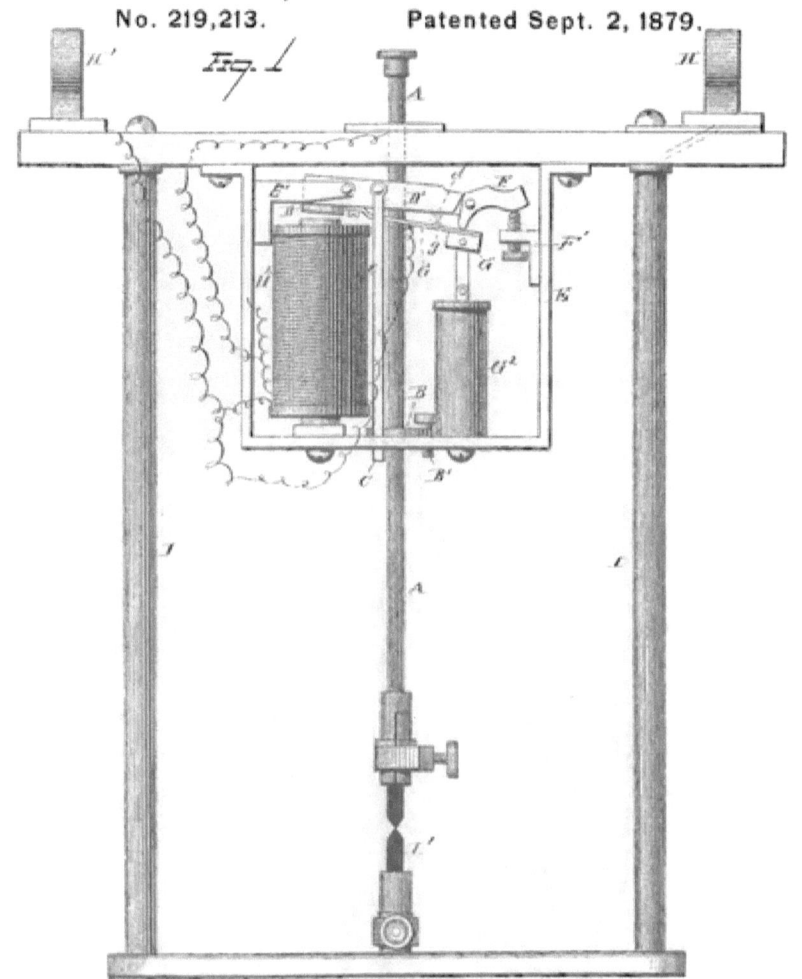

UNITED STATES PATENT OFFICE.

CHARLES F. BRUSH, OF CLEVELAND, OHIO.

IMPROVEMENT IN REGULATING DEVICES FOR ELECTRIC LAMPS.

Specification forming part of Letters Patent No. 219,213, dated September 2, 1879; application filed October 24, 1878.

To all whom it may concern:

Be it known that I, CHARLES F. BRUSH, of Cleveland, in the county of Cuyahoga and State of Ohio, have invented certain new and useful Improvements in Apparatus for Producing Electric Light; and I do hereby declare the following to be a full, clear, and exact description of the invention, such as will enable others skilled in the art to which it pertains to make and use it, reference being had to the accompanying drawings, which form part of this specification.

My invention relates to electric lighting apparatus; and it consists in a lamp or regulator, or a system of lamps or regulators on a single circuit, adapted, by any suitable means, to separate the carbons to any given or adjusted degree, and at intervals independent of the influence of the electric current operating the lamp or lamps, to bring said carbons into contact with each other, allow them to feed, as necessary, and then immediately to separate them to said given or adjusted distance, which distance is to be previously gaged according to the amount of the electric current. This may be accomplished by a combination of mechanical and electric apparatus which may be used to perform these functions, and this, probably, would be my preferred construction; and I will herein specify one such form of device, though it is understood that I do not limit myself to any given mechanism whatever.

In the drawings, Figure 1 represents, in side elevation, one form of device according to my invention. Fig. 2 shows detached and detail views of some of the parts of such a device as set forth in Fig. 1. Fig. 4 shows another modified form of device according to my invention. Fig. 5 represents a form and arrangement of my invention where, instead of each lamp being separately and independently governed, two or more, or an entire system of lamps, are simultaneously controlled from any single point on the circuit between the lamps and source of current. Fig. 6 comprehends several figures, showing a modified form of my invention, wherein the clamp operating to separate the carbons is either attached directly to, or in fact is, the armature of an electro-magnet. Fig. 7 shows a new construction of contact points or surfaces wherein carbon is employed as a facing.

A is a carbon-holder, in the form of a metallic rod or tube, provided at its lower end with any suitable arrangement for receiving and retaining a carbon, and this rod or tube is designed to be lifted or moved in any suitable manner, preferably, however, by a clamping device, that may be made automatically to gripe, move, and release said rod, as may be required.

Many forms of clamping device may be adopted; but that which I find to be as simple and effective as any is a loose ring or washer, B, surrounding the rod, which, when lifted from any single point, is tilted, and thereby made to firmly gripe and retain the rod A. By the use of an adjustable stop, B', the upward movement of the clamp, and thereby the separation of the carbons, is limited to any predetermined degree. Now, supposing that it is desired to maintain substantially a one-eighth-inch voltaic arc, the apparatus is adjusted so that the carbon-holder A can only be raised to separate the carbons that distance, when it is positively stopped and there held. If retained in this position too long, the carbons would consume to such a degree that the light would be extinguished. To prevent this I cause the carbons, at intervals of suitable length, to be brought into contact independent of the influence of the current operating the lamp, by which operation the gripe of the clamp B is released and the carbons allowed to feed to the amount consumed, after which they are immediately separated one-eighth of an inch, as before, and firmly held in that relation until again made to come in contact with each other, as already specified.

It will be remembered that these operations are performed without any breaking of the electric current, while at the same time, by causing the intervals of contact of the carbons to be sufficiently frequent, there will be no probability of the light becoming extinguished.

This arrangement enables me to successfully operate more than one light upon a single electric circuit, while it also serves a useful purpose in single lights, especially in places where the lamp must be subjected to much jolting—as, for instance, if employed for a locomotive head-light.

Having now pointed out the main features

and functions of my invention, I will specify means whereby these peculiar movements of the carbons may be accomplished.

Referring to Fig. 1 of the drawings, C is a lifter for raising one edge of the clamp B. This lifter is pivoted to the rocking lever D', which lever is pivoted to the metallic frame or casing E'.

To one end of the lever D' is fixed an armature, D, placed in proper relation with its electro-magnet H² to be attracted, and thus moved by said magnet, as will hereinafter appear.

Fixed to the opposite end of the lever D' is the tilting piece F, formed, substantially as shown, from suitable insulating material. Attached also to, but insulated from, said lever D' is the flat spring G, headed with a block, G¹, of insulating material. The block G affords a journal-connection to the piston of a dash-pot, G².

The piston-head of the dash-pot is provided with suitable valve contrivance G³, so arranged and constructed that the piston-head shall move slowly in one direction, preferably upward, and freely and quickly in the other.

H H¹ in the device here shown are hooks or other equivalents, for suspending or attaching the lamp at the locality where it is intended to be used, and these hooks represent, and are placed in electric connection respectively with, the positive and negative poles of the lamp, as and for the purpose shown in United States Patent No. 203,411, granted to me May 7, 1878.

I is a metallic rod connecting the hook H with the lower carbon, I'. d g are contact-points, fixed, respectively, to the lever D' and spring G; or, as will hereinafter appear, these contact-points d g may be placed anywhere in the electric circuit, and made to come into occasional contact by any contrivance whatever.

Electric connections by wire or other suitable means are made as follows: First, between hook H and rod I; second, between spring G and hook H¹; third, between carbon-holder A and helix of magnet H²; fourth, between carbon-holder A and metallic frame or casing E; fifth, between hook H¹ and helix H².

The device just specified will operate as follows: Before the passage of the electric current the carbons will rest in contact by the gravity of the upper carbon-holder, A, and in this position the circuit is from hook H, through rod I, carbons, carbon-holder A, frame E, helix H², and from thence to hook H¹. Immediately upon the passage of the electric current the armature is drawn down, thus operating to raise the lifter C, clamp B, and carbon-holder A to a height limited by the adjustable stop B'. This separates the carbons and produces the electric light. At the time the armature D is drawn down the opposite end of the lever D' is raised and the contact-point d raised with it. The resistance offered by the dash-pot G², however, prevents the contact-point g from immediately following. The result is that the points d g are separated; but the spring G is now called into play, and it acts to slowly raise the contact-point g, and during the time that the points d g are separated is when the carbons will be held steadily and firmly apart their adjusted distance by the force of the current passing through the helix H². After a time, however, the spring G will bring the points d g into contact, and thus afford a free passage for the current independent of the helix H², thus diverting the greater portion of the current from said helix, without, however, affecting its passage through the carbons.

The armature D, which is thus released, allows the rod A to drop, thereby loosening the gripe of the clamp B and permitting the upper carbon to feed forward to the amount consumed during the approach of the points d g. A quick drop motion of the carbon-holder A is effected by the peculiar construction of the piston-head of the dash-pot, whose valvular character, as already pointed out, is such as to permit a quick free movement in one direction and a slow movement in the other.

At the moment of contact between the points d g the current is principally from hook H, through rod I, carbons, rod A, frame E, lever D', contact-points d g, to hook H¹—a circuit offering far less resistance than one including the helix H². It will therefore be seen that the main portion of the current is diverted from the helix H², thus suddenly weakening its magnet and allowing the carbon-holder A to drop and feed its carbon forward. By this movement, however, the tilting piece F, striking against the adjustable stop F', is, by the weight of the lever D' and its attachments C B A, made to push down upon the spring G and separate the contact-points d g, thus reestablishing the main current through the helix H², drawing down its armature D, and separating the carbons again to their fixed limit.

The operations just described are constantly repeated in regular rotation, and the light produced is uniform and steady, excepting a slight wink or flicker at the moments when the carbons are brought in contact. When multiple lights are employed this winking, if occurring in but one lamp at a time, as may be the case, if desired, is not noticeable; and in cases where but one light is used, as in a locomotive headlight, this occasional wink is not at all objectionable, as the disturbance is but momentary, and the light only lessened, not extinguished.

In the form of device just specified the spring G is the element operating to bring the contact-points d g together, and thus to practically demagnetize the magnet H²; but this function of short-circuiting the magnet H² may be accomplished by many devices besides the spring G; also, may the contact-points d g be placed in the circuit at any convenient place whatever, so long as their contact, effected as may be, operates to short-circuit the

helix H² or allow the carbons to come together, as already specified.

Instead of this contact being accomplished by the spring G and dash-pot arrangement, it may be done by any appropriate clock-work mechanism that shall (at suitable intervals (that may, if desired, be made adjustable) operate to make and break said contact, and thus bring the carbons together, feed, and separate them, as already shown.

Fig. 3 of the drawings shows one form that might be adopted wherein a disk or wheel, g^2, is made to revolve either with a regular or an intermitting motion. A point, d, on its circumference is placed in the electric circuit, which, when brought into contact with the stationary point g, shall operate to the same effect as a contact between $d\ g$ in Fig. 1; or, instead of this disk or wheel g^2 being moved by clock-work, it may be revolved by suitable belt-connection with any driving-shaft of a machine shop or factory where the lamp is used.

Another effective device for occasionally making and breaking the short circuit heretofore referred to would be by means of two revolving arms or disks, $p\ p'$, made either of different lengths or diameters, or caused to revolve with differing velocities, or both. Each arm or disk $p\ p'$ is provided with one or more projecting contact-surfaces, $d\ g$. Owing to the differing velocity of rotation of these contact-surfaces $d\ g$, they would be brought together regularly, and at intervals of suitable length, regulated by the relative sizes of the arms or disks $p\ p'$, or their velocities, or both, and when they met their contact would be sufficiently short, thus not materially disturbing the light.

The arms or disks $p\ p'$ may be revolved by clock-work or in any other way, and each lamp may be separately provided with a device, $p\ p$, or two or more lamps of a system; or, indeed, an entire system of lamps on a single circuit, as shown in Fig. 5 of the drawings, may be simultaneously and effectively governed by one pair of arms or disks, $p\ p'$, by locating said pair anywhere on the circuit between the lamps and source of current.

Each contact $d\ g$ is placed respectively in electrical connection with the positive and negative poles of the lamp, or the positive and negative wires of the circuit, and their contact, as already sufficiently specified, will operate to cause the carbons to come together and feed.

Still another modified form of my invention is shown in Fig. 6 of the drawings.

Thus far I have shown intermediate mechanism between the magnet and clamp, whereby the magnet operates said clamp as I have shown. All this intermediate mechanism may be dispensed with, and the clamp be directly attached to, or in fact be, the armature of the electro-magnet. In this form of device the position of the magnet or the floor upon which the clamp rests, or both, should be made adjustable, so as to regulate and determine the separating motion of the carbons. When this construction is adopted, I recommend the employment of a spring, J, the office of which shall simply be to insure the griping function of the clamping device by bearing down at or near a point opposite from where the lifting-finger raises the clamp. This will prevent a liability of any loosening of the clamping contrivance on account of jolting.

In this last-named form of device either the adjustable magnet or the adjustable floor, as above specified, or both, will operate as the adjustable stop B', to limit the separation of the carbons, as may be desired.

Fig. 7 of the drawings represents an effective form of construction of the contact-points $d\ g$. In this construction the said contact-points are either formed entirely from carbon or are faced with this material. Thus formed the points $d\ g$ will be cheap, durable, and effective.

I have sufficiently demonstrated the fact that carbon contact-points, such as $d\ g$, are not only superior to, but in many essential respects different from, the ordinary contact-points of platinum and similar substances heretofore in common use.

In contact-points as heretofore made the electric spark which is apt to be created by interruption of the current much more rapidly destroys even a platinum-surface than it will a carbon surface.

Another and equally important advantage that I have discovered in favor of carbon contact-points is the fact that grease and dirt are far less liable to be deposited upon a carbon than upon a metallic surface, and this deposition of foreign matter between the contact-points is a well-recognized cause of faulty and unreliable operation. Moreover, besides the inherent superiority and advantage of carbon over any metallic substance for contact-points, it can be produced and applied at a greatly-reduced expense, and is, moreover, more readily renewed when necessary than contact-points as hitherto constructed.

What I claim is—

1. In combination with the carbons, or their equivalent, of an electric lamp, a device for governing and controlling the carbons in the following manner, to wit: to separate said carbons to a distance required for the desired length of voltaic arc, and to maintain them in a separated relation excepting at momentary intervals of suitable frequency, when the said carbons are arbitrarily caused to feed and come into contact with each other by the shunting of a portion or the whole of the electric current from the magnet operating to separate said carbons, substantially as and for the purpose specified.

2. In combination with the carbons, or their equivalent, of an electric lamp, a device for governing and controlling the carbons in the following manner, to wit: to separate said carbons to a distance required for the desired length of voltaic arc, and to maintain them in

a separated relation excepting at momentary intervals of suitable frequency, when the said carbons are arbitrarily caused to feed and come into contact with each other without an interruption of the passage of the electric current through the carbons by the shunting of a portion or the whole of the electric current from the magnet operating to separate said carbons, substantially as shown.

3. In combination with the carbons, or their equivalent, of an electric lamp, a device for governing and controlling the carbons in the following manner, to wit: to separate said carbons to a distance required for the desired length of voltaic arc, and to maintain them in a separated relation excepting at momentary intervals of suitable frequency, when the said carbons are arbitrarily caused to feed and come into contact with each other without interruption of the electric current in the battery or other source of current by the shunting of a portion or the whole of the electric current from the magnet operating to separate said carbons, substantially as shown.

4. An electric lamp wherein the combined clamp and lifting device B', or its equivalent, is directly attached to, or in fact is, the armature of an electro-magnet, substantially as shown.

5. In an electric lamp wherein the clamp B', or its equivalent, is directly attached to, or in fact is, the armature of an electro-magnet, a vertically adjustable floor or rest for said clamp, substantially as and for the purpose specified.

6. In an electric lamp wherein the clamp B', or its equivalent, is directly attached to, or in fact is, the armature of an electro-magnet, a suitable arrangement and device for making said electro-magnet adjustable in its position, substantially as and for the purpose shown.

7. The contact points or surfaces d g, placed in electrical connection respectively with the positive and negative wires (or other conductors) of a circuit upon which one or more electric lamps are placed, in combination with suitable device for occasionally bringing said points or surfaces into momentary electrical connection, for the purpose, at the times of said contact or connection, of permitting the carbons or illuminating points of said lamp or lamps, as consumed, to feed, substantially as shown.

8. In combination with the mechanism of an electric lamp, the contact points or surfaces d g, or their equivalent, and a suitable device for effecting an occasional momentary electrical connection between said points or surfaces, for the purpose, at the times of said connection, of permitting the illuminating points or carbons of said lamp, as consumed, to feed, substantially as shown.

9. The contact points or surfaces d g, consisting of or faced with carbon, substantially as and for the purpose shown.

In testimony whereof I have signed my name to this specification in the presence of two subscribing witnesses.

CHARLES F. BRUSH.

Witnesses:
JNO. CROWELL, Jr.,
LEVERETT L. LEGGETT.

Assigned to Brush Electric Co. -- Jan 8 [...]

THE UNITED STATES OF AMERICA.

TO ALL TO WHOM THESE PRESENTS SHALL COME:

Whereas Charles F. Brush of Cleveland, Ohio

_____ has presented to the Commissioner of Patents a petition praying for the grant of Letters Patent for an alleged new and useful improvement in Dynamo Electric Machines

a description of which invention is contained in the Specification of which a copy is hereunto annexed and made a part hereof, and has complied with the various requirements of law in such cases made and provided, and

Whereas upon due examination made the said Claimant is adjudged to be justly entitled to a Patent under the law.

Now therefore these LETTERS PATENT are to grant unto the said _____ his heirs or assigns for the term of _____ years from the _____ day of _____ one thousand eight hundred and eighty the exclusive right to make, use and vend the said invention throughout the United States and the Territories thereof.

In testimony whereof I have hereunto set my hand and caused the seal of the Patent Office to be affixed at the City of Washington this _____ day of _____ in the year of our Lord one thousand eight hundred and eighty and of the Independence of the United States of America the one hundred and _____.

Countersigned:
Commissioner of Patents.

Acting Secretary of the Interior.

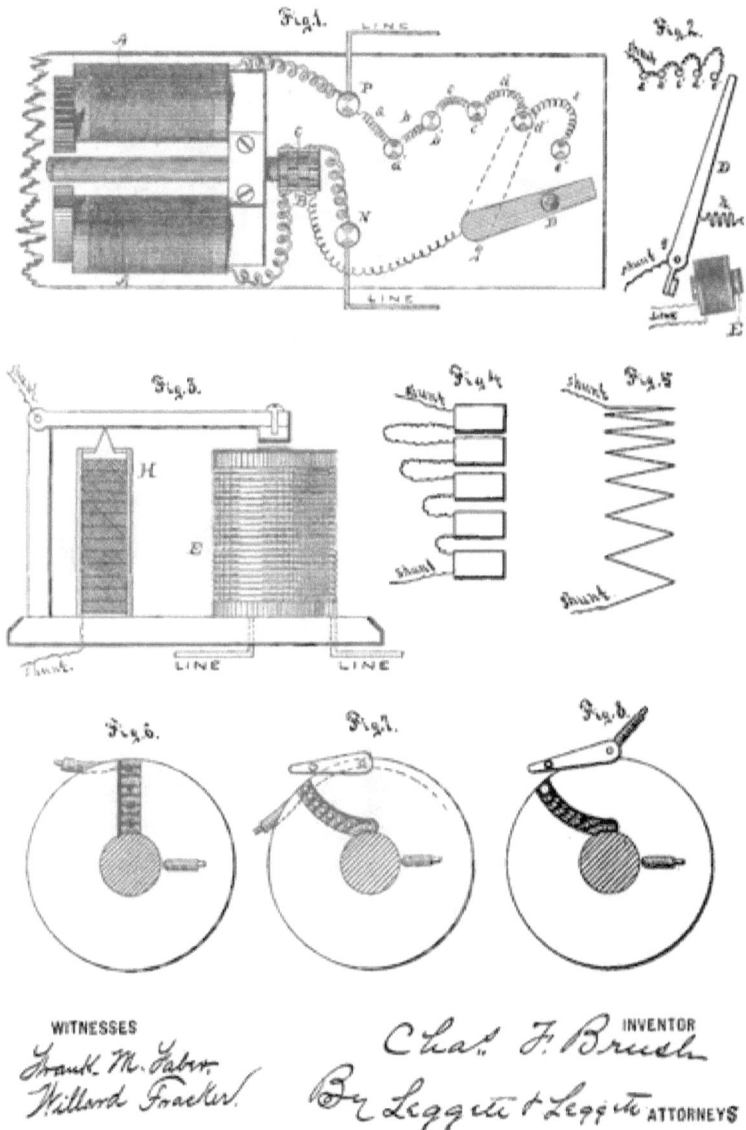

United States Patent Office.

CHARLES F. BRUSH, OF CLEVELAND, OHIO.

DYNAMO-ELECTRIC APPARATUS.

SPECIFICATION forming part of Letters Patent No. 224,511, dated February 17, **1880.**

Application filed November 21, 1879.

To all whom it may concern:

Be it known that I, CHARLES F. BRUSH, of Cleveland, in the county of Cuyahoga and State of Ohio, have invented certain new and useful Improvements in Dynamo-Electric Apparatus; and I do hereby declare the following to be a full, clear, and exact description of the invention, such as will enable others skilled in the art to which it pertains to make and use it, reference being had to the accompanying drawings, which form part of this specification.

My invention relates to dynamo-electric machines, and has for its object the adaptation of such machines to variable external conditions without variation of the speed at which their armatures are rotated, but by variation of the intensity of the magnetic field, and this by means not directly depending on the volume of current circulating in the external circuit.

When dynamo-electric machines of usual construction are driven at a normal speed, the external or working resistance must be of certain amount in order to secure a normal volume of current in circulation. Any addition to the work to be performed or increase of external resistance is attended by a diminution of the current strength, while any decrease in the resistance of the external circuit is productive of an increased volume of current. In other words, the current produced by these machines varies inversely as the work they are called upon to perform.

It is generally desirable and often necessary that the volume of current maintained in circulation by a machine should remain nearly constant, while the external or working resistance is varied within reasonable limits to conform to variable requirements. This end has heretofore been attained by varying the speed at which the armature of the machine is rotated. This method is generally impracticable, especially when many variations of external conditions are encountered.

I effect my object by varying the intensity of the magnetic field in which the armature rotates. Suppose a machine driven at its normal speed maintains its normal current through a certain external resistance. Now, if this resistance is diminished, and at the same time the intensity of the magnetic field of the machine is also diminished a certain amount, then the current in circulation will remain the same as before, because its electro-motive force has been lowered.

The magnetic field of the machine is weakened either by shunting away from the coils of the field-magnets a portion of the current which excites them, or by cutting out or short-circuiting some portion of one or more of the coils, so that the current shall make a less number of convolutions about the cores of the magnets. By varying the resistance of the shunt which diverts a portion of the current from the magnet-coils, or by varying the number of convolutions of the coils cut out or short-circuited, any number of variations in the intensity of the magnetic field of the machine may be produced.

In the drawings, Figure 1 represents a portion of a dynamo-electric machine provided with a shunt of manually-adjustable resistance around the field-magnet circuit. Fig. 2 represents a modified embodiment of my invention, wherein its operations are performed in an automatic manner. Figs. 3, 4, and 5 show other similar modifications. Fig. 6 represents a field-magnet coil adapted to have various portions of itself short-circuited. Fig. 7 shows a modification of the same. Fig. 8 represents a magnet-helix adapted to have various portions of itself cut out of the circuit.

In Fig. 1, A A represent the two helices of one of the magnets of a dynamo-electric machine. They are joined together in single circuit, and one end of the conductor so formed is attached to the commutator-brush B, while the other end is attached to the binding-post P, forming one terminal of the machine. The other binding-post or terminal, N, is connected with the remaining commutator-brush C.

a b c d e are resistance-coils connected with each other in series by means of the studs or buttons a' b' c', &c., the coil a being also connected with one end of the field-magnet conductor at P.

D is a switch-arm, pivoted at g, and adapted to connect g with a' b' c', &c., at pleasure. The stud g is connected with the commutator-brush B, and thus with the other end of the magnet-circuit.

Now, when the terminals P N are connected by means of the external or working circuit

(not shown) all of the current developed by the machine in operation will circulate in the helices A A so long as the switch-arm D is not in contact with any of the buttons a' b' c', &c.; but when the arm D is moved into contact with the button a', then a portion of the current developed by the machine will be diverted from the helices A A, and will flow through the shunt-circuit P a a' D g B, the amount so shunted being determined by the resistance of the shunt-circuit as compared with that of the magnet-circuit. The machine will now be in a condition to develop its normal current through a small external resistance only, because its field-magnets are greatly weakened through the decrease of the current exciting them.

The coil a is made of such resistance that when it only is included in the shunt-circuit the machine shall be adapted to operate normally the smallest external resistance met with in practice.

When the arm D is moved to the button b' the resistance b is added to the shunt-circuit, whereby less current is diverted from the magnet-circuit, the intensity of the magnetic field is increased, and the machine is adapted to operate an increased external resistance. By moving the arm D to c', &c., and thus adding the resistances c, &c., to the shunt-circuit, the machine will in like manner become adapted to operate more and more external resistance, until, finally, when the arm D is moved off from the last button, e, (the resistance of the shunt-circuit being now infinitely great,) the machine will have attained its full power.

In order to adapt the machine to regularly-increasing external resistances the resistances b c d e are made successively greater, because each one, in order to increase the total resistance of the shunt in a given proportion, must obviously be larger than the one preceding it. Thus the last resistance after e (circuit open) is infinitely great.

Obviously one or more (preferably all) of the magnet-helices of a machine may be included in that part of the circuit of the machine affected by the shunt.

In practice I find it convenient to arrange the resistances a b c, &c., on metal cores in a metal case, and connect the piece of apparatus with the dynamo-machine by means of suitable wires. The metal of the cores and case absorbs the heat developed in the resistance-coils, and dissipates it by radiation and convection. I also provide the metal case surrounding and protecting the resistance-coils with suitable openings above and below to allow a circulation of air about the coils, which arrangement materially aids in keeping them cool.

My invention is well adapted for use with dynamo-electric machines operating several electric lights in single circuit, since by means of this device such machines may operate normally any number of lights from one (the other lights being short-circuited) up to their full capacity without change of speed, and with an absorption of driving-power varying (though not proportionally) with the number of lights used. It may also be applied to electroplating-machines, and with excellent results.

Fig. 2 of the drawings illustrates a method of operating the switch-arm D automatically, according to the varying requirements of the working circuit of the machine.

The arm D is held in the position shown in the figure by means of the spring H, so that the shunt-resistances are open-circuited when the machine is operating its highest external resistance. An armature is attached to a short prolongation of the arm D in front of an electro-magnet, E, which is excited by the working current from the machine, as shown. The tension of the spring H is so adjusted that it shall be just sufficient to hold the arm D in the position shown when the current exciting the opposing magnet E is of normal amount.

Now, if the external or working resistance of the machine is diminished, the first effect will be an augmentation of the volume of current in circulation; but this will at once increase the attraction of the magnet E for its armature, and the arm D will be thrown successively into contact with the buttons e', d', &c., until the shunt-resistance is sufficiently reduced to effect the reduction of the general current nearly to its normal condition in the manner already specified. Conversely, an increase of resistance in the working circuit will first diminish the current in circulation, the magnet E will become weakened, and the opposing spring H will throw the arm D in the other direction until the increasing resistance of the shunt produces a sufficiently-increased working current to enable the magnet E to arrest the action of the spring.

Fig. 3 shows a modified form of automatic shunt-resistance. The resistances a, b, c, &c., of Figs. 1 and 2 are here replaced by a pile, H, of carbon disks or plates, the resistance of which is varied by varying pressure brought to bear on the pile through the agency of the magnet E, the latter being excited by the working current from the dynamo-machine, as described in connection with Fig. 2.

The operation of the device is obvious without further explanation.

Figs. 3, 4, and 5 show obvious modifications of the resistance-pile H, Fig. 3.

Instead of employing a fixed magnet-core and movable armature in these automatic devices, the magnet-helix may be made hollow, and a movable core may be substituted for the armature.

Means other than magnetism may also be employed to effect these automatic operations—such, for instance, as varying expansion in wires, bars, or ribbons of metal, produced by varying temperatures of such bodies, due to varying currents passing through them.

Automatic variations of the magnetic field

of a dynamo-electric machine corresponding to varying external or working resistances may also be effected by means of a device shown and described in Letters Patent No. 217,677, granted to me July 22, 1879, and known as a "teaser." The action of this device for this purpose is obvious: the greater the resistance of the working circuit of the machine the greater amount of current will be shunted through the teaser, thus strengthening the magnetic field of the machine accordingly.

Instead of shunting away a portion of the current used to excite the magnets of a dynamo-electric machine, in order to reduce the magnetic field of the latter, some of the convolutions of the magnet-helices may be short-circuited, or cut out of the circuit altogether, thus reducing the magnetism by reducing the number of current convolutions. This method may be applied to one or several of the field-of-force helices of a machine.

Fig. 6 of the drawings shows an end view of a field-magnet core and helix. A portion of the magnet-head is represented as cut away, thus exposing the convolutions of helix-conductor to view. Now, by inserting one or more metallic pins or plugs between the convolutions of wire, as shown in the figure, a suitable number of layers of the wire may be short-circuited (and thus rendered inactive) to effect the purpose in view.

Fig. 7 shows a modification of Fig. 6, wherein the short-circuiting plugs are replaced by a switch-arm connected with the outer convolution of wire, and adapted to make contact with various other convolutions, thus short-circuiting all of those convolutions or layers of wire which lie between.

Fig. 8 shows a modification of the device shown in Fig. 7, wherein the switch-arm itself forms the terminal of the helix-conductor, thus determining the number of convolutions of the working helix according to its position, the remaining idle convolutions being open-circuited.

The devices shown in Figs. 6, 7, and 8 may be rendered automatic in their action by means analogous to that shown in Fig. 2.

What I claim is—

1. A dynamo-electric machine constructed or combined with suitable device for primarily varying the strength of the current exciting its field-of-force electro-magnets.

2. In a dynamo-electric machine, the combination, with one or more of its inducing or field-of-force electro-magnets, of an adjustable resistance, whereby the strength of the current applied to said magnets may be determined, and governed, and varied, substantially as and for the purpose shown.

3. In a dynamo-electric machine, the combination, with one or more of its inducing or field-of-force electro-magnets, of a shunt-circuit, within which is included an adjustable resistance for varying the strength of the current applied to said magnets.

In testimony whereof I have signed my name to this specification in the presence of two subscribing witnesses.

CHARLES F. BRUSH.

Witnesses:
JNO. CROWELL, Jr.,
LEVERETT L. LEGGETT.

Assigned to Brush Electric Co. — JAN 8 18__

UNITED STATES OF AMERICA

No. 234,456.

To all to whom these presents shall come:

Whereas *Charles F. Brush,* of *Cleveland, Ohio,* has presented to the Commissioner of Patents a petition praying for the grant of Letters Patent for an alleged new and useful improvement in *Automatic Cut=Out Apparatus for Electric Lights or Motors,* a description of which invention is contained in the Specification of which a copy is hereunto annexed and made a part hereof, and has complied with the various requirements of Law in such cases made and provided, and

Whereas upon due examination made the said Claimant is adjudged to be justly entitled to a Patent under the Law.

Now therefore these **Letters Patent** are to grant unto the said *Charles F. Brush,* his heirs or assigns for the term of *seventeen* years from the *sixteenth* day of *November* one thousand eight hundred and *eighty* the exclusive right to make, use and vend the said invention throughout the United States and the Territories thereof.

In testimony whereof I have hereunto set my hand and caused the seal of the Patent Office to be affixed at the City of Washington this *sixteenth* day of *November* in the year of our Lord one thousand eight hundred and *eighty* and of the Independence of the United States of America the one hundred and fifth.

Countersigned

Commissioner of Patents.

Acting Secretary of the Interior.

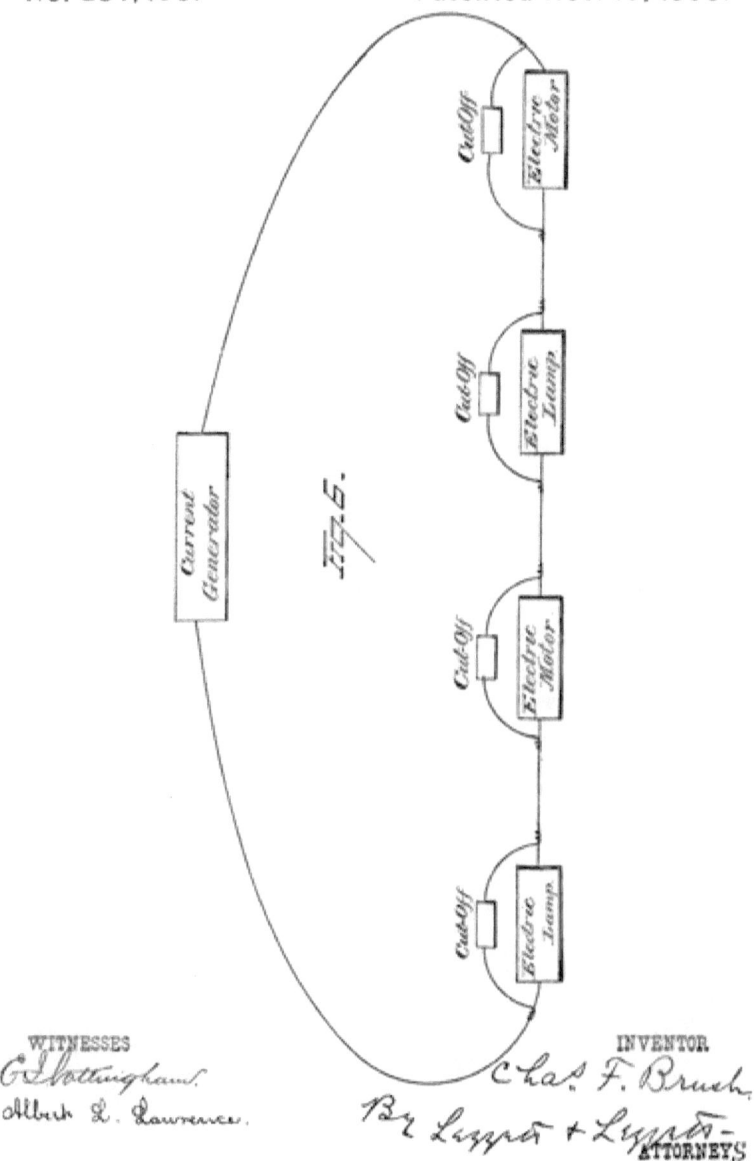

C. F. BRUSH.
Automatic Cut-Out Appparatus for Electric Lights or Motors.

No. 234,456. Patented Nov. 16, 1880.

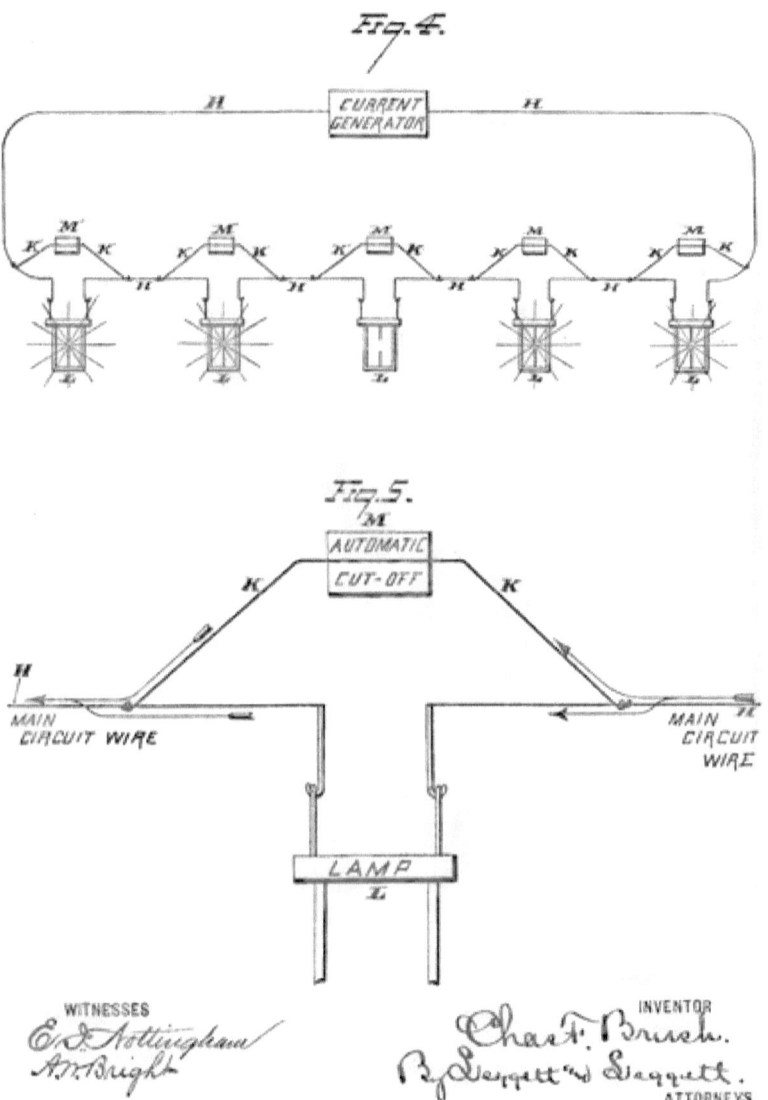

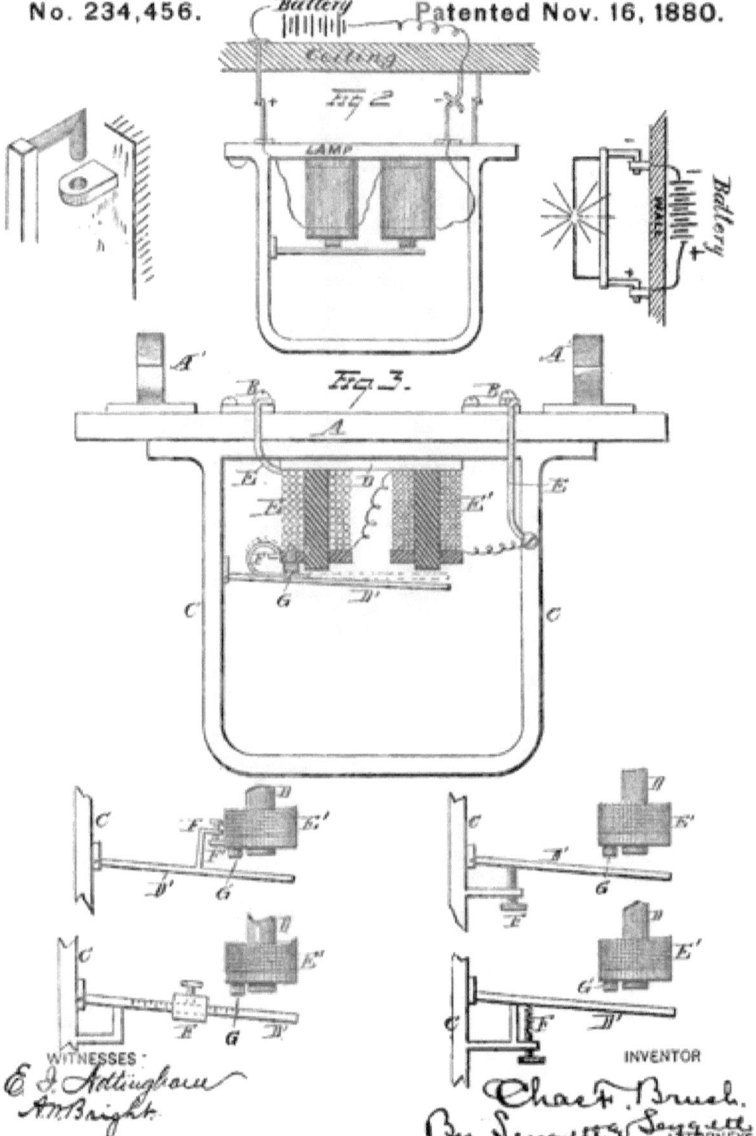

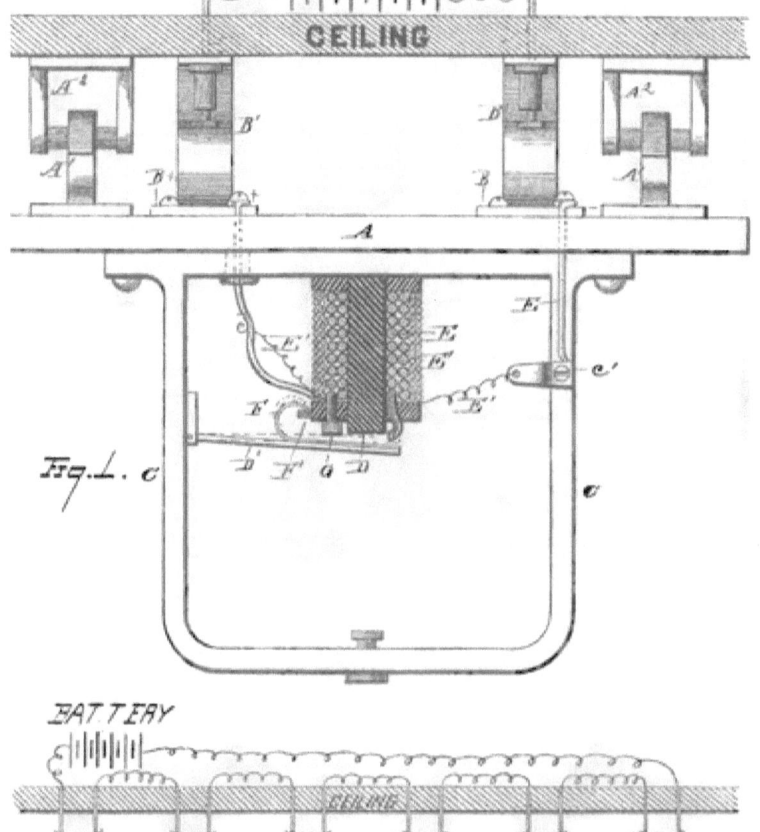

UNITED STATES PATENT OFFICE.

CHARLES F. BRUSH, OF CLEVELAND, OHIO.

AUTOMATIC CUT-OUT APPARATUS FOR ELECTRIC LIGHTS OR MOTORS.

SPECIFICATION forming part of Letters Patent No. 234,456, dated November 16, 1880.

Application filed September 30, 1879.

To all whom it may concern:

Be it known that I, CHARLES F. BRUSH, of Cleveland, in the county of Cuyahoga and State of Ohio, have invented a certain new and useful Method and Means of Employing Electricity for Lighting and other Purposes; and I do hereby declare the following to be a full, clear, and exact description of the invention, such as will enable others skilled in the art to which it pertains to make and use it, reference being had to the accompanying drawings, which form a part of this specification.

My invention relates to the employment of electricity for lighting and other purposes, and especially to a system where more than one electric lamp, electro-motor, or any other electro-receptive device—that is, a device to be operated upon or actuated by an electric current—are located within a common or continuous circuit; and said invention consists in a system wherein two or more electric lamps, electro-motors, or other electro-receptive devices are placed within a single or common circuit, each of said electro-receptive devices associated with a closed shunt-circuit, within which is included a cut-off or short-circuiting contrivance, the whole being constructed, arranged, connected, and adjusted in such a manner that if any of the said electro-receptive devices should offer too great an electrical resistance the current in its individual shunt will be so affected that its cut-off shall be called into operation to automatically short-circuit that particular electro-receptive device, cutting it out of circuit without interrupting or breaking the current in the general circuit or in the remaining electro-receptive devices.

My invention also consists in the combination, with a single electric lamp, motor, or other electro-receptive device, of a closed shunt-circuit, within which is included a cut-off or short-circuiting contrivance, the whole being so constructed, arranged, connected, and adjusted that the electric current shall, during the operation of said electro-receptive device, divide itself between it and its said shunt, and so that if, from any cause, said receptive device shall offer a too great electrical resistance, said resistance shall so affect the current in said shunt that said cut-off shall be called into operation to automatically short-circuit said electro-receptive device.

My invention also consists in a system for the employment of electricity for lighting and for other purposes, said system consisting of a suitable electric-current generator, and connected therewith a general-circuit conductor, said conductor being divided at each point where the current is to be utilized into more than one closed path or circuit, one containing a machine or device to be operated upon or actuated by the electric current and another containing a cut-off or short-circuiting contrivance for automatically cutting said machine or device out of the circuit whenever, from any cause, said machine or device shall offer too great an electrical resistance.

My invention also consists in a peculiar construction and arrangement of the electrical-contact surfaces between the general-circuit conductor and an electric lamp, electro-motor, or other electro-receptive device that is designed to be hung or attached to a wall, ceiling, or support, whereby said lamp, motor, or electro-receptive device is placed in circuit by the simple act of fixing it in the locality where it is desired to be used.

I shall describe my invention as applied to electric lamps, and to a system where more than one lamp are placed within the same circuit and each provided or associated with its individual short-circuiting apparatus.

When several electric-light regulators are operated by a single electric current it is evident that the failure of any one of the regulators to feed its carbons forward will, by ultimately interrupting the current, not only extinguish itself, but also the lights of all the other regulators. It is to guard against this accident that I have designed my present invention.

My device operates to close the electric circuit through the regulator by affording a passage for the current independent of the carbon points when the latter fail to move forward properly. This short-circuiting may be made to occur either before or after the interruption of the current by the too great separation of the carbons.

I accomplish my design by shunting from the main current that passes through the regulator a small portion of said main current by means of a helix of suitably high resistance. The ends of this helix are connected to the main

circuit of the regulator at points on opposite sides of the voltaic arc. Hence, as is well known, the amount of current through this helix must vary with the resistance of said voltaic arc. If, now, the regulator to which this helix is applied fails to advance its carbons, their increasing separation due to their combustion or other cause will constantly increase the resistance of the voltaic arc, and thus shunt more and more of the whole current through the helix, whose resistance remains constant. This action may continue until the voltaic arc finally ceases, in which case the resisting helix, affording the only circuit through the regulator, may convey even more current than before the cessation of the arc.

I inclose within the helix a core of iron and place near the lower end of this core an armature at such a distance that the magnetism of the core induced by the current in the helix shall be insufficient to raise it when the normal amount of current is passing through the helix; but when, owing to the too great separation of the carbons in the regulator or the cessation of the voltaic arc, this current increases beyond a certain strength, the armature is attracted and drawn toward the core, thus making a contact between suitable metallic surfaces suitably connected, and affording a free passage for the current through or around the regulator independent of the carbons. But it will be obvious that when the device has operated as just described, the current will be greatly lessened in the said helix, and consequently, without some retaining device the armature would fall back in its old position, thus opening the electric circuit. Residual magnetism may be utilized for this purpose, and a number of mechanical devices also readily suggest themselves; but I prefer for this purpose the device shown in the drawings. It consists of the second helix of coarse wire surrounding the core, which helix forms part of the short circuit which is established when the core lifts its armature. This helix, coming into action at the instant when the helix of high resistance, before described, ceases to be efficient, maintains the magnetism of the core, and consequently the integrity of the short circuit, until the faulty regulator is removed or the current stopped.

My whole device may be combined with and form part of an electric-light regulator, as shown in the drawings, or it may be constructed as a separate piece of mechanism and applied to any regulator, either near or at a distance, by means of suitable conducting-wires.

Two cores may be employed instead of one, as described, thus forming an ordinary horseshoe electro-magnet, and the two helices described (or more than one of each) may be arranged in many obvious ways in relation to each other while still performing their peculiar functions; or the second helix of coarse wire may be dispensed with, as above indicated.

In the drawings, Figure 1 shows one form of device embodying my invention and one method of placing several lamps on a single circuit, also one method of attaching a pendent lamp to a ceiling. Fig. 2 shows a few of various modifications to which my invention is susceptible as relates to the method of attaching a lamp to a wall or ceiling. Fig. 3 shows a few of various modifications to which my invention is susceptible as regards mechanism for automatically accomplishing the shunting or short-circuiting hereinbefore mentioned.

The form in which I shall describe my invention is that of the pendent or swinging lamp, which, as appears in United States Patent No. 203,411, granted to me May 7, 1878, is but one of several varieties; but I wish it to be understood that I do not limit the application of my present invention to any specific form of lamp or regulator whatever, inasmuch as it may be adaptable without any material variation to electric-light regulators of many kinds other than I have shown.

A is a plate of wood, gutta-percha, or any suitable non-conducting material. To this plate are attached the suspending hooks, loops, or their equivalent, A'. These hooks are simply designed to suspend the lamp, and are not placed in electrical connection with any part of the apparatus. A² are loops or hooks attached to the wall or ceiling, with which the hooks A' engage.

B B are contact-plates, springs, or their equivalents, representing and placed in electrical connection respectively with the positive and negative poles of the lamp.

B' B' are stationary plates, springs, or other suitable equivalent contact-surfaces fixed stationary at that locality in the wall or ceiling where the lamp is intended to be used. These contact-surfaces B' represent and are placed respectively in electrical connection with the battery, dynamo-electric machine, or other source of electric current.

The contact-surfaces B and B' may be constructed in any manner, so that by the act of placing the lamp in position they shall be brought together in such a way that the lamp is put in the electric circuit.

I do not limit myself to any special design or construction of the contact-surfaces B B', as they may be indefinitely varied without in any degree departing from my invention.

C is a frame, preferably constructed of iron or other electro-conducting material, and this frame is formed in any proper manner to hold and accommodate the various parts of the regulator.

D is the magnet-core hereinbefore described. D' is its armature. Around the magnet-core is wound the helix E, of coarse wire, and the helix E', of fine wire.

It will be observed that the armature is made movable by pivoting it to the frame C. The armature and frame C are placed in electrical connection with each other. The position of the armature D' during the time that the lamp is properly acting is in its dropped position

away from the core D. The distance of the armature's drop may be regulated in any desired way by means of the curved piece F, which may be bent at pleasure to adjust the desired drop of the armature. The piece F rests upon any suitable stop F'.

G is a contact-point of any suitable conducting material, so placed that the armature as it is lifted will impinge against it before coming into contact with the core D, thus always preventing any actual union between the core and armature. This contact-point G connects with the coarse-wire helix E. The coarse helix is arranged and connected as follows: Commencing from the contact-plate B, it describes a helix around the core D and terminates with the contact-point G. Thus it will be seen that until connection is made between the contact-point G and armature D' the coarse helix E does not constitute a completed circuit. The fine-wire helix E', commencing from its attachment to the coarse wire, as shown at c, proceeds directly to describe a helix about the core D, and then connects with the frame at c', and also with the pole B opposite from that to which the coarse helix E is primarily connected, as above specified.

It is obvious that the device just specified is susceptible of an indefinite number of modifications. For instance, instead of the magnet, as described, a horseshoe or two-legged magnet may be used, one leg carrying the coarse-wire and the other the fine-wire helix, and the connections be made substantially as before shown. Likewise the armature and its adjustment may be indefinitely varied, as indicated in the drawings.

During the time that the lamp is properly performing, the current through the fine-wire helix E' will not be sufficient to lift the armature D'; but when it is desirable to "short-circuit" the lamp, as above set forth, then the current will be sufficiently strong to draw this armature. The degree of strength of current required to lift the armature is determined entirely by the adjustment of the armature, and this degree may be greater or less as circumstances may require.

It will be borne in mind that during the time the armature is in its dropped position the main portion of the current is passing through the carbons; but when the armature is drawn into its contact position, then the carbons are cut out of the electric circuit, and the current takes the following course: Beginning from the pole B, it passes down through coarse helix E, thus strongly magnetizing the core D and thus securely maintaining the contact position of the armature, then through the contact-points G and through the armature D' to the frame C, and from thence to the opposite pole B', with which the frame C is now in electrical connection.

Instead of constructing the magnet and armature as shown in the drawings, these parts may be adapted to operate by the force of axial magnetism. In such case the helix or helices E or E' are wound upon a hollow spool, within which extends a core attached to a lever similar to the armature D'. The attractive effect of the current in such a construction would be to draw the core up within the hollow of the helix-spool, thus to make a contact between part G and frame C, as already specified.

As already mentioned, the shunting or cut-off mechanism, being an independent structure, need not of necessity be coupled with a lamp in a single device. Its character and functions would in no manner or degree be changed were the lamp proper to constitute one separate structure and the cut-off mechanism another so long as the two are so arranged and electrically connected with the main-circuit conductor that the current shall divide itself between said lamp and cut-off, as already hereinbefore shown.

Fig. 4 of the drawings illustrates, in a diagrammatic manner, a system wherein the lamps and their individual short-circuiting devices are separate structures and located apart from each other. Fig. 5 is an enlarged view of a single lamp and its cut-off arranged as shown in Fig. 4. We here see five lamps, L, included within a single circuit, H. At each lamp the main-circuit conductor H is split, so that the current not only passes through the lamp L to operate it, but also through the conductor K and the shunting or short-circuiting device M. Thus arranged and connected the lamps and their individual shunting devices may be located in different places, if it should be desired, and it is plainly evident that when thus arranged all the parts will operate in identically the manner and to the effect already specified.

I have now disclosed in detail one manner of embodying and applying my invention, from which it will clearly appear that it is equally applicable, without material change or modification, to other electro-receptive devices than lamps; and Fig. 6 of the drawings illustrates diagrammatically a system wherein two electric lamps and two electro-motors are placed upon a single circuit, and in association with each is shown its individual short-circuiting device, which, as already shown, may be a separate structure or not, as desired. In such a system as indicated and suggested in Fig. 6, if a lamp or a motor from any cause should offer a too great electrical resistance, it will cause an increased amount of current to be sent to the short-circuiting apparatus connected therewith, and the faulty lamp or motor will be automatically cut out of circuit, and this without a breaking of the general circuit or any material disturbance of the current therein, so that all the remaining lamps or motors on said circuit are practically unaffected.

What I claim is—

1. An electric-lighting apparatus constructed to offer two conducting-paths to the electric current at the same time, one path including the illuminating-electrodes and the other

path including a shunting or short-circuiting device, substantially as and for the purpose shown.

2. An electric-lighting apparatus combining the following instrumentalities, to wit: illuminating-electrodes and an automatic shunting or short-circuiting device for extinguishing the light of said electrodes, said shunting or short-circuiting device constructed to be called into its light-extinguishing function through the agency of an increased proportion of the electric current diverted to it by reason of any undue electrical resistance offered by the said illuminating-electrodes or the mechanism operating them.

3. A system wherein two or more electric lamps are included within a single circuit, with a short-circuiting device associated with each lamp, the said circuit-conductor so arranged and constructed that the current shall divide itself at each lamp between said lamp's electrodes (and the mechanism operating them) and that lamp's individual shunt or short-circuiting device, the whole so constructed, connected, and adapted to operate that if from any cause any lamp shall offer an abnormally great electrical resistance an increased proportion of the current will be diverted to that lamp's particular short-circuiting device, which increased proportion of current through said short-circuiting device shall automatically call it into operation to extinguish the light of said faulty lamp, and at the same time to transmit the current so as not to extinguish or materially affect any other lamp upon the circuit, substantially as shown.

4. An electro-magnet, D, having a fine-wire helix, E', and a coarse-wire helix, E, combined and electrically connected substantially as shown, and constructed to shunt the current from an electric lamp with which it is associated when said lamp shall offer an abnormally great electrical resistance, substantially as and for the purpose shown.

5. The combination, with an electric-lighting apparatus, of the helix E', of comparatively high resistance, said helix E' constructed to automatically operate a shunting or short-circuiting device that shall extinguish the light whenever said apparatus shall offer an abnormally great electrical resistance, substantially as and for the purpose shown.

6. An automatic cut-off or short-circuiting apparatus adjusted and electrically connected with an electric lamp, electro-motor, or other electro-receptive device, substantially as indicated, so that the electric current from the main-circuit-conductor will be divided between said cut-off and electro-receptive device, the cut-off being constructed to automatically short-circuit and cut out said electro-receptive device through the influence of an increased amount of current diverted to said cut-off by reason of a too great electrical resistance offered by said electro-receptive device.

7. The combination, with any suitable electric-current generator and an electric-circuit conductor connected therewith, of shunt-circuits connected with the conductor on opposite sides of any point or points therein from which the current or a portion thereof is to be utilized for any purpose, and a device located in said shunt-circuit and adapted to interpose any desired resistance in the shunt-circuit and to automatically put in circuit a supplemental electric conductor whenever the main conductor or machine connected therewith offers a too great electrical resistance.

8. A system for the employment of electricity for lighting and for other purposes, said system consisting of a suitable electric-current generator and connected therewith a general circuit-conductor, said conductor being divided at each point where the current is to be utilized into more than one closed path or circuit, one path or circuit containing a machine or device to be operated upon or actuated by the electric current and another path containing a cut-off or short-circuiting contrivance for automatically cutting said machine or device out of the circuit whenever from any cause said machine or device shall offer too great an electrical resistance.

9. An electro-receptive device, in combination with a constantly-closed shunt electrically connected with the main-circuit conductor upon both sides of said electro-receptive device, said shunt constructed or provided with suitable contrivance for automatically putting in circuit and around said electro-receptive device a supplemental conductor for receiving and transmitting the main-circuit current whenever from any cause said electro-receptive device shall offer too great an electrical resistance.

10. In combination with a suitable device for attaching an electric lamp to a wall, ceiling, or support, one or more suitable contact-surfaces, B B, electrically connected with said lamp, and contact-surfaces B' B', representing and placed in electric connection respectively with the positive and negative poles of the battery or other source of electric current, said contact-surfaces B' placed stationary at the locality where said lamp is intended to be used.

In testimony whereof I have signed my name to this specification in the presence of two subscribing witnesses.

CHARLES F. BRUSH.

Witnesses:
  LEVERETT L. LEGGETT,
  JNO. CROWELL, Jr.

Assigned to Brush Electric Co. — JAN 8 18

UNITED STATES OF AMERICA

No. 237,511

To all to whom these presents shall come:

Whereas Charles F. Brush of Cleveland, Ohio has presented to the Commissioner of Patents a petition praying for the grant of Letters Patent for an alleged new and useful improvement in

Reflectors

a description of which invention is contained in the Specification of which a copy is hereunto annexed and made a part hereof, and has complied with the various requirements of Law in such cases made and provided, and

Whereas upon due examination made the said Claimant is adjudged to be justly entitled to a Patent under the Law.

Now therefore these **Letters Patent** are to grant unto the said Charles F. Brush his heirs or assigns for the term of seventeen years from the twenty-fifth day of March one thousand eight hundred and eighty-one the exclusive right to make, use and vend the said invention throughout the United States and the Territories thereof.

In testimony whereof I have hereunto set my hand and caused the seal of the Patent Office to be affixed at the City of Washington this twenty-fifth day of March in the year of our Lord one thousand eight hundred and eighty-one and of the Independence of the United States of America the one hundred and fifth.

Countersigned
E. M. Marble
Commissioner of Patents.

A. Bell
Acting Secretary of the Interior.

782

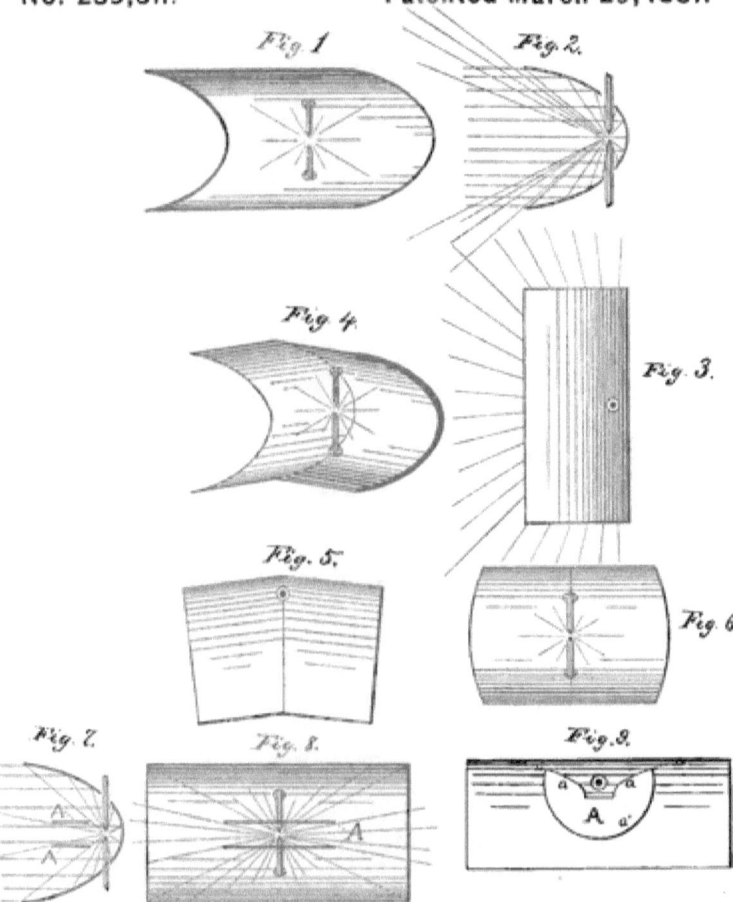

UNITED STATES PATENT OFFICE.

CHARLES F. BRUSH, OF CLEVELAND, OHIO.

REFLECTOR.

SPECIFICATION forming part of Letters Patent No. 239,311, dated March 29, 1881.

Application filed August 9, 1880. (No model.)

To all whom it may concern:

Be it known that I, CHARLES F. BRUSH, of Cleveland, in the county of Cuyahoga and State of Ohio, have invented certain new and useful Improvements in Reflectors; and I do hereby declare the following to be a full, clear, and exact description of the invention, such as will enable others skilled in the art to which it pertains to make and use it, reference being had to the accompanying drawings, which form part of this specification.

My invention relates to light-reflectors; and it consists in the form of same, substantially as hereinafter specified.

In the drawings, Figure 1 represents a front quarter-view of a reflector constructed according to my invention. Fig. 2, a side elevation of same; Fig. 3, a plan view of same; Fig. 4, a view similar to that shown in Fig. 1, illustrating a modified form of my invention. Fig. 5 is a plan view of the device shown in Fig. 4; Fig. 6, a front view of the said modified device; Fig. 7, a view of my device in side elevation, showing the position and relation of the cut-off plates; Fig. 8, a front view of the device shown in Fig. 7, and Fig. 9 a combined section and plan view of the same, showing the shape of the cut-off plates.

As sufficiently indicated in the drawings, my reflector combines the characteristics of a cylinder and parabola, such as could be produced by curving a flat sheet of metal to the form of a parabola, as shown in Figs. 1 and 2. When a light is placed in the focus of this parabola the reflection will be in the form, substantially, of a horizontal sheet extending through an arc of one hundred and eighty degrees, more or less, according to the adjustment or peculiar construction of the reflector. This is indicated in Figs. 2 and 3 of the drawings, which show the direction of the light-rays.

I have designed this reflector for use more particularly with the electric light, although I do not limit its use thus narrowly. I have, therefore, shown in the drawings, the usual carbons and their voltaic arc as the luminous agent.

In the form of reflector shown in Figs. 1, 2, and 3, the illuminating carbons will cast their shadow and where this would be undesirable the modified form illustrated in Figs. 4, 5, and 6 may be adopted. This modification consists merely in constructing the back of the reflector in an angular fashion, as shown in Figs. 4, 5, and 6, instead of straight, as shown in Figs. 1 and 3.

In many places where this type of reflector is designed for use, it is important to cut off as far as possible all the rays of light excepting such as are reflected, and the direct rays that proceed in substantially the same direction as those reflected. For this purpose the cut-off plates A are provided. They are held, by any suitable attachments or supports, in substantially the position and relation indicated in the drawings. In Fig. 2, which shows these cut-off plates omitted, it will be seen how the direct rays of light diverge in front of the reflectors, and Fig. 7 illustrates how these rays are cut off by the provision of the cut-off plates A. These plates, in order to intercept no more rays than desirable, should have a form substantially as shown in plan view in Fig. 9; but this form will vary with different curves given the reflector, to accord with reflectors of varying depths.

The shape of the edges a should conform suitably with the definite parabolic curve imparted to the reflecting surface, as these edges of the plates A intercept the direct lateral rays.

The front edge a' may be made circular in form, and this will intercept the direct rays that would escape beyond the upper and lower front edges of the reflector, which are straight.

If it is desired to intercept the light-rays in one direction only, then a single cut-off plate—say the upper one—will be sufficient to arrest the rays in that direction.

I am aware that reflectors have been constructed with faces such as would be formed by bending a flat sheet in one direction into a circular or analogously-curved shape; but I lay no claim to such an invention, as a reflector thus shaped would totally defeat the only object of my invention, which is to reflect light into the form of a flat sheet, and

this can only be effected by the employment of a reflector such as illustrated and described herein.

What I claim is—

1. A reflector having a concave face such as would be formed by bending a flat sheet, substantially as shown, so that it would have in cross-section the form of a parabola.

2. The combination, with a reflector having a concave face such as would be formed by curving a flat sheet in one direction only, of one or more cut-off plates, A, suitably shaped to accord with the curve of said reflector, substantially as and for the purpose shown.

In testimony whereof I have signed my name to this specification, in the presence of two subscribing witnesses.

CHARLES F. BRUSH.

Witnesses:
LEVERETT L. LEGGETT,
JNO. CROWELL, Jr.

Assigned to Brush Electric Co. -- JAN 8 13

UNITED STATES AMERICA

No. 139,312

To all to whom these presents shall come:

Whereas Charles F. Brush of Cleveland Ohio has presented to the Commissioner of Patents a petition praying for the grant of Letters Patent for an alleged new and useful improvement in

Electrics

a description of which invention is contained in the Specification of which a copy is hereunto annexed and made a part hereof, and has complied with the various requirements of Law in such cases made and provided, and *Whereas* upon due examination made the said Claimant is adjudged to be justly entitled to a Patent under the Law.

Now therefore these **Letters Patent** are to grant unto the said Charles F. Brush, his heirs or assigns for the term of _seventeen_ years from the _twenty ninth_ day of _March_, one thousand eight hundred and _eighty one_, the exclusive right to make, use and vend the said invention throughout the United States and the Territories thereof.

In testimony whereof I have hereunto set my hand and caused the seal of the **Patent Office** to be affixed at the City of Washington this _twenty ninth_ day of _March_ in the year of our Lord one thousand eight hundred and _eighty one_ and of the Independence of the United States of America the one hundred and fifth.

Countersigned
Marble
Commissioner of Patents.

A. Bell
Acting Secretary of the Interior.

(No Model.)

C. F. BRUSH.
Reflector.

No. 239,312.   Patented March 29, 1881.

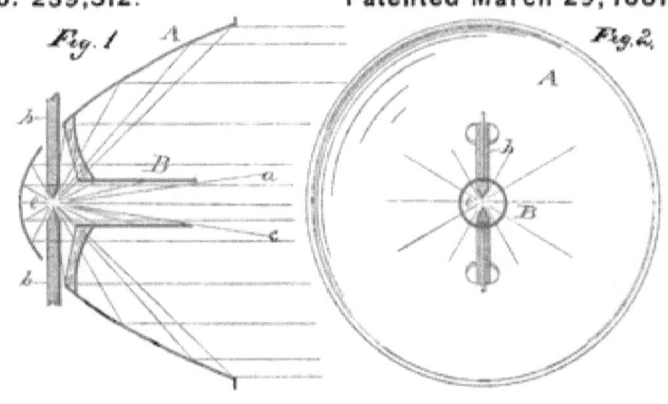

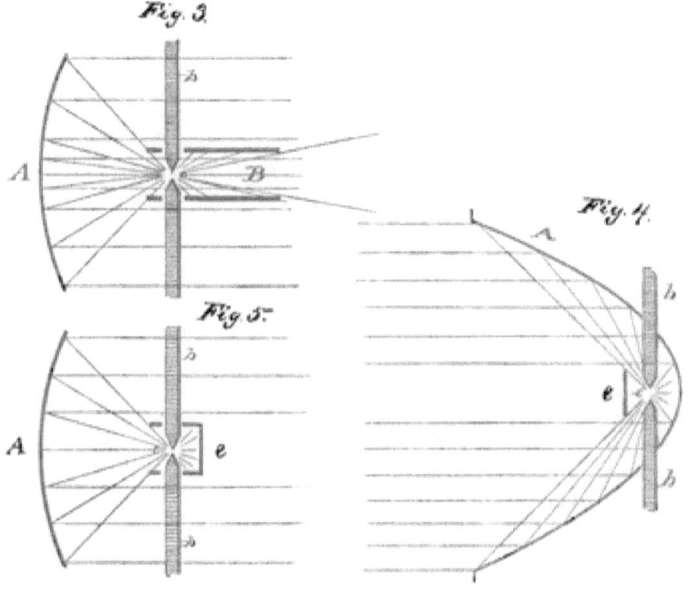

WITNESSES
F. M. Fabir.
Jno. Crowell Jr.

INVENTOR
Chas. F. Brush
By Leggitt & Leggitt ATTORNEYS

United States Patent Office.

CHARLES F. BRUSH, OF CLEVELAND, OHIO.

REFLECTOR.

SPECIFICATION forming part of Letters Patent No. 239,312, dated March 29, 1881.

Application filed August 6, 1880. (No model.)

To all whom it may concern:

Be it known that I, CHARLES F. BRUSH, of Cleveland, in the county of Cuyahoga and State of Ohio, have invented certain new and useful Improvements in Reflectors; and I do hereby declare the following to be a full, clear, and exact description of the invention, such as will enable others skilled in the art to which it pertains to make and use it, reference being had to the accompanying drawings, which form part of this specification.

My invention relates to reflectors for electric and other lights, and has for its object the suppression of the direct or unreflected light issuing from the luminous source, without interfering materially with the reflected rays. The desirability of this suppression is very apparent when electric lights are used with parabolic or other reflectors on board ships. Here the object of the reflector and light is to illuminate distant objects while the ship remains in comparative darkness, so that the pilot may clearly see the distant objects illuminated without being himself blinded by the light. When an electric light is used with even a very deep parabolic reflector in the ordinary manner, the wide cone of unreflected light escaping from the mouth of the reflector illuminates the mist, which is always present in greater or less quantity in the atmosphere near the surface of water, so as to present the appearance of a luminous fog-bank of greater or less density and of large size. The water is also rendered distinctly luminous where the light strikes it, especially when rough. This luminosity of the water and atmosphere is very annoying to the pilot, often making the electric light an annoyance rather than a benefit; but when the cone of unreflected light is suppressed these evils disappear, and the great utility of the light becomes manifest. The unreflected light may evidently be suppressed by adapting a tube of suitable size (cylindrical or slightly conical) to the mouth of the reflector and extending it a sufficient distance forward; but it is equally evident that this method is impracticable.

I accomplish my object by placing a short tube of comparatively small diameter very near the light, with its axis coincident with that of the reflected beam.

In the drawings, Figure 1 shows a cross-section through its axis of an ordinary parabolic reflector provided with my device. Fig. 2 shows a front view of the same. Fig. 3 shows a shallow spherical reflector provided with my device. Figs. 4 and 5 show disks substituted for the tubular device.

A, Figs. 1 and 2, is a parabolic reflector, provided with openings in the usual manner, through which the carbons b b of an electric lamp pass, uniting at or near the focus c of the reflector.

B is a tube of thin metal, open at both ends, and having its axis coincident with the axis of the reflector. This tube is placed sufficiently near the luminous point to obstruct the cone of light a c which would otherwise issue unreflected from the parabola, but not sufficiently near to intercept rays of light which would fall within the reflector. The tube B evidently does not interfere with the reflected light, since the latter may all pass through and outside of it. The unreflected light issuing from the tube is so slightly divergent as to be unobjectionable.

The tube B may be supported in position by any suitable means, one method being shown in the figures. In practice I prefer to attach the tube to guides through which the carbons b b pass, so that the relative position of the tube and luminous center may remain constant, while the position of the light is changed backward or forward to make the reflected beam slightly divergent or parallel, as may be required.

Fig. 3 shows my device adapted to a shallow reflector. Here the tube B necessarily extends slightly back of the carbons, and is provided with suitable openings through which the carbons pass, as shown.

The tube B should not have a reflecting surface inside, because, if reflecting, the cone of light entering it will, after several reflections, emerge as the same cone diminished in intensity, however, by the reflections it has undergone.

Evidently a small disk suitably placed would oppose the unreflected cone of light, Figs. 1 and 2, as well as does the tube B; but it would also intercept more or less of the reflected light, according to its size. If made very small this loss of light would not be no-

ticeable, but the necessary proximity of the disk to the luminous point and the mal-adjustment attending a slight change in position of the latter render its use objectionable.

Fig. 4 shows a disk, c, substituted for the tube B, Fig. 1.

Fig. 5 shows a disk and tube, c, substituted for the tube B, Fig. 3. This disk c, while it may be employed as an inferior substitute for the tube, I do not consider to be an equivalent thereof. I have merely referred to the disk in this specification by way of explanation; but as it is my intention hereafter to make separate application for Letters Patent upon said disk, I do not intend, by anything disclosed in this specification, to waive any right of hereafter applying for and securing a patent upon the disk c referred to.

What I claim is—

The combination, with a concave reflector, of a cut-off tube having a non-reflecting inner surface, said tube located in such proximity to the light or flame as to intercept and cut off the direct rays of light, substantially as shown and described.

In testimony whereof I have signed my name to this specification in the presence of two subscribing witnesses.

CHARLES F. BRUSH.

Witnesses:
LEVERETT L. LEGGETT,
JNO. CROWELL, Jr.

assigned to Brush Electric Co. — JAN 8 1887

UNITED STATES AMERICA

No. 239,313

To all to whom these presents shall come:

Whereas Charles F. Brush of Cleveland, Ohio has presented to the Commissioner of Patents a petition praying for the grant of Letters Patent for an alleged new and useful improvement in

Current Governors for Dynamo Electric Machines

a description of which invention is contained in the Specification of which a copy is hereunto annexed and made a part hereof, and has complied with the various requirements of Law in such cases made and provided, and

Whereas upon due examination made the said Claimant is adjudged to be justly entitled to a Patent under the Law.

Now therefore these **Letters Patent** are to grant unto the said Charles F. Brush his heirs or assigns for the term of seventeen years from the twenty-ninth day of March one thousand eight hundred and eighty one the exclusive right to make, use and vend the said invention throughout the United States and the Territories thereof.

In testimony whereof I have hereunto set my hand and caused the seal of the Patent Office to be affixed at the City of Washington this twenty-ninth day of March in the year of our Lord one thousand eight hundred and eighty one and of the Independence of the United States of America the one hundred and fifth.

Acting Secretary of the Interior

Countersigned:
M. Noble
Commissioner of Patents

(No Model.)

C. F. BRUSH.
Current Governor for Dynamo Electric Machines.

No. 239,313. Patented March 29, 1881.

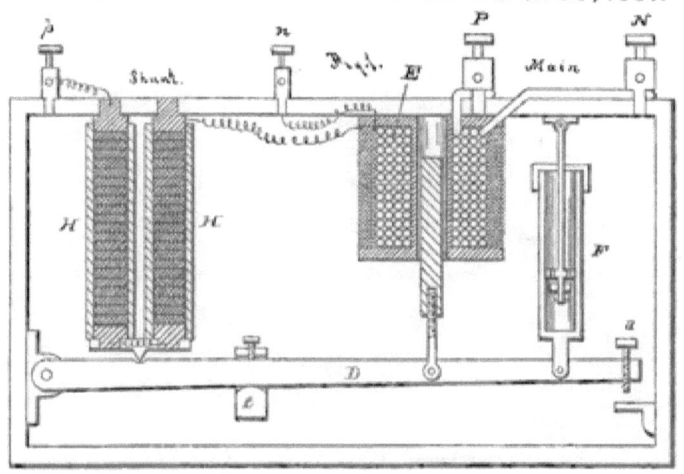

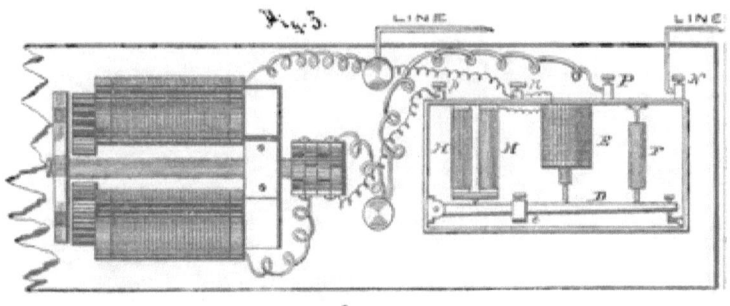

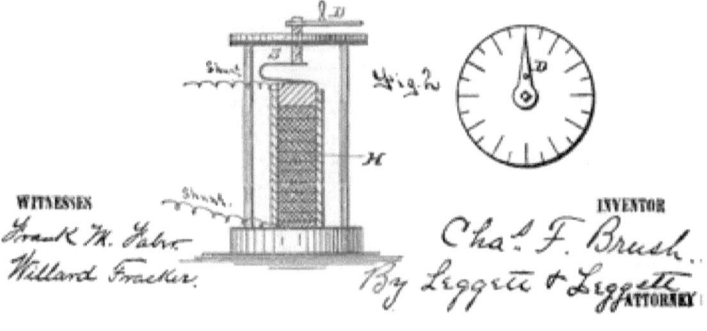

WITNESSES
Frank M. Fabr.
Willard Fracker.

INVENTOR
Chas. F. Brush.
By Leggett & Leggett
ATTORNEY

UNITED STATES PATENT OFFICE.

CHARLES F. BRUSH, OF CLEVELAND, OHIO.

CURRENT-GOVERNOR FOR DYNAMO-ELECTRIC MACHINES.

SPECIFICATION forming part of **Letters Patent** No. 239,313, dated **March 29, 1881.**

Application filed May 26, 1880. (No model.)

To all whom it may concern:

Be it known that I, CHARLES F. BRUSH, of Cleveland, in the county of Cuyahoga and State of Ohio, have invented certain new and useful Improvements in Current-Governors for Dynamo-Electric Machines; and I do hereby declare the following to be a full, clear, and exact description of the invention, such as will enable others skilled in the art to which it pertains to make and use it, reference being had to the accompanying drawings, which form part of this specification.

My invention relates to dynamo-electric machines, and has for its object the adaptation of such machines to variable external conditions without variation of the speed at which their armatures are rotated, but by variation of the intensity of the magnetic field, and this by means not directly depending on the volume of current circulating in the external circuit. In Letters Patent No. 224,511, granted to me February 17, 1880, I have shown and described several methods for effecting this object, and it is the improvement or further development of some of these methods which forms the subject of this my present invention.

I shall assume that the broad principle of shunting away a portion of the current employed to excite the field-magnets of a dynamo-electric machine for the purpose of weakening the magnetic field has been sufficiently well enunciated in the Letters Patent above referred to to require no further explanation; also, that the function of the main or external current in operating the automatic forms of the apparatus has been clearly shown.

In the improvement of the apparatus shown in Fig. 3 of the drawings forming part of the Letters Patent No. 224,511, I use two or more piles of carbon plates, H, connected in series, so that the shunt-circuit includes them successively. This is to render the apparatus more compact by obviating the necessity of an inconveniently long pile of carbon. I further employ the shunt-current itself to assist the main current in operating the magnet E, and thus render the apparatus more sensitive in its operation. I also employ a dash-pot to prevent sudden movements of the magnet-armature, and thus avoid abrupt variations of resistance in the carbon pile.

Figure 1 of the present drawings shows these modifications of and additions to my former device. Fig. 2 shows a form of apparatus wherein a pile of carbon plates, H, or similar resistance, is employed in a manual apparatus. Fig. 3 represents my present device as connected and applied to a dynamo-electric machine.

In Fig. 1 of the drawings, H H are piles of carbon or other suitable plates, inclosed loosely within glass, porcelain, or other suitable insulating tubes or supports. The piles rest upon blocks of carbon or metal electrically connected, carried by a bar of wood or metal, which is pivoted to and supported by the lever D. The upper ends of the insulating-tubes are loosely closed by plugs of carbon or metal supported by the frame of the apparatus and insulated from each other. Obviously three or more piles, H, may be employed, all connected in series, as are the two shown, and this is advisable when a compact apparatus of high resistance is required. The tubes or supports inclosing the piles H may be of metal (to absorb and radiate the heat generated) lined with mica or other insulator.

The magnet-helix E consists of two separate coils of wire—one located in the shunt-circuit, the other in the main circuit, both as shown. These two coils or helices may be arranged in various manners in relation to each other. Either may occupy the outer position, or may cover exclusively one end of the spool. Two compound helices, E, with corresponding cores of iron, may be employed to increase the effect.

Within the helix E is a movable iron core pivoted to the lever D. This lever, pivoted at one end, as shown, also carries a movable, and therefore adjustable, weight, c. (An adjustable spring may be substituted.) The free end of the lever D also carries the body of a dash-pot, F, and a thumb-screw, d, by which the downward movement of the lever is adjusted. The piston of the dash-pot F is attached to the frame-work of the apparatus by means of its rod, as shown, and is provided with a valve opening downward. When the dash-pot is filled with glycerine or other suitable liquid, its piston and valve allow the lever D to move downward freely, but retard its upward movement. The valve in the pis-

ton is not essential, but is desirable, as will be shown later.

The operation of the whole device is as follows: The binding-posts *p n*, forming the terminals of the shunt-circuit, are connected with the field-magnets of a dynamo-electric machine in the manner explained in the previous Letters Patent referred to. The course of the shunt-current is then from the post *p*, through the piles H H, outer portion of helix E, to post *n*. The binding-posts P N are put in the main or working circuit of the machine, as was also explained in my said prior patent, but in such a manner that the main current shall pass through the helix E in the same direction as the shunt-current. The weight *c* is so adjusted that when the machine is working to its full capacity, and the normal working-current is passing through its portion of the helix E, the inclosed iron core, lifted by the axial magnetism developed in the helix, shall just sustain the lever D, and parts connected therewith, while subjecting the piles H to little or no pressure. Since in this condition of affairs the piles H H perform no function, the circuit through them may be entirely broken by dropping the lever D sufficiently. This, however, is not essential. The office of the thumb-screw *d* is now apparent. If, now, the resistance of the working-circuit of the dynamo-machine be lessened from any cause, the current will be correspondingly increased in the helix E, and the inclosed core will be drawn upward, raising the lever D and subjecting the resistance-piles H to a pressure corresponding to the increase of current in the main circuit. Current will then be shunted from the field-magnets of the dynamo-machine until the main current is reduced to nearly its original strength. Some increase of current strength is, however, required, in order to maintain a suitable pressure in the piles H H. It is in order to render this necessary excess of main current as small as possible that the shunted current is made to pass through a portion of the helix E. The shunted current thus assists in maintaining a suitable pressure on the resistance-piles H H, and the apparatus is thereby enabled to respond to very much smaller variations in the strength of the main current than it otherwise could do. When the carbon piles H H are subjected to pressure their conducting power increases less rapidly than the pressure applied. Hence the apparatus is not liable to get into the condition of "unstable equilibrium."

The office of the dash-pot F has already been described; but the function of the valve in its piston has not been indicated. Suppose a number of voltaic-arc lamps are operated in the main circuit, and the latter, as often occurs in practice, becomes for an instant broken, then, owing to the valve in the piston-rod of the dash-pot, the lever D drops at once, and the shunt resistance increases, so that when the carbons in the lamps have come together and completed the main circuit again the full power of the dynamo-machine will be available to separate the carbons in the lamps, and, owing to the slow upward motion of the lever D allowed by the dash-pot, sufficient time is given for the carbons in the lamps to become fully separated before the shunt can act; but if the lever D had not been allowed to fall materially during the instant the main circuit was broken, the abnormally-great current developed when the circuit was closed, and before the carbons in the lamps had time to separate, would further raise the lever D and unfit the dynamo-machine for developing its normal current. An appreciable length of time would then be required for the resistance apparatus and the lamps to again adjust themselves. Again, if the resistance of the main circuit is suddenly increased, the valve in the dash-pot allows the lever D to fall at once, and thus the dynamo-machine is quickly adapted to the new condition of circuit.

Instead of the piles of carbon plates H H, other forms of resistance capable of being varied by the movement of the lever D may be employed; also, in place of the helix E and movable core, an ordinary electro-magnet, with fixed core and movable armature, may be used, with or without the compound helix or helices.

Fig. 2 shows a method whereby a pile of carbon plates, H, or similar resistance, may be employed in a manual apparatus. Pressure is applied to the pile by means of a screw actuated by the lever D, as shown. This lever moves over a graduated circle, and acts as an index of the pressure applied to the carbon pile H, so that a pressure suitable for a given condition of external resistance having been once determined, it may be found again without experiment.

A spring, S, may be interposed between the screw and the pile, as shown, to allow greater movement of the screw than might otherwise be admissible.

Obviously more than one pile H may be employed in this apparatus, as is done in Fig. 1.

From its function in determining and governing the current evolved by a dynamo-electric machine, I will call the device herein referred to a "current-governor."

What I claim is—

1. In a current-governor constructed to operate in connection with a dynamo-electric machine, an electro-magnet excited by two helices, one helix included within the main circuit and the other within a shunt-circuit, within which said shunt-circuit is placed an adjustable resistance, substantially as shown.

2. The combination, in an electric-current governor, of an adjustable or variable resistance, mechanism to vary said resistance, substantially as specified, and a dash-pot, or equivalent, for modifying the motion of said resistance-varying mechanism, substantially as shown.

3. In a current-governor constructed to operate in connection with a dynamo-electric

machine, as shown, a dash-pot or any equivalent device or mechanism that shall interpose a retarding influence or action in one direction only, substantially as shown.

4. In a current-governor constructed to operate in connection with a dynamo-electric machine, an arm or lever, D, in combination, first, with an adjustable resistance constructed to be varied through the movement of said lever; second, with an electro-magnet, through the influence of which motion is imparted to said arm or lever; and, third, with any suitable mechanism (such as the dash-pot or its equivalent) for governing or modifying the movements of said arm or lever, substantially as shown.

5. In a current-governor constructed to operate in connection with a dynamo-electric machine, two or more resistance-piles, H, or their equivalents, electrically connected in series, and a device associated with each pile for varying its electrical resistance, substantially as shown.

In testimony whereof I have signed my name to this specification in the presence of two subscribing witnesses.

CHARLES F. BRUSH.

Witnesses:
LEVERETT L. LEGGETT,
JNO. CROWELL, Jr.

Assigned to Brush Electric Co. — JAN 8 13

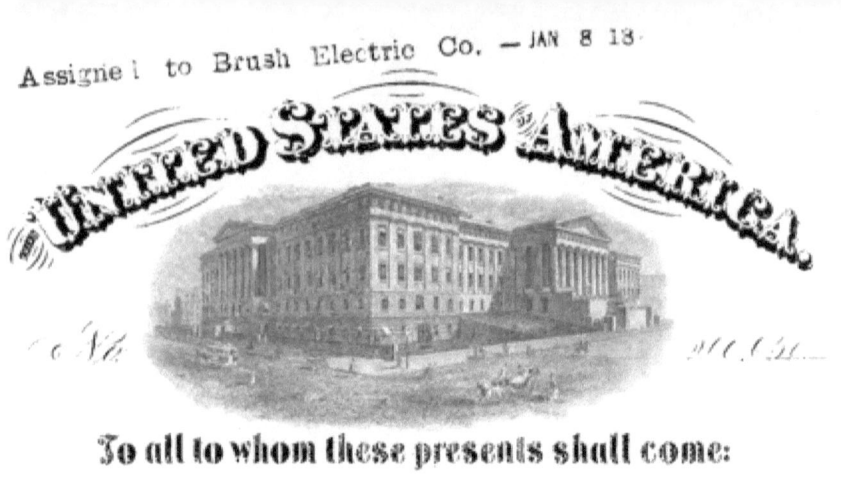

UNITED STATES AMERICA

To all to whom these presents shall come:

Whereas Charles F. Brush of Cleveland Ohio has presented to the Commissioner of Patents a petition praying for the grant of Letters Patent for an alleged new and useful improvement in

Current Surveyors Dynamo Electric Machines

a description of which invention is contained in the Specification of which a copy is hereunto annexed and made a part hereof, and has complied with the various requirements of Law in such cases made and provided, and

Whereas upon due examination made the said Claimant is adjudged to be justly entitled to a Patent under the Law.

Now therefore these **Letters Patent** are to grant unto the said Charles F. Brush his heirs or assigns for the term of seventeen years from the _____ day of _____ one thousand eight hundred and eighty two the exclusive right to make, use and vend the said invention throughout the United States and the Territories thereof.

In testimony whereof, I have hereunto set my hand and caused the seal of the **Patent Office** to be affixed at the City of Washington this _____ day of _____ in the year of our Lord one thousand eight hundred and eighty two and of the Independence of the United States of America the one hundred and seventh.

Countersigned M. Marble
Commissioner of Patents

Secretary of the Interior

(No Model.) 3 Sheets—Sheet 3.

C. F. BRUSH.
CURRENT GOVERNOR FOR DYNAMO ELECTRIC MACHINES.

No. 260,650. Patented July 4, 1882.

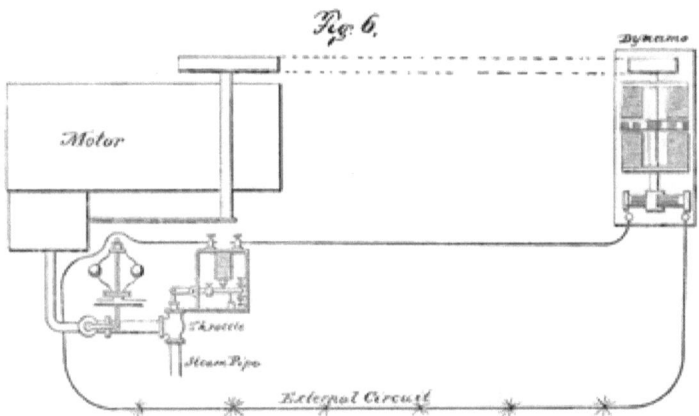

WITNESSES

INVENTOR
Chas. F. Brush.
By Liggett & Liggett
Attorney

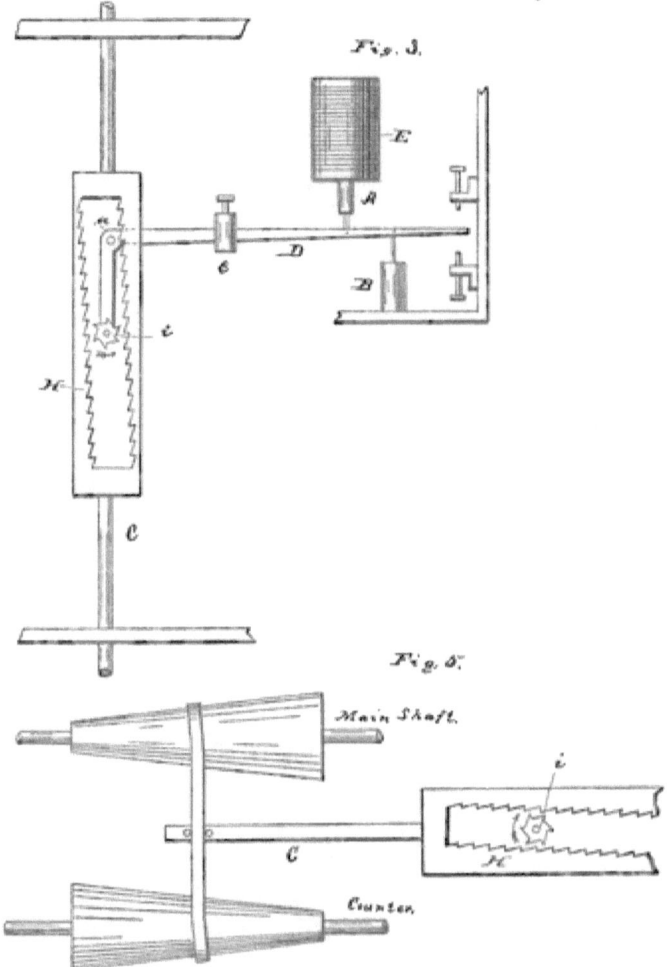

(No Model.) 3 Sheets—Sheet 1.

C. F. BRUSH.
CURRENT GOVERNOR FOR DYNAMO ELECTRIC MACHINES.

No. 260,650. Patented July 4, 1882.

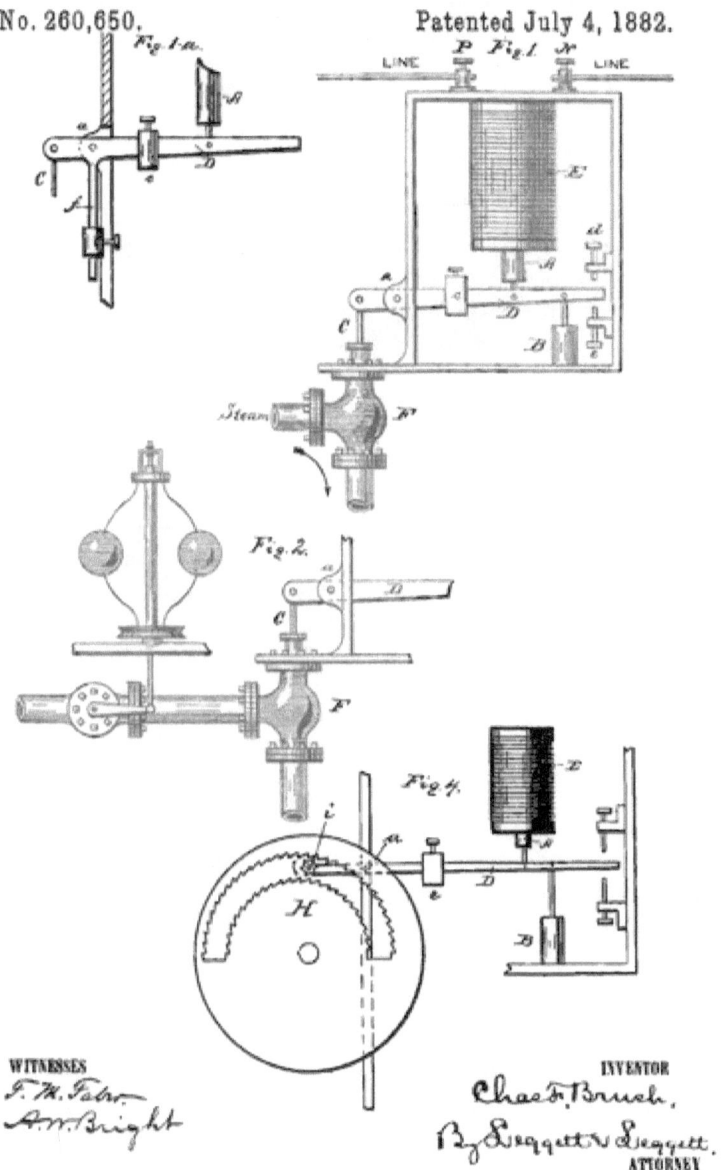

WITNESSES
F. W. Fabro
A. W. Bright

INVENTOR
Chas. F. Brush,
By Leggett & Leggett,
ATTORNEY

United States Patent Office.

CHARLES F. BRUSH, OF CLEVELAND, OHIO.

CURRENT-GOVERNOR FOR DYNAMO-ELECTRIC MACHINES.

SPECIFICATION forming part of Letters Patent No. 260,650, dated July 4, 1882.

Application filed June 29, 1880. (No model.)

To all whom it may concern:

Be it known that I, CHARLES F. BRUSH, of Cleveland, in the county of Cuyahoga and State of Ohio, have invented certain new and useful Improvements in Electrical Governors for Dynamo-Electric Machines; and I do hereby declare the following to be a full, clear, and exact description of the invention, such as will enable others skilled in the art to which it pertains to make and use it, reference being had to the accompanying drawings, which form part of this specification.

My invention relates to dynamo-electric machines, and has for its object the automatic control of the driving-power applied to such apparatus, whereby the speed of armature rotation is regulated in accordance with the requirements of the external circuit, so that a uniform, or nearly uniform, current-strength may be maintained while the circuit-resistance varies.

I accomplish my object by employing a magnetic apparatus actuated by the external current of the machine to regulate the admission of steam or water, as the case may be, to the driving-engine. Increase of current in the circuit acts to diminish the supply of motive agent, and thus to decrease the speed of the dynamo-machine until the normal current volume is restored, while decrease of current produces the contrary effect.

In the drawings, Figure 1 shows my automatic apparatus applied as a governor to a steam-engine. Fig. 2 shows my electrical governor combined with a centrifugal governor. Fig. 3 illustrates a modification of my device adapted to overcome the mechanical resistance of the regulating valves or gates in the cases of large steam-engines and water-wheels. Fig. 4 shows another modification similar to Fig. 3. Fig. 5 illustrates a method of governing the speed of a dynamo-machine while that of the primary driving power remains constant. Fig. 6 illustrates an electric lighting system embodying one form of my improvement.

In Fig. 1, E is a hollow helix, having its terminals connected with the binding-posts P N, and thus with the line or external circuit of the dynamo-electric machine whose speed is to be governed. Within this helix is a movable iron core, A, pivoted to the lever D, as shown. The lever D is pivoted again to the frame of the apparatus at a. The lever has also pivoted to it the piston-rod of a dash-pot, B. The piston of this dash-pot may or may not be provided with a valve to free the motion of the lever D in one direction. c is a weight, movable and therefore adjustable on the arm or lever D. d e are screws for adjusting the limits to the movements of the lever D. At the other end of the lever D is pivoted a valve-stem, C, forming part of an ordinary steam-governor valve, F. This valve controls the admission of steam to the engine (not shown) which drives the dynamo-electric machine or machines (not shown) in whose working-circuit the helix E is located.

In practical operation the weight c is so adjusted that when the normal electric current circulates in the helix E the attraction of the latter for its core A shall be just sufficient to sustain the core, together with the movable parts attached thereto. If, now, the valve-stem C is not in the right position—is raised too high, for instance—too much steam will be admitted to the engine through the valve F, and the engine and dynamo-machine attached will have their speed of rotation increased. This will augment the current in the helix E, drawing upward the core A and depressing the valve-stem C until the speed of the engine is properly reduced. If the line-resistance is reduced from any cause, the increase of current thereby produced in the circuit, including the helix E, will act as before, further throttling the steam at the governor-valve F, and thus reduce the speed of the engine and dynamo-machine until the current in the circuit is nearly or quite reduced to its normal strength. If, on the other hand, the circuit-resistance is increased by inserting more electric lights or otherwise, the weakening of the current thereby occasioned allows the helix E to drop its core A and raise the valve-stem C, thus admitting more steam to the engine, which accordingly increases its speed until the normal current strength in the circuit is restored.

The office of the dash-pot B is to prevent the too sudden opening or closing of the valve F. Two helices, E, with corresponding cores A united in the customary manner, may be employed instead of the single one shown.

Any suitable form of throttle-valve may be employed at F, and, if desirable, the valve may be so constructed that the upward motion of the stem C shall operate to close it, thus allowing of a change of position in the fulcrum of the lever D.

Instead of utilizing the motion of the stem C to throttle the steam admitted to the engine to be controlled, it may be employed to regulate the point of "cut-off" of the steam in the cylinder by any of the methods customary with engines of the "automatic cut-off" class. This of course is the more desirable manner of applying my invention, especially in the case of large engines, since the same economy of steam will be effected that obtains when the engines are governed by centrifugal action in the ordinary manner.

I have illustrated my invention applied as a throttling-governor instead of as a cut-off governor for the sake of simplicity merely, and do not in any manner limit myself to the particular form or application shown.

In the construction of my apparatus it will of course be necessary to so arrange or shape the helix E and core A that the latter shall not be attracted with increasing force as it moves upward through the distance allowed it, since a neglect of this precaution would evidently leave the apparatus in a state of unstable equilibrium. On the contrary, it is advisable to so arrange matters that the attraction of the helix for its core shall diminish slightly as the latter ascends. The same ultimate result may be obtained by attaching a suitably-weighted pendulum-lever to the arm D at its fulcrum, as shown in Fig. 1ª. Here, as the core A rises, the pendulum f is thrown out of the vertical position, and more or less of its weight is added to that of the lever D, according to the position of the core A, so that the latter will have a constantly-increasing load to carry as it ascends.

In order to prevent the engine "racing" when the working-circuit of the dynamo machine or machines which it is driving becomes of abnormally-high resistance or is broken, an ordinary centrifugal governor may be employed in combination with my electrical governor, as shown in Fig. 2. Here the centrifugal governor is so adjusted that it does not begin to control the flow of steam until the engine has passed beyond its normal maximum rate of speed. Thus when conditions arise, accidentally or otherwise, under which the electrical governor cannot properly perform its function this auxiliary centrifugal governor comes into action.

I have thus far described my apparatus as applied to the automatic control of the speed of dynamo-electric machines driven by steam-power only, but that it is equally applicable when water-power is employed must be obvious. In the case of water-power, the available mechanical force of the helix E and its core will not be sufficient to operate the gate controlling the flow of water, and some auxiliary mechanism furnishing the required mechanical power, but controlled by the electrical apparatus, must be employed. This auxiliary mechanism I do not here claim as my invention; but I shall show and describe the same for the purpose, merely, of setting forth one or two of various methods whereby the axial magnet of my governor can be employed to control a water-gate or belt-shifting apparatus. In omitting, however, any attempt herein to claim said auxiliary mechanism, I do not waive the right in any future application to more particularly show, specify, and claim this auxiliary mechanism, if I so elect, inasmuch as it is here introduced for the sake of convenience in setting forth the full application of my invention, hereinabove specified. Fig. 3 shows one convenient form of such mechanism. Here the valve or gate stem C is made of suitable size and strength, and, instead of being attached directly to the arm D, is attached to a frame, H. The sides of this frame form two toothed racks parallel with each other, but not so with the line of motion of the frame. The lever D carries at its working end a ratchet-wheel, i, of such size that it can just revolve between the racks forming the sides of the frame H without engaging with either. This ratchet-wheel is attached to the end of a jointed or flexible shaft or spindle (not shown) passing through the arm D. By means of its flexible shaft the wheel i is connected with the motive power which is to be governed, or with other motive power from which it receives a slow rotary motion in the direction indicated by the arrow, while at the same time it is free to be carried to the right or left by the lever D. Now, when the core A rises the ratchet-wheel i engages with the right-hand rack of the frame H, and the latter, together with the stem C, is carried upward until the rack, owing to its oblique motion, ceases to engage the ratchet-wheel i. When the core A falls the wheel engages with the other rack and the stem C is depressed. Thus the stem C is caused to rise and fall (much or little) with the core A, and may overcome great mechanical resistance without taxing the magnetic part of the apparatus. By inclining the racks H in the other direction and reversing the motion of the wheel i the stem C will be caused to move upward when the core A moves downward, and the contrary. This auxiliary mechanism may also be employed to work the governing-valves or cut-off mechanism of large steam-engines where the friction of parts is considerable.

In the case of water-wheels, as with steam-engines, it is always advisable to employ an auxiliary governor, as and for the purpose already specified in connection with the steam apparatus.

Fig. 4 shows a modification of the device shown in Fig. 3, wherein the frame H is curved, so that angular or rotary motion is produced instead of rectilinear motion.

Other auxiliary governing apparatus con-

trolled by the helix E and core A, Fig. 3, may be employed, either of electrical or of purely mechanical nature; but, as I have sufficiently indicated the principle involved, I will not describe further modifications.

The application of my invention to gas and other heat engines, wind-wheels, &c., when employed to drive dynamo-electric machines is too obvious to require explanation.

The mechanism shown in Fig. 3, or its equivalent, may further be employed to control and vary the speed of dynamo-electric machines while the speed of the primary driving power remains constant. One method of accomplishing this result is illustrated in Fig. 5. Here power is transmitted from the main shaft to the counter-shaft by means of a belt traveling on oppositely-coned pulleys, as shown. The belt is shifted, as required, by means of the stem or rod C, actuated in the manner already specified in connection with Fig. 3, so that while the speed of the main shaft remains constant that of the counter-shaft and dynamo-machine driven therefrom may be suitably varied and controlled.

I have described the helix E as being located in and operated by the main or working current of the dynamo-machine whose speed is to be governed; but it may evidently be located in a shunt or derived circuit wherein the current strength is dependent on that in the working-circuit. Such a modification obviously does not affect the principles involved in my invention.

When the helix E and core A are replaced by an ordinary electro-magnet with fixed core and movable armature it is difficult to obtain sufficient movement of the latter with uniformity of action to effect the object in view. Therefore the magnet E of my governor is of the type termed "axial"—that is, one having a hollow helix inclosing a loosely-fitting core that is drawn within the helix with a force proportionate to the strength of current traversing said helix. The employment of this axial type of magnet in an electrical governor, as herein specified, I believe to be entirely novel with this my invention, and by its use many essential advantages and functions are secured.

I am aware that effort has heretofore been made to produce a governor that would, through the influence of the electric current generated by a dynamo-electric machine, operate to determine and control the speed at which said dynamo-electric machine is driven. Nothing, however, up to the present time has been produced that has ever been susceptible of any practical application, inasmuch as the complexity of mechanism employed and the erroneous principles and ideas proceeded upon have defeated the object sought.

What I claim is—

1. In a system for generating and applying an electric current, the combination of the following-named instrumentalities, to wit: A dynamo-electric machine, a motor for driving said dynamo-electric machine, an external or working circuit upon which is placed one or more electric lamps, electro-motors, or any device to be operated upon or actuated by the electric current, and a governor consisting of a hollow or axial magnet that is energized by current from said dynamo-electric machine, and that is associated with suitable valve or cut-off mechanism, said governor constructed and adjusted to control the speed at which the dynamo-electric machine is driven according to the varying condition of the current in said external or working circuit, substantially as shown.

2. In an electrical governor for regulating the speed at which a dynamo-electric machine is driven, an axial magnet for imparting motion to the moving parts of said governor, said axial magnet being energized by the current of the dynamo-electric machine to be controlled.

3. The combination, with a motor for driving a dynamo-electric machine, of a hollow or axial magnet influenced by the current of said dynamo-electric machine and a valve mechanism controlled by said axial magnet to govern the admission of steam, water, or equivalent driving agent to said motor, and thus to govern its speed in accordance with the varying condition of the said current, substantially as shown.

4. The combination, with a motor for driving a dynamo-electric machine, of two governors, one for controlling the speed at which said dynamo-electric machine is driven and answering to the variations in the condition of the external or working circuit, and the other constructed to act only when said speed tends to exceed a given and prescribed maximum.

5. In combination with an electric governor for regulating the speed at which a dynamo-electric machine is driven, the pendent weight f, substantially as and for the purpose shown.

In testimony whereof I have signed my name to this specification in the presence of two subscribing witnesses.

CHARLES F. BRUSH.

Witnesses:
LEVERETT L. LEGGETT,
JNO. CROWELL, Jr.

Assigned to Brush Electric Co. —JAN 8 18

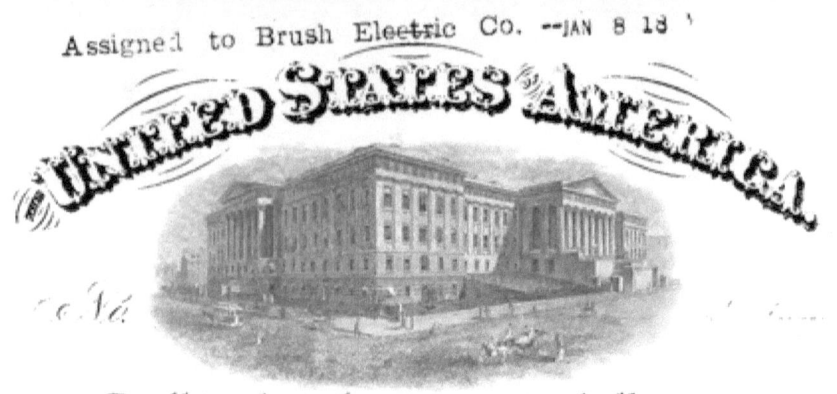

UNITED STATES AMERICA

No.

To all to whom these presents shall come:

Whereas _____

ha__ presented to the *Commissioner of Patents* a petition praying for the ____ of *Letters Patent* for an alleged new and useful improvement in _____

a description of which invention is contained in the *Specification* of which a copy is hereunto annexed and made a part hereof, and ha__ complied with the various requirements of Law in such cases made and provided, and

Whereas upon due examination made the said Claimant __ adjudged to be justly entitled to a Patent under the Law.

Now therefore these **Letters Patent** are to grant unto the said _____ heirs or assigns for the term of ____ years from the _____ day of _____ one thousand eight hundred and eighty ___ the exclusive right to make, use and vend the said invention throughout the United States and the Territories thereof.

In testimony whereof, I have hereunto set my hand and caused the seal of the **Patent Office** to be affixed at the City of Washington this ____ day of _____ in the year of our Lord one thousand eight hundred and eighty ___ and of the Independence of the United States of America the one hundred and seventh.

Countersigned: Marble
Commissioner of Patents.

Secretary of the Interior.

(Model.)

C. F. BRUSH.
THERMIC REGULATOR FOR ELECTRIC CURRENT GENERATORS.

No. 260,651. Patented July 4, 1882.

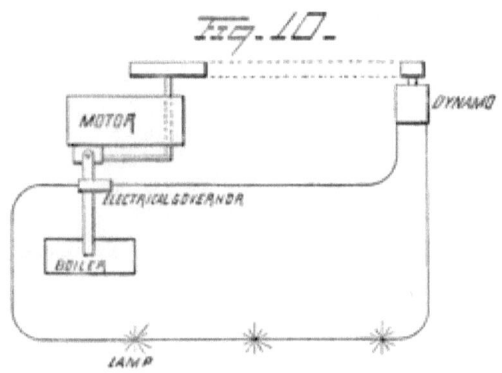

WITNESSES
Herman Moran
A W Bright

INVENTOR
Chas. F. Brush.
By Leggett & Leggett
Attorney

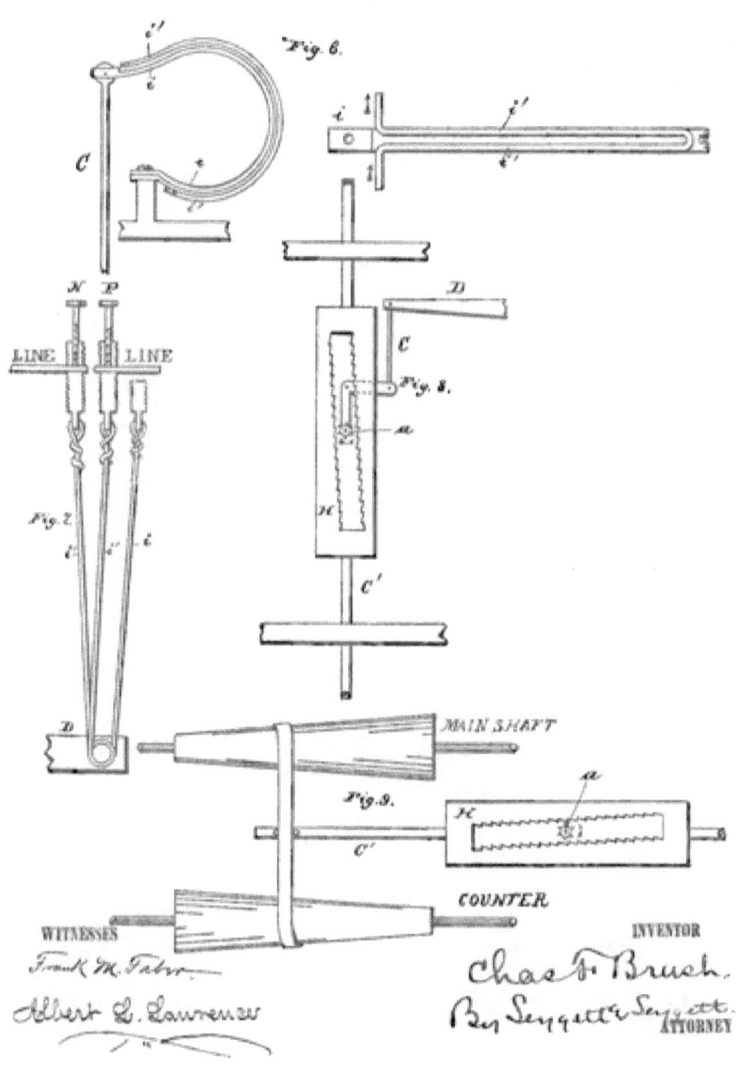

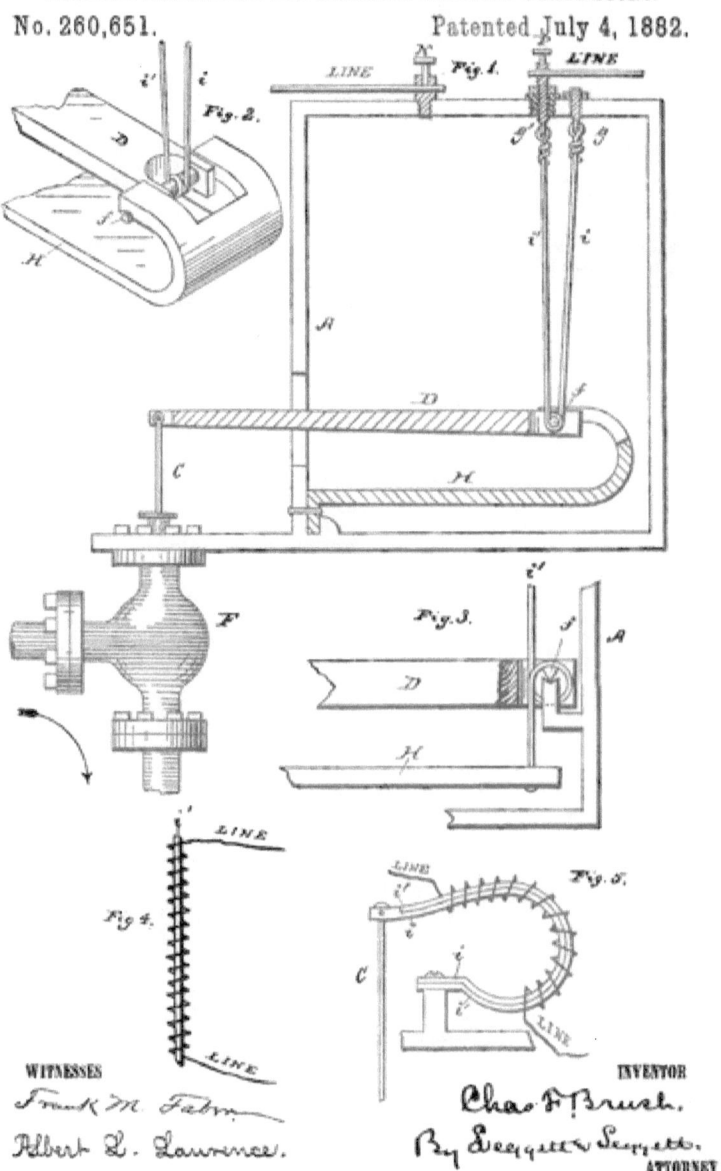

UNITED STATES PATENT OFFICE.

CHARLES F. BRUSH, OF CLEVELAND, OHIO.

THERMIC REGULATOR FOR ELECTRIC-CURRENT GENERATORS.

SPECIFICATION forming part of Letters Patent No. 260,651, dated July 4, 1882.

Application filed July 15, 1880. (Model.)

To all whom it may concern:

Be it known that I, CHARLES F. BRUSH, of Cleveland, in the county of Cuyahoga and State of Ohio, have invented certain new and useful Improvements in Thermic Regulators for Electric-Current Generators; and I do hereby declare the following to be a full, clear, and exact description of the invention, such as will enable others skilled in the art to which it pertains to make and use it, reference being had to the accompanying drawings, which form part of this specification.

My invention relates to dynamo-electric machines, and has for its object the automatic control of the driving-power applied to such apparatus, whereby the speed of armature-rotation is regulated in accordance with the requirements of the external circuit, so that a uniform, or nearly uniform, current strength may be maintained while the circuit-resistance varies.

I accomplish my object by employing an electro-thermal apparatus actuated by the external current of the machine to regulate the admission of steam or water, as the case may be, to the driving-engine. Increase of current in the circuit acts to diminish the supply of motive agent, and thus to decrease the speed of the dynamo-machine until the normal current-volume is restored, while decrease of current produces the contrary effect.

In the drawings, Figure 1 shows my automatic apparatus applied as a governor to a steam-engine. Fig. 2 is an enlarged view of a portion of the mechanism shown in Fig. 1. Fig. 3 shows a device wherein a single wire, i', is employed instead of two, as before. Fig. 4 shows the wire i' heated indirectly by the passage of current through a helix surrounding it. Fig. 5 shows a combination of two unequally-expansible metals heated indirectly by the current. Fig. 6 shows a combination of two strips of metal, one of them being heated directly by the passage of current through it. Fig. 7 shows how the wire i', Fig. 1, may be duplicated to increase the strength of the apparatus. Fig. 8 shows auxiliary motor mechanism for working large valves, water-gates, &c., the whole controlled by my electro-thermal apparatus. Fig. 9 shows my auxiliary mechanism adapted to shift belts on coned pulleys. Fig. 10 shows a dynamo-electric machine with its external circuit containing working devices, a motor for driving the dynamo-machine, and a regulator.

In Fig. 1, D is an arm or lever, provided at one end with a cylindrical cross-piece of steel or other suitable material, f, as shown enlarged in Fig. 2. The projecting ends of this cross-piece are formed into blunt knife-edges, as shown.

A wire, $i\ i'$, of suitable size and preferably of soft steel, is passed through a small hole in the central part of the cross-piece or fulcrum f, and each half of the wire is then passed once or twice around the cylindrical portion of the cross-piece in opposite directions. The ends of this wire are then carried up and attached to the studs $g\ g'$, as shown in Fig. 1. These studs are threaded and provided with nuts above the frame A, as shown. The stud g' is insulated from the frame A by means of a bushing, through which it passes, and its upper end forms the binding-post P. The lower end of the wire i' is electrically connected with the binding-post N through the fulcrum f, spring H, and frame A. Thus, by means of the binding-posts P N, the wire i' is included in the line or external circuit of the dynamo-electric machine whose speed is to be governed.

H is a very stiff spring, of steel or other metal, attached to the frame A and split at its free end so as to engage with and form a support for the knife-edges at the extremities of the fulcrum f. The wires $i\ i'$, being sufficiently strained by means of the screw-studs $g\ g'$, hold the lever D firmly against the spring H, and in the position shown in the figure. At the other end of the lever D is pivoted a valve-stem, C, forming part of an ordinary steam governor-valve, F. This valve controls the admission of steam to the engine which drives the dynamo-electric machine or machines in whose working-circuit the wire i' is located.

When my device is in operation the wire i' will become more or less heated by the passage of current through it, and will expand accordingly, while the wire i remains as before. The cylindrical portion of the fulcrum f, being partially relieved of its support on one side, will be carried downward by the powerful spring H, the free end of the lever D will be depressed,

and with it the valve-stem C. The length of the wires $i\ i'$ is so adjusted by means of the screw-studs $g\ g'$ that when i' is expanded by the passage of the normal volume of current through it the valve-stem C shall be in a position to admit just sufficient steam through the valve F to drive the engine and dynamo-machine attached thereto at a sufficient speed to maintain the aforesaid normal volume of current in circulation. If now the line-resistance is reduced from any cause, the increase of current thereby produced in the circuit including the wire i', will further heat the latter, allowing the valve-stem C to be depressed by the lever D and spring H, thus throttling the steam at the governor-valve F and reducing the speed of the engine and dynamo-machine until the current in the circuit is nearly or quite reduced to its normal strength. If, on the other hand, the circuit-resistance is increased by inserting more electric lights or otherwise, the weakening of the current thereby occasioned allows the wire i' to partially cool and contract, thus raising the stem C and admitting more steam to the engine, which accordingly increases its speed until the normal current strength in the circuit is nearly or quite restored.

A notable feature of the mechanism shown in Fig. 1 is the use of two wires, $i\ i'$, of the same metal. This feature I have styled my "compensating device." It insures the normal working of the apparatus at all temperatures, since it is the difference in temperature between the wires $i\ i'$ and not the actual temperature of i' which determines the working of the apparatus. In ordinary working the temperature of the whole apparatus gradually rises considerably, and of course the absolute temperature of the wire i' augments accordingly without any increase of current through it; and were it not for my compensating device the operation of the governor would be seriously affected from this cause.

Fig. 7 indicates how two or more wires, i', may be employed instead of one, as before shown, the current passing through them successively. Thus greater available working strength may be secured to the apparatus. The wire may likewise be multiplied or increased in size.

Fig. 3 shows one of several forms of device in which but one wire, i', is employed. This device will evidently perform all the functions described in connection with Fig. 1, except compensation for changes of general temperature.

The wires $i\ i'$ may be replaced by thin ribbons of metal, and this is even desirable, so far as that portion which passes around the fulcrum f is concerned, on account of greater flexibility; or this part may be ribbon and the rest wire.

The wire i' may be surrounded by a long helix, through which the current passes, while being itself insulated from the current, and thus be heated indirectly by the latter. Fig. 4 shows such a modification.

Instead of employing wires $i\ i'$, as in Fig. 1, I may use narrow sheets of metal connected rigidly together, side by side, and insulated from each other both thermally and electrically. The pair may be used straight, curved, or coiled, as in Fig. 6, which shows this form of device. Here the expansion of the outer strip of metal, i', by the heat due to the passage of current through it, while the inner strip, i, remains unheated, operates to depress the valve-stem C. This arrangement of parts evidently embodies my compensating device, and is a mere modified form thereof.

Fig. 5 shows a device similar to Fig. 6; but the strips $i\ i'$ are of different metals, expanding unequally on the application of heat. They are riveted or soldered together, the metal i' being the more expansible of the two, and both are heated either by the passage of current through them or by the passage of current through a helix surrounding them, as shown in the figure. The operation of the device is evident, but it lacks the compensating feature, which was retained in the device shown in Fig. 6.

My invention is equally useful with rapidly intermittent, alternating, or continuous currents, and I do not limit myself to any particular manner of applying current to heat the wire i' or its equivalent. Any suitable form of throttle-valve F, Fig. 1, may be employed.

Instead of utilizing the motion of the stem C to throttle the steam admitted to the engine to be controlled, it may be employed to regulate the point of cut-off of the steam in the cylinder by any of the methods customary with engines of the automatic cut-off class. This of course is the more desirable manner of applying my invention, especially in the case of large engines, since the same economy of steam will be effected that obtains when the engines are governed by centrifugal action in the ordinary manner.

I have illustrated my invention applied as a throttling-governor instead of as a cut-off governor for the sake of simplicity merely, and do not in any manner limit myself to the particular form or application shown.

In order to prevent the engine racing when the working-circuit of the dynamo machine or machines which it is driving becomes of abnormally-high resistance or is broken, an ordinary centrifugal governor may be employed in combination with my electrical governor. The centrifugal governor is so adjusted that it does not begin to control the flow of steam until the engine has passed beyond its normal maximum rate of speed. Thus when conditions arise, accidentally or otherwise, under which the electrical governor cannot properly perform its function this auxiliary centrifugal governor comes into action.

I have thus far described my apparatus as applied to the automatic control of the speed

of dynamo-electric machines driven by steam-power only; but that it is equally applicable when water-power is employed must be obvious. In the case of water-power the available mechanical force of the lever D will not be sufficient to operate the gate controlling the flow of water, and some auxiliary mechanism furnishing the required mechanical power, but controlled by the electrical apparatus, must be employed. Fig. 8 shows one convenient form of such mechanism. Here the valve or gate stem C' is made of suitable size and strength, and instead of being attached directly to the arm D is attached to a frame, H. The sides of this frame form two toothed racks parallel with each other, but not so with the line of motion of the frame. The lever D and stem C control the lateral position of a ratchet-wheel, a, of such size that it can just revolve between the racks forming the sides of the frame H without engaging with either. This ratchet-wheel is attached to the end of a jointed or flexible shaft or spindle, (not shown,) by means of which it is connected with the motive power which is being governed, or with other motive power, from which it receives a slow rotary motion in the direction indicated by the arrow, while at the same time it is free to be carried to the right or left by motion of the lever D. Now, when the lever D rises the ratchet-wheel a engages with the right-hand rack of the frame H, and the latter, together with the stem C', is carried upward until the rack, owing to its oblique motion, ceases to engage the ratchet-wheel a. When the arm D falls the wheel engages with the other rack, and the stem C' is depressed. Thus the stem C' is caused to rise and fall much or little with the arm D, and may overcome great mechanical resistance without taxing the electro-thermal part of the apparatus. This auxiliary mechanism may also be employed to work the governing-valves or cut-off mechanism of large steam-engines where the friction of parts is considerable.

In the case of water-wheels, as with steam-engines, it is always advisable to employ an auxiliary governor, as and for the purpose already specified in connection with the steam apparatus.

Other auxiliary governing apparatus controlled by my electro-thermal device may be employed either of electrical or of purely mechanical nature; but as I have sufficiently indicated the principle involved I will not describe further modifications.

The application of my invention to gas and other heat engines, wind-wheels, &c., when employed to drive dynamo-electric machines, is too obvious to require explanation.

The mechanism shown in Fig. 8, or its equivalent, may further be employed to control and vary the speed of dynamo-electric machines, while the speed of the primary driving-power remains constant. One method of accomplishing this result is illustrated in Fig. 9. Here power is transmitted from the main shaft to the counter-shaft by means of a belt traveling on oppositely-coned pulley, as shown. The belt is shifted as required by means of the stem or rod C', actuated in the manner already specified in connection with Fig. 8, so that while the speed of the main shaft remains constant that of the counter-shaft and dynamo-machine driven therefrom may be suitably varied and controlled.

What I claim is—

1. In a system for generating and applying an electric current, the combination of a dynamo-electric machine, a motor for driving said dynamo-electric machine, an external or working circuit, upon which is placed one or more electric lamps, electric motors, or any devices to be operated upon or actuated by the electric current, and a governor consisting of an electro-thermal device energized by the said electric current associated with suitable valve or cut-off mechanism, said governor constructed and adjusted to control the speed at which the said dynamo-electric machine is driven, substantially as shown.

2. The combination, with a dynamo-electric machine and devices for regulating the speed of the dynamo-electric machine, of an electro-thermal device arranged and adapted to be energized by the electric current, and to actuate or control the speed-regulating devices of said dynamo-electric machine, substantially as set forth.

3. The combination, with a motor for driving a dynamo-electric machine, of an electro-thermal device influenced by the current of said dynamo-electric machine, and a valve mechanism controlled by said electro-thermal device to govern the admission of steam, water, or equivalent driving agent to said motor, and thus to govern its speed in accordance with the varying requirements or resistance of the circuit of the said current, substantially as shown.

4. The combination, with the working-circuit of a dynamo-electric machine and devices for regulating the speed of the dynamo-electric machine, of the wires i i', or their equivalents, adapted by their difference in temperature to actuate or control said speed-regulating devices, substantially as set forth.

In testimony whereof I have signed my name to this specification in the presence of two subscribing witnesses.

CHARLES F. BRUSH.

Witnesses:
 LEVERETT L. LEGGETT,
 JNO. CROWELL, Jr.

Assigned to Brush Electric Co. — JAN 8 '3

UNITED STATES AMERICA

To all to whom these presents shall come:

Whereas _____

ha__ presented to the Commissioner of Patents a petition praying for the _____ of Letters Patent for an alleged new and useful improvement in _____

a description of which invention is contained in the Specification of which a copy is hereunto annexed and made a part hereof, and ha__ complied with the various requirements of Law in such cases made and provided, and Whereas upon due examination made the said Claimant __ adjudged to be justly entitled to a Patent under the Law.

Now therefore these **Letters Patent** are to grant unto the said _____ heirs or assigns for the term of _____ years from the _____ day of _____ one thousand eight hundred and eighty __ the exclusive right to make, use and vend the said invention throughout the United States and the Territories thereof.

In testimony whereof I have hereunto set my hand and caused the seal of the Patent Office to be affixed at the City of Washington this _____ day of _____ in the year of our Lord one thousand eight hundred and eighty ___ and of the Independence of the United States of America the one hundred and seventh.

Countersigned: _____ Marble
Secretary of the Interior.
Commissioner of Patents.

(No Model.)
C. F. BRUSH.
DYNAMO ELECTRIC MACHINE.

No. 260,652. Patented July 4, 1882.

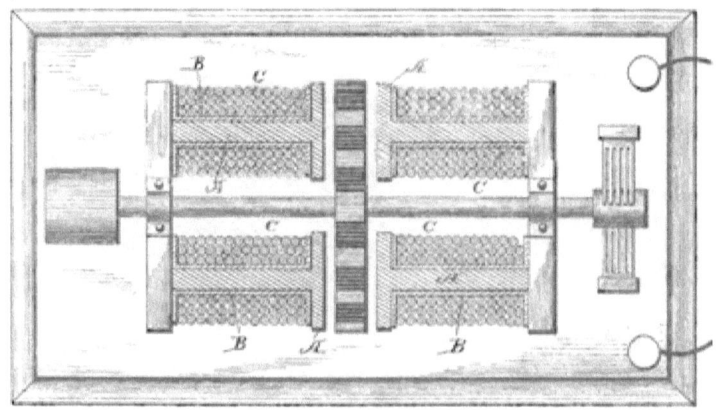

Fig. 5.

WITNESSES

INVENTOR
Chas F. Brush.
By Leggett & Leggett
Attorney

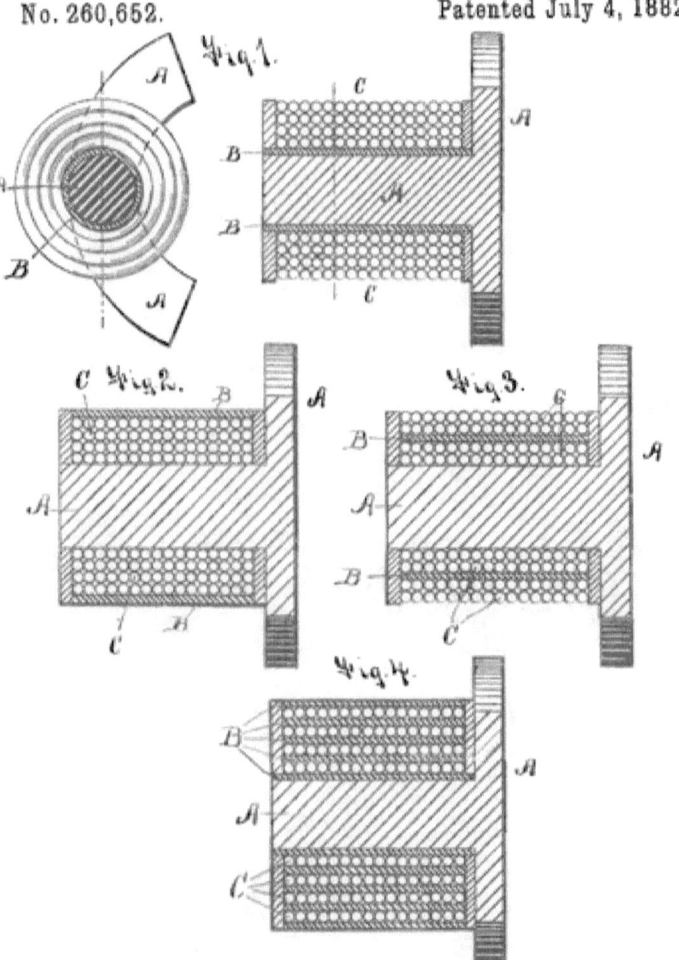

UNITED STATES PATENT OFFICE.

CHARLES F. BRUSH, OF CLEVELAND, OHIO.

DYNAMO-ELECTRIC MACHINE.

SPECIFICATION forming part of Letters Patent No. 260,652, dated July 4, 1882.

Application filed June 1, 1880. (No model.)

To all whom it may concern:

Be it known that I, CHARLES F. BRUSH, of Cleveland, in the county of Cuyahoga and State of Ohio, have invented certain new and useful Improvements in Dynamo-Electric Machines; and I do hereby declare the following to be a full, clear, and exact description of the invention, such as will enable others skilled in the art to which it pertains to make and use it, reference being had to the accompanying drawings, which form part of this specification.

My invention relates to dynamo-electric machines, and has for its object the suppression to a considerable extent of the "extra current" induced in the helices of the field-of-force magnets of such machines when from any cause fluctuations of magnetic intensity occur. The advantages arising from the suppression of this extra current obtain with dynamo-electric machines of all capacities and in all applications, but are more especially prominent in those machines which are adapted to produce currents of high electro-motive force and considerable volume. The conspicuous evils attending the presence of the extra current in such machines are danger to the insulation of the apparatus and exaggeration of accidental or unavoidable current fluctuations.

In dynamo-electric machines producing currents of high tension the number of convolutions of the helices exciting the field-magnets must be large on account of the comparatively small volume of current in circulation. Now, when the current from such a machine is suddenly diminished by sudden increase of resistance to its passage, or when it is stopped altogether by the breaking of its circuit, the extra current produced by the discharge of the magnetism of the field-magnets and by the inductive action of the different convolutions of the exciting helices on each other is of very high tension, capable of bursting through heavy insulation or traversing a very considerable air-space. Again, when one or more voltaic-arc lamps are operated in the circuit of a machine a peculiar rythmical fluctuation of the current strength, as indicated by corresponding motion in the mechanism of the lamp or lamps, may often be observed, while the speed at which the armature of the machine is rotated remains perfectly constant. By preventing motion of the mechanism of the lamps for a short time this action may cease, but is liable to appear again upon any disturbance of the circuit-resistance. Thus a state of unstable equilibrium is indicated either in the lamps, dynamo-machine, or both. Although this condition of affairs may obtain in the lamps where it is easily remedied, it may also appear in the machine, as is proven by the success of the remedy applied, consisting in the suppression, as far as is practicable, of the extra current in the field-magnet helices and the absorption of the opposing or inverse electro-motive force caused by rising magnetism of the inclosed cores. The exact manner in which the elimination of the inverse and direct currents in the helices of the field-magnets due to the rising or falling of the magnetism of their cores acts as a remedy for the evil last indicated is not easy to explain. I have developed several theories concerning the phenomenon, but, as none are entirely satisfactory, I will not state them.

I accomplish my object by surrounding the cores of the field-magnets of a dynamo-electric machine with a continuous band of sheet copper or other suitable conductor wound in the direction of the magnetising-helices. Over these bands are coiled the said magnetising-helices in the customary manner.

Figure 1 of the drawings shows this form of my invention. Figs. 2, 3, 4 show various modifications of the same. Fig. 5 illustrates a dynamo-machine provided with my improvement.

In Fig. 1, A is the iron core of one of the field-magnets of a dynamo-electric machine.

B is a tube, of copper or other suitable conductor, surrounding the core A.

C is the usual magnetising-helix.

The function of the tube or envelope B in affording a free path for both the inverse and direct currents, due to rising or falling magnetism of the core A, and thus absorbing the greater part of the inductive influence of the latter, is too obvious to require further explanation.

Obviously the tube or band B may envelop both core A and helix C, as shown in Fig. 2, or it may inclose a portion only of the helix, as shown in Fig. 3.

For the purpose of further absorbing the inverse and direct currents induced directly by

Assigned to Brush Electric Co. -- JAN 8 18

UNITED STATES OF AMERICA

No. _____   _____

To all to whom these presents shall come:

Whereas Charles F. Brush, Cleveland, Ohio has presented to the Commissioner of Patents a petition praying for the grant of Letters Patent for an alleged new and useful improvement in

Electric Circuit Systems

a description of which invention is contained in the Specification of which a copy is hereunto annexed, and made a part hereof, and has complied with the various requirements of Law in such cases made and provided, and

Whereas upon due examination made the said Claimant is adjudged to be justly entitled to a Patent under the Law.

Now therefore these **Letters Patent** are to grant unto the said Charles F. Brush, his heirs or assigns for the term of _____ years from the _____ day of _____ one thousand eight hundred and eighty ___ the exclusive right to make, use and vend the said invention throughout the United States and the Territories thereof.

In testimony whereof I have hereunto set my hand and caused the seal of the **Patent Office** to be affixed at the City of Washington this _____ day of _____ in the year of our Lord one thousand eight hundred and eighty ___ and of the Independence of the United States of America the one hundred and seventh.

Countersigned: _____ Marble, Secretary of the Interior
Commissioner of Patents

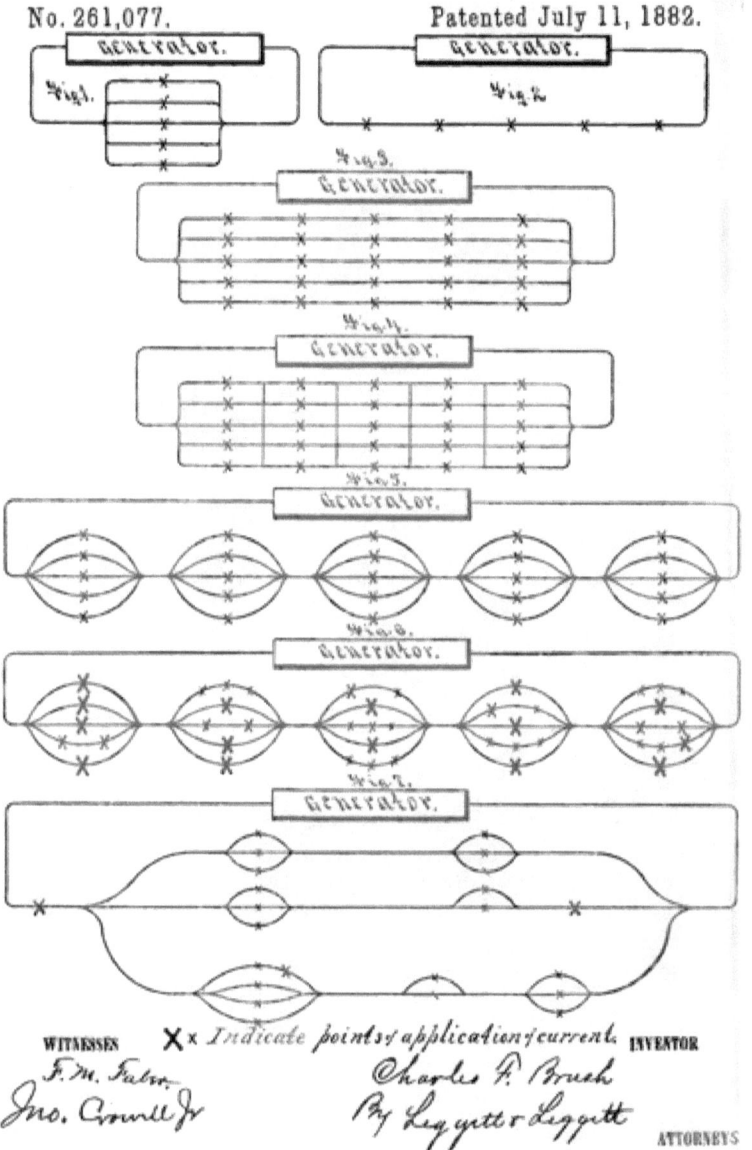

UNITED STATES PATENT OFFICE.

CHARLES F. BRUSH, OF CLEVELAND, OHIO.

ELECTRIC-CIRCUIT SYSTEM.

SPECIFICATION forming part of Letters Patent No. 261,077, dated July 11, 1882.

Application filed June 4, 1880. (No model.)

To all whom it may concern:

Be it known that I, CHARLES F. BRUSH, of Cleveland, in the county of Cuyahoga and State of Ohio, have invented certain new and useful Improvements in Electric-Circuit Systems; and I do hereby declare the following to be a full, clear, and exact description of the invention, such as will enable others skilled in the art to which it pertains to make and use it, reference being had to the accompanying drawings, which form part of this specification.

My invention relates to a system of electric circuits for electric-lighting and electric-engineering purposes.

Figure 1 of the drawings indicates a common method of dividing an electric current so as to utilize its energy simultaneously at several points. Fig. 2 illustrates another well-known method of arriving at the same result. Fig. 3 shows a well-known combination of the two preceding methods. Fig. 4 shows the arrangement of circuits constituting my invention. Fig. 5 shows an arrangement of circuits equivalent to that in Fig. 4. Fig. 6 shows two or more minor applications of current at one or several principal points. Fig. 7 indicates how my invention may be modified and indefinitely extended.

The well-known method shown in Fig. 1 of dividing an electric current so as to utilize its energy simultaneously at several points possesses the advantage that if one or more of the branches of the electric circuit become broken the remaining branches remain intact, while it has the disadvantage of requiring a current of comparatively-low electro-motive force and large volume, necessitating large conductors and entailing much loss of energy when the points of application are far removed from the source of current. The plan shown in Fig. 2 has the merit of requiring a current of comparatively-high electro-motive force and small volume, capable of traversing long conductors of small size with comparatively little loss of energy, while it entails the disadvantage that if the circuit is broken at one of the points of application of the current the latter is interrupted at all points.

Fig. 3 shows a combination of the methods already described, consisting of a multiplication of the second method. This plan is evidently a compromise between the advantages and disadvantages of the two former ones, and is superior to either. It is the one commonly employed in telegraphy, where several lines, each operating several instruments or electric engines, are worked by a single battery.

My invention consists in the improvement of the third method described, whereby the full advantage of the first method is secured to it.

Fig. 4 illustrates my arrangement of circuits for and of points of application of an electric current. This system is evidently a multiplication of the first method; but it possesses advantages not heretofore obtained in any system of circuits. By this method currents of high electro-motive force and of consequent easy transportation may be utilized simultaneously at many points, while the interruption of the current at any one or several of these points (provided they be not all in any one vertical series of points, indicated in the diagram Fig. 4, which is a remote contingency) will not materially affect the current at any other point.

Fig. 5 shows my invention in more intelligible form and as practically employed.

The current may be utilized at any of its points of application in the development of light, heat, chemical action, motive power, or any purpose for which a current is desired; and it may be employed for different purposes at different points, or for several different purposes at any or each of its principal points of application. Such an arrangement as last indicated is shown in Fig. 6, wherein two or more minor applications of the current are made in one or several of its branches. Obviously the total consumption or utilization of current need not be the same in all branches of the circuit, but may differ widely at different points.

As already indicated, Fig. 7 shows how my invention may be modified and extended indefinitely.

My system of electric circuits may be employed in the distribution of electricity for lighting or other purposes in rooms, buildings, blocks of buildings, streets, and whole cities. By its means portions of the same current may be independently and simultaneously employed, for the same or different purposes, in

many different and widely-separated localities.

What I claim is—

1. A system for transmitting electric currents to translating devices, consisting essentially in an electrical conductor divided along its length into two or more series of paths or branches, each path or branch of each series being electrically connected at opposite ends with the main conductor and translating devices interposed in said branch circuits, substantially as set forth.

2. A system for transmitting electric currents to translating devices arranged in multiple-arc series, consisting of a single conductor split or divided into two or more branches electrically connected at their ends with the main conductor and electrically connected with each other at one or more intermediate points, substantially as set forth.

In testimony whereof I have signed my name to this specification in the presence of two subscribing witnesses.

CHARLES F. BRUSH.

Witnesses:
LEVERETT L. LEGGETT,
JNO. CROWELL, Jr.

Assigned to Brush Electric Co. - JAN 8 13

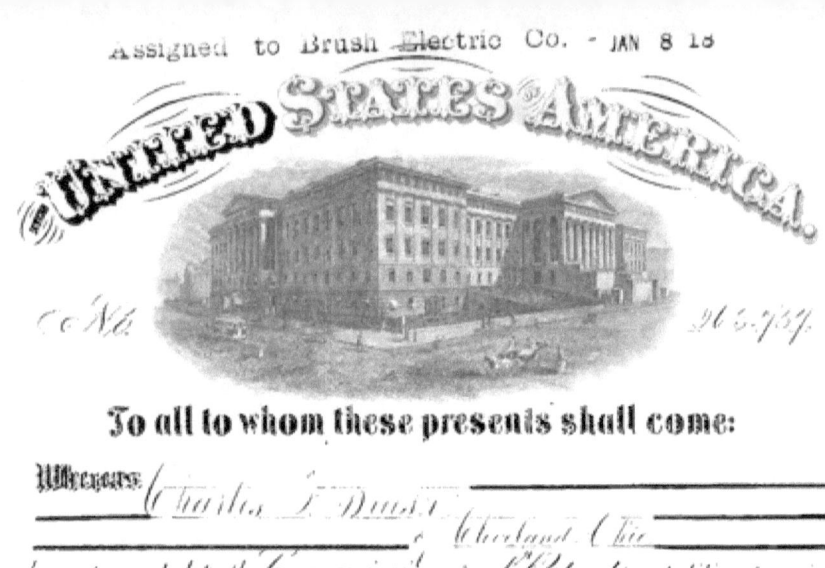

United States of America

No. 263,757

To all to whom these presents shall come:

Whereas Charles F. Brush _____ of Cleveland, Ohio _____ ha_ presented to the Commissioner of Patents a petition praying for the grant of Letters Patent for an alleged new and useful improvement in

Process & Apparatus of straightening Carbons, &c. _____

a description of which invention is contained in the Specification of which a copy is hereunto annexed, and made a part hereof, and ha_ complied with the various requirements of Law in such cases made and provided, and

Whereas upon due examination made the said Claimant _ adjudged to be justly entitled to a Patent under the Law.

Now therefore these **Letters Patent** are to grant unto the said Charles F. Brush _____ heirs or assigns, for the term of seventeen years from the fifth day of September one thousand eight hundred and eighty two the exclusive right to make, use and vend the said invention throughout the United States and the Territories thereof.

In testimony whereof I have hereunto set my hand and caused the seal of the **Patent Office** to be affixed at the City of Washington this fifth day of September in the year of our Lord one thousand eight hundred and eighty two and of the Independence of the United States of America the one hundred and seventh.

Countersigned _____   _____ Secretary of the Interior
                        _____ Commissioner of Patents

(No Model.)

C. F. BRUSH.

PROCESS OF AND APPARATUS FOR STRAIGHTENING CARBON RODS.

No. 263,757. Patented Sept. 5, 1882.

Fig. 1.

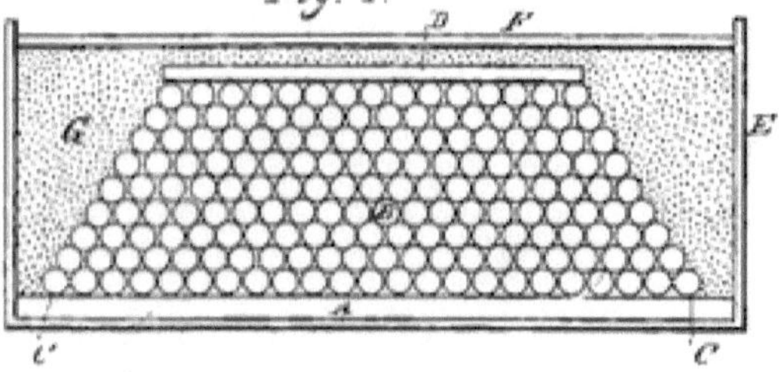

Fig. 2

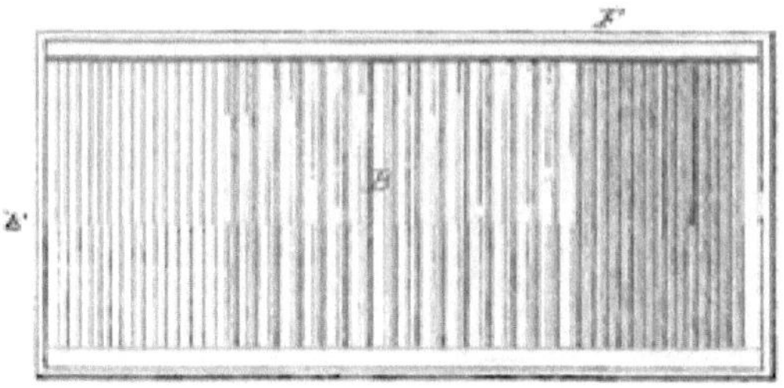

WITNESSES

W. Engel

Jno. Crowell Jr

Charles F. Brush INVENTOR

By Leggett & Leggett

ATTORNEYS

UNITED STATES PATENT OFFICE.

CHARLES F. BRUSH, OF CLEVELAND, OHIO.

PROCESS OF AND APPARATUS FOR STRAIGHTENING CARBON RODS.

SPECIFICATION forming part of Letters Patent No. 263,757, dated September 5, 1882.

Application filed June 4, 1881. (No model.)

To all whom it may concern:

Be it known that I, CHARLES F. BRUSH, of Cleveland, in the county of Cuyahoga and State of Ohio, have invented certain new and useful Improvements in Process of and Mechanism for Straightening Carbon Sticks; and I do hereby declare the following to be a full, clear, and exact description of the invention, such as will enable others skilled in the art to which it pertains to make and use it, reference being had to the accompanying drawings, which form part of this specification.

My invention relates to the manufacture of the carbon rods or sticks used in electric lighting by the voltaic arc; and it consists in the method or process of straightening carbons which have become bent or distorted during the process of manufacture. Such distortion (easy to prevent before the baking or calcining) often occurs during this part of the manufacture, and since the carbons after this operation are eminently rigid and more or less brittle it has heretofore been considered impracticable to straighten them, and their value has been greatly reduced or entirely destroyed. I have observed that however long or whatever number of times artificially-prepared carbons are calcined they continue to shrink in length, although to a less and less extent as the operation proceeds. During this continued process of calcination and shrinkage I find that the carbons are very slightly plastic, but sufficiently so to allow of their being straightened, if previously distorted, by the application of moderate but long-continued stress in suitable directions while they are maintained at a high temperature. I attribute the long-continued shrinking and slight plasticity of the carbons to the continued but very gradual elimination of hydrogen, which element I think can never be entirely expelled.

I have in view several processes for the more complete elimination of hydrogen from carbon used in electric lighting, both by the arc and by the incandescent plan, for which I intend to apply for Letters Patent in due time, and I do not hereby waive the right to embody and claim in such application any matter pertaining to these processes which may appear in this specification.

I accomplish my object of straightening carbons previously distorted during calcination by packing them in a peculiar manner in suitable pots or boxes and recalcining them. I place in the bottom of a rectangular pot of adequate dimensions and of suitable material a flat slab or plate of slate, stone, or other suitable material not liable to become bent or warped at a high temperature. On this slab is placed, horizontally and side by side, a layer of carbon rods to be straightened, nearly or quite touching each other, and preferably with their principal curvature or distortion in a vertical plane. This precaution, although desirable in this and subsequent layers of carbons, is not always essential. Directly on the first layer of carbons another layer is placed in quincunx order, having one less carbon than the layer below, and so on, until the pot is sufficiently filled. A slab or plate similar to the one at the bottom of the pile of carbons is placed on the top layer to act as a weight and a protection against the entrance of sand into the pile. This weight is not absolutely essential to the success of the process, but is generally desirable. The pot is of such size that a space of an inch or more is left between its sides and the ends of the carbons forming the pile. The space at the sides, ends, and top of the pile of carbons is filled with clean sand; but any tilting of the pot, by reason of which sand would be caused to flow into the spaces between the carbons, is very carefully avoided. The sand is used simply to protect the carbons from access of air during the subsequent baking, and hence any other suitable material, capable or not of flowing like sand—such, for instance, as pulverized coke—may be used in its stead. A lid or cover over the pot is advisable as a further protection.

In order to preserve the integrity of the pile or pyramid of carbons, both during its building and subsequently, it is necessary to prevent lateral motion of the end carbons of the bottom layer. If these carbons are simply blocked against the ends of the pot or are confined by placing a foreign body between them and the ends of the pot, they are sure to become displaced when the pot expands in heating, and the sand or other filling material flows to fill the increased space. In such a case the whole pile of carbons is liable to become displaced. It is necessary, then, to anchor the end carbons of the bottom layer into

the pile itself in order to prevent this accident. I overcome this difficulty by employing double or triple carbons for the ends of the first layer.

In molding the carbons many parallel rods are formed at once, all joined together by a thin web. I break up these sets ordinarily into single rods; but for the purpose described I leave two or more still joined by their webs and use these preferably, after being baked, for the ends of the first layer of carbons in the calcining-pot. Thus rolling or sliding of the end members of this layer is effectually prevented, and the stability of the whole pile is assured.

It will be evident that all the members of the pile of carbons I have described will, by the weight of those above or of the slab at top, or both, and in the absence of sand or other packing material between them, tend to become parallel and straight, and will assume this disposition when rendered sufficiently plastic by heat, and will retain it when subsequently cooled. Of course some members of the pile will remain more or less distorted after passing through the straightening process. These may be again treated with others, so that the number of carbons finally lost through distortion is very small indeed compared with the number found crooked after the ordinary baking process is completed.

In the drawings, Figure 1 shows in vertical section, transverse to the carbons, a pot filled and ready for the furnace. Fig. 2 is a plan view of the pot and carbons, Fig. 1, with the cover F, slab D, and sand G removed.

In Fig. 1, A is the plate or slab on which the pile or pyramid of carbons B rests. The ends of the lowest row of carbons consist of twin carbons, C C. D is the slab or weight placed at the top of the pile B. E is the containing-pot, of cast-iron or other suitable material, of which F is a cover. G represents the protecting-filling of sand or other suitable material.

Obviously the pot E and its contents may be heated rapidly and to a high temperature at once, instead of receiving the very slowly increasing heat found necessary when freshly-molded carbons are being baked, and hence the time required for the straightening process may be very much less than required for the original baking.

What I claim is—

1. In the method or process of straightening deformed or bent carbon rods or sticks, arranging bent carbon rods or sticks in a pyramidal pile in a receptacle, inserting packing material at the sides and ends of the pile, and leaving the spaces between the carbon rods vacant, substantially as set forth.

2. The method of straightening deformed or bent carbon rods or sticks, consisting in arranging the bent carbon rods or sticks in a pyramidal pile in a receptacle and on a supporting slab formed of suitable material to withstand warping and inserting packing material at the sides and ends of the pile and leaving the spaces between the carbon rods vacant, substantially as set forth.

3. The method of straightening deformed or bent carbon rods or sticks, consisting in arranging them in pyramidal form within a suitable receptacle, inserting packing material at the sides and ends of the pile and leaving the interspaces vacant, and subjecting the pile to the pressure of a superior cumbent weight while it is being heated, substantially as and for the purpose set forth.

4. A pyramidal pile of bent or deformed carbon sticks or rods, having its lower course provided at its opposite ends with twin or compound carbons, substantially as and for the purpose set forth.

5. The combination, with the inclosing-box E and slab A, of the pyramidal pile of bent or deformed carbons B, the slab D, and packing G, substantially as and for the purpose set forth.

In testimony whereof I have signed my name to this specification in the presence of two subscribing witnesses.

CHARLES F. BRUSH.

Witnesses:
JNO. CROWELL, Jr.,
ALBERT E. LYNCH.

Assigned to Brush Electric Co.   JAN 8 15

UNITED STATES OF AMERICA

No. 165,413

To all to whom these presents shall come:

Whereas Charles F. Brush of Cleveland, Ohio has presented to the Commissioner of Patents a petition praying for the grant of Letters Patent for an alleged new and useful improvement in

Process-making Carbons, &c.

a description of which invention is contained in the Specification of which a copy is hereunto annexed and made a part hereof, and has complied with the various requirements of Law in such cases made and provided, and

Whereas upon due examination made the said Claimant is adjudged to be justly entitled to a Patent under the Law.

Now therefore these **Letters Patent** are to grant unto the said Charles F. Brush his heirs or assigns for the term of seventeen years from the fifth day of September one thousand eight hundred and eighty two the exclusive right to make, use and vend the said invention throughout the United States and the Territories thereof.

In testimony whereof I have hereunto set my hand and caused the seal of the **Patent Office** to be affixed at the City of Washington this fifth day of September in the year of our Lord one thousand eight hundred and eighty two and of the Independence of the United States of America the one hundred and seventh.

Countersigned:

Commissioner of Patents.

Acting Secretary of the Interior

(No Model.)

C. F. BRUSH.
PROCESS OF BAKING CARBON RODS.

No. 263,758. Patented Sept. 5, 1882.

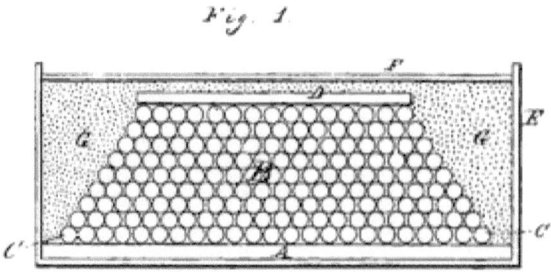

UNITED STATES PATENT OFFICE.

CHARLES F. BRUSH, OF CLEVELAND, OHIO.

PROCESS OF BAKING CARBON RODS.

SPECIFICATION forming part of Letters Patent No. 263,758, dated September 5, 1882.

Application filed May 27, 1881. (No model.)

To all whom it may concern:

Be it known that I, CHARLES F. BRUSH, of Cleveland, in the county of Cuyahoga and State of Ohio, have invented certain new and useful Improvements in Processes for Baking Carbon Rods; and I do hereby declare the following to be a full, clear, and exact description of the invention, such as will enable others skilled in the art to which it pertains to make and use it, reference being had to the accompanying drawings, which form part of this specification.

My invention relates to the manufacture of the carbon rods or sticks used in electric lighting with the voltaic arc; and it consists in a method or process of baking or calcining such carbons, whereby great economy of space is effected and deformation of the carbons during the baking largely prevented.

I place in the bottom of a rectangular pot of adequate dimensions and suitable material a flat slab or plate of slate, stone, carbon, or other suitable material not liable to become bent or warped at a high temperature. On this slab is placed horizontally and side by side a layer of carbon rods nearly or quite touching each other. Directly on this layer of carbons is placed another layer in quincunx order, having one less carbon than the layer below, and so on until the pot is sufficiently filled with carbons. The pot is of such size that a space of an inch or more is left between its sides and the ends of the carbons forming the pile. The space at the sides and ends of the pile of carbons is then filled with clean sand of a suitable size of grain, and sifted, if necessary. Next the pot is tilted in the direction of the length of the carbons sufficiently to cause the sand at their higher ends to flow into the spaces between them, while the carbons are prevented from sliding out of position by the packing of sand at their lower ends. Fresh sand is added as required until the spaces between the carbons are entirely filled. During the filling process the top of the pile of carbons may be confined, if found necessary, to prevent the vertical displacement of the upper layers. A flat slab or weight may be placed on top of the pile of carbons to prevent the warping of the upper layers during baking; but this is often unnecessary. Finally, the box or pot is filled with sand to a sufficient extent to protect the carbons from access of air during baking. A lid or metal cover over all is advisable as a further protection.

In order to preserve the integrity of the pile or pyramid of carbons, both during its building and subsequently, it is necessary to prevent lateral motion of the end carbons of the bottom layer by rolling or sliding. If these carbons are simply blocked against the ends of the pot, or are confined by placing a foreign body between them and the ends of the pot, they are sure to become displaced when the pot expands in heating and the sand flows to fill the increased space. In such case the whole pile of carbons becomes more or less displaced, and many or all of the carbons are distorted. It is necessary, then, to anchor the end carbons of the first layer into the pile itself in order to prevent this accident. I overcome this difficulty by employing double or triple carbons for the ends of the first layer.

In molding the carbons many parallel rods are formed at once, all joined together by a thin web. I break up these sets ordinarily into single rods; but for the purpose described I leave two or more still joined by their webs, and use these, preferably after being baked, for the ends of the first layer of carbons in the calcining-pot. Thus rolling or sliding of the end members of this layer is effectually prevented and the stability of the whole pile is assured.

It will be seen that by my method of packing carbons the greatest possible economy of space is effected, and displacement and consequent distortion of individual carbons cannot be caused by the flowing of the surrounding sand due to the expansion of the containing vessel, or the ultimate shrinking of the pile itself, except in the latter case, so far as the top layer or layers are concerned.

If carbons are packed in the vertical position, the flowing of the sand at their upper ends when the containing pot expands spreads them apart and bends the greater portion of them.

In the drawings, Figure 1 shows in vertical section transverse to the carbons a pot filled and ready for baking. Fig. 2 is a plan view

of the pot and carbons, Fig. 1, with the cover F, slab D, and sand G removed.

In Fig. 1, A is the plate or slab on which the pile or pyramid of carbons B rests. The ends of the lowest row of carbons consist of twin carbons C C. D is the slab or weight, which may or may not be placed at the top of the pile B.

E is the containing pot, of cast-iron or other suitable material, of which F is a cover. G represents the filling-sand.

What I claim is—

1. In the process of baking or calcining carbon rods or sticks, arranging the carbon rods or sticks in pyramidal form in a receptacle and filling the interspaces and the spaces at the sides and ends of the pyramidal pile with suitable packing material, substantially as set forth.

2. In the process of baking or calcining carbon rods or sticks in a receptacle, arranging the carbon rods or sticks in pyramidal form on a slab or plate of suitable material to withstand warping and filling the interspaces and the spaces at the sides and ends of the pyramidal pile with suitable packing, substantially as set forth.

3. In the process of baking or calcining carbon rods or sticks, arranging the carbon rods or sticks in pyramidal form on a slab or plate of suitable material to withstand warping, filling the interspaces and the spaces at the sides and ends of the pyramidal pile with suitable packing, and subjecting the pile to a superior cumbent weight during the process of baking, substantially as and for the purpose set forth.

4. A pyramidal pile of carbons having the ends of its lower course formed of twin or connected carbons to prevent displacement, substantially as and for the purpose set forth.

5. The combination, with the pyramidal pile of carbon rods or sticks, of the supporting-slab, the packing, and the inclosing box, substantially as and for the purpose set forth.

6. The combination, with the pyramidal pile of carbon rods or sticks packed in suitable material, of the supporting-slab A, upper slab, D, and inclosing box E, substantially as and for the purpose set forth.

In testimony whereof I have signed my name to this specification in the presence of two subscribing witnesses.

CHARLES F. BRUSH.

Witnesses:
JNO. CROWELL, Jr.,
HERMAN MORAN.

Assigned to Brush Electric Co. -- JAN 8 18

United States of America

No. 272,514

To all to whom these presents shall come:

Whereas Charles F. Brush of Cleveland, Ohio, has presented to the Commissioner of Patents a petition praying for the grant of Letters Patent for an alleged new and useful improvement in Carbon, and Sticks, & Mechanism for using same,

a description of which invention is contained in the Specification of which a copy is hereunto annexed and made a part hereof, and has complied with the various requirements of Law in such cases made and provided, and

Whereas, upon due examination made the said Claimant is adjudged to be justly entitled to a Patent under the Law.

Now therefore these **Letters Patent** are to grant unto the said Charles F. Brush his heirs or assigns for the term of seventeen years from the First day of May one thousand eight hundred and eighty three the exclusive right to make, use and vend the said invention throughout the United States and the Territories thereof.

In testimony whereof I have hereunto set my hand and caused the seal of the **Patent Office** to be affixed at the City of Washington this First day of May in the year of our Lord one thousand eight hundred and eighty three and of the Independence of the United States of America the one hundred and seventh.

Countersigned:
M. E. Marble
Acting Secretary of the Interior.

Commissioner of Patents.

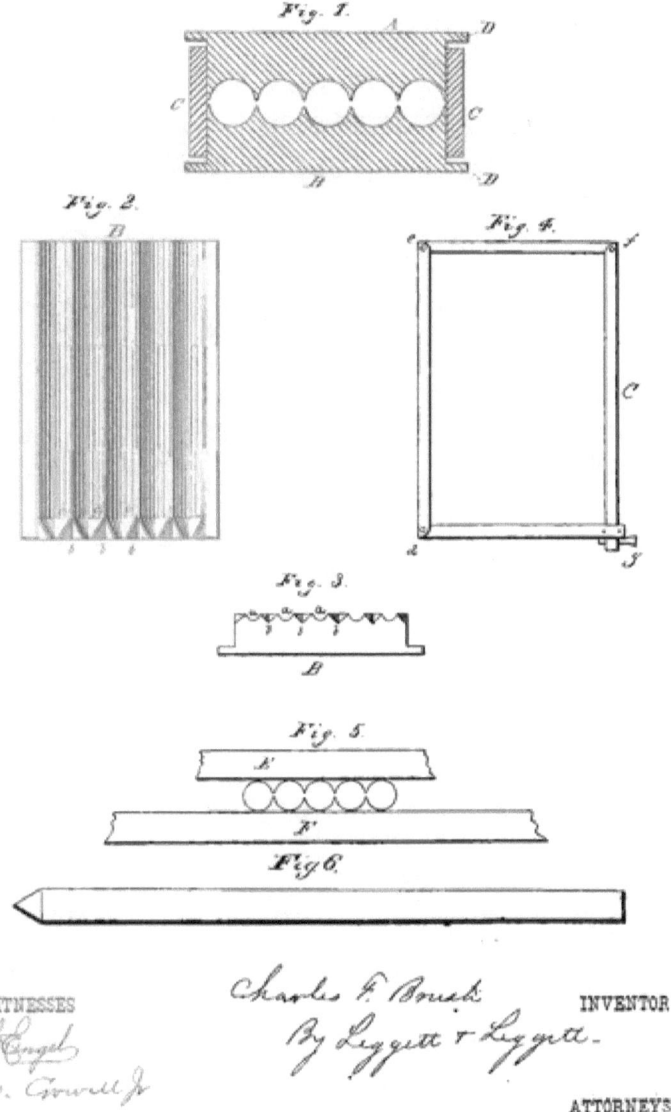

UNITED STATES PATENT OFFICE.

CHARLES F. BRUSH, OF CLEVELAND, OHIO.

CARBON ROD OR STICK AND MECHANISM FOR MAKING THE SAME.

SPECIFICATION forming part of Letters Patent No. 274,904, dated April 3, 1883.

Application filed June 4, 1881. (No model.)

To all whom it may concern:

Be it known that I, CHARLES F. BRUSH, of Cleveland, in the county of Cuyahoga and State of Ohio, have invented certain new and useful Improvements in Carbon Rods or Sticks and Mechanism for Making the Same; and I do hereby declare the following to be a full, clear, and exact description of the invention, such as will enable others skilled in the art to which it pertains to make and use it, reference being had to the accompanying drawings, which form part of this specification.

My invention relates to an improvement in carbon rods or sticks for electric lights and mechanism for making the improved carbon rods; and the invention consists in a carbon rod or stick formed with a molded or compressed pointed end.

It further consists in improved mechanism for making carbon rods or sticks, as will hereinafter be described, and pointed out in the claims.

The advantages of pointed carbons over those not so shaped are obvious. The electric light between a fresh pair of carbons previously pointed assumes its normal condition almost immediately, while if the carbons have not been pointed the light is very unsatisfactory for several minutes during the time the ends of the carbons are burning to a proper shape.

It has heretofore been customary to mold carbons with unpointed ends and point them afterward by grinding. This operation is expensive and tedious, owing to the hardness of the material.

I employ a set or gang of molds consisting of a pair of metal plates, one side of each having parallel grooves milled into it, the cross-section of each groove being nearly half that of the carbon to be produced. These plates are fitted into a metal frame, hinged at three corners and secured at the fourth by means of a key. One of the plates, being placed with its grooved side upward, is surrounded by the frame, which projects a suitable distance above the plate. The space thus formed is filled with the pulverized carbon mixture. The latter being spread uniformly over the lower plate, the upper plate is placed in the frame grooved side downward. The whole is then heated sufficiently to render the carbon mixture slightly plastic, and then the plates are pressed together with great force by hydraulic or other means, whereby the carbon mixture is pressed into smooth and uniform bars of a shape corresponding to the interior of the molds. Then the frame is removed by extracting the key at one corner and opening the frame, and the plates are removed from the inclosed carbons. The latter are allowed to cool and become hard between flat plates of stone or metal, whereby crookedness is prevented.

In the drawings, Figure 1 shows in cross-section my form of molds, consisting of plates A B and frames C. Fig. 2 is a plan view of plate B. Fig. 3 is an end view of plate B, showing depressions $b\,b$. Fig. 4 is a plan view of frame C, showing joints $d\,e\,f$ and key-fastening g. Fig. 5 illustrates the method of cooling and straightening the carbons by confining them between two flat surfaces. Fig. 6 represents one of my improved carbon rods or sticks.

In Fig. 1, A B are the grooved plates I have referred to, shown in sectional elevation. C is the frame surrounding the plates, which frame is shown in plan in Fig. 4. It will be noticed that when the plates A B are brought nearly together the grooves in them form cylindrical and nearly separate cavities. D D are lugs formed on the plates A B to facilitate handling them.

Fig. 2 is a plan view of the plate B. It will be seen that the grooves in the plate are contracted at one end, forming, when the other plate is applied, hollow truncated cones $a\,a$, which, when filled with the carbon mixture, form the pointed ends of the carbon rods; but the contraction of the grooves at one end of the plate B would leave triangular flat places on the face of the plate. Now, when the plates are pressed together, the carbon mixture between the opposed flat portions of the two plates, having no escape except by flowing laterally, which it is very slow to do, especially when the plates are near together, would greatly resist the pressure and relieve other portions of the molds from their due amount. I overcome this difficulty by hollowing out the flat spaces b, as shown in Fig. 3, to a sufficient extent to accommodate, when under pressure, that portion of the carbon mixture lying between the

triangular parts of the plates, so as to prevent undue opposition to the pressure forcing the plates together.

Obviously other forms of point than the conical one shown may be given to the carbons by my process; or the carbons may be pointed at both ends, if desired, and in this case two sets of carbons might be molded at once by suitably increasing the length of the molds and afterward cutting the long rods in two.

Fig. 4 shows the frame C jointed at the corners $d\ e\ f$, and finally secured at the corner g by a key, as shown, one side of the frame, through which the key is inserted, being reduced in size and passing through the adjoining side of the frame. The joints d and f may be suppressed and these parts made rigid, if desired, the joint e being often sufficient. When a set or sheet of carbons is removed from the molds in a warm and somewhat plastic condition and placed on a cold surface to cool and harden, that portion of the carbons touching the cool surface hardens and contracts while the remainder is still soft. Now, when the remaining portions contract, although the amount of contraction is very small, it is often sufficient to raise the ends of the carbons, and thus render them crooked. I overcome this difficulty by placing another flat plate of metal or stone on the top of the carbons, as shown in Fig. 5, whereby they are simultaneously cooled on opposite sides. The upper plate also acts by its weight to prevent crookedness.

After a set of carbons has cooled and become rigid the thin web joining the different members is broken and the carbons are ready to be trimmed, if necessary, and baked.

What I claim is—

1. As a new article of manufacture, a carbon stick or rod having a compressed pointed end, substantially as set forth.

2. Molds for forming electric-light carbons, provided with depressions $b\ b$, substantially as and for the purpose specified.

3. The frame C, provided with one or more hinged corners and a key-fastening, g, the key of said fastening being wedge-shaped, substantially as set forth.

4. Molds for forming electric-light carbons, provided with grooves having contracted ends $a\ a$, in combination with depressions $b\ b$, substantially as and for the purposes set forth.

5. Molds for forming electric-light carbons, consisting of plates A B, provided with grooves, in combination with a jointed frame, C, substantially as and for the purposes specified.

6. Molds for forming electric-light carbons, consisting of plates A B, provided with grooves having contracted ends $a\ a$, in combination with a jointed frame, C, substantially as and for the purposes set forth.

7. Molds for forming electric-light carbons, consisting of grooved plates A B, in combination with a jointed frame, C, having a key-fastening, g, the key of said fastening being wedge-shaped, substantially as set forth.

In testimony whereof I have signed my name to this specification in the presence of two subscribing witnesses.

CHARLES F. BRUSH.

Witnesses:
JNO. CROWILL, Jr.,
ALBERT E. LYNCH.

Assigned to Brush Electric Co. - JAN 8 18[?]

UNITED STATES OF AMERICA

No. _____   _____

To all to whom these presents shall come:

Whereas Charles F. Brush, of Cleveland, Ohio

ha_ presented to the Commissioner of Patents a petition praying for the grant of Letters Patent for an alleged new and useful improvement in

Armatures of Dynamo Electric Machines

a description of which invention is contained in the Specification of which a copy is hereunto annexed and made a part hereof, and ha_ complied with the various requirements of Law in such cases made and provided, and

Whereas upon due examination made the said Claimant is adjudged to be justly entitled to a Patent under the Law.

Now therefore these **Letters Patent** are to grant unto the said

Charles F. Brush, _____ heirs, or assigns for the term of seventeen years from the twenty-____ day of _____ one thousand, eight hundred and eighty ___, the exclusive right to make, use and vend the said invention, throughout the United States, and the Territories thereof.

In testimony whereof I have hereunto set my hand and caused the seal of the **Patent Office** to be affixed at the City of Washington this _____ day of _____ in the year of our Lord one thousand eight hundred and eighty ___, and of the Independence of the United States of America the one hundred and eighth.

Countersigned: _____   _____
                                           Secretary of the Interior

(No Model.)

C. F. BRUSH.
ARMATURE FOR DYNAMO ELECTRIC MACHINES.

No. 285,457.   Patented Sept. 25, 1883.

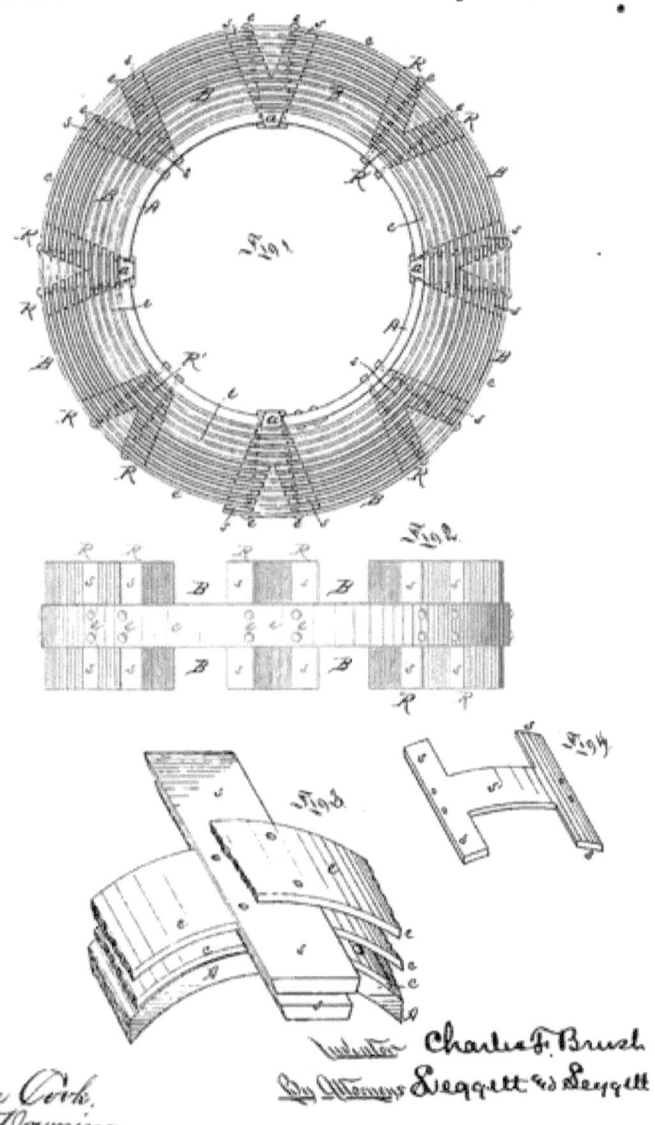

UNITED STATES PATENT OFFICE.

CHARLES F. BRUSH, OF CLEVELAND, OHIO.

ARMATURE FOR DYNAMO-ELECTRIC MACHINES.

SPECIFICATION forming part of Letters Patent No. 285,457, dated September 25, 1883.

Application filed July 25, 1883. (No model.)

To all whom it may concern:

Be it known that I, CHARLES F. BRUSH, of Cleveland, in the county of Cuyahoga and State of Ohio, have invented certain new and useful Improvements in Armatures for Dynamo-Electric Machines; and I do hereby declare the following to be a full, clear, and exact description of the invention, such as will enable others skilled in the art to which it pertains to make and use the same.

Figure 1 is a side view, or a view in elevation, of my improved armature, but without the bobbins. Fig. 2 is a top or edge view thereof. Fig. 3 is an enlarged view, in perspective, of a detached portion of the armature; and Fig. 4 shows a modified form of plate which may be employed.

My present invention relates to certain improvements in the construction of the revolving armatures of electric-current-generating machines, and more particularly to armatures of the kind or class such as is shown and described in Letters Patent No. 189,997, granted to me August 24, 1877, and reissued October 12, 1880, by reissue No. 9,410, and also in Letters Patent No. 203,413, granted to me May 7, 1878. The armature of the present invention is an improvement on the armatures of said patents, chiefly in the fact that the laterally-projecting portions thereof, between which the wires are wound to form the bobbins, are formed or built up of a series of comparatively thin and distinct metallic plates interposed between the coils or folds of a metallic ribbon, which, when coiled, forms, either alone or in connection with an inner or base ring on which it is wound, the annular portion of the armature. Preferably, and chiefly for convenience in mechanical construction, I employ the base-ring, and coil or wind the band thereon very much as ribbon is spooled; but in the operation of winding I interpose between the coils, on either side of the point or place where bobbins are desired, thin soft-metal plates, the ends of which project out laterally beyond the sides of the band-formed ring a distance equal or about equal to the thickness of the bobbin or bundle of wires to be wound around the band-formed ring, so that both the bobbins and the plates, when the armature is revolved in the machine, shall just clear the pole-pieces of the field-magnets.

In the drawings, A indicates the base or inner ring, made thick enough to give a suitable support to the flexible band wound thereon; and I also employ it as a device by which—say through lugs *a a* or otherwise—to make connection between the armature and the hub of the driving-shaft. Its breadth should be exactly or approximately that desired in the body of the armature-ring, of which the band *c* forms a part. This band *c*, of any desired length, and of iron or other suitable magnetizable material, is secured at one end to the ring A, and then wound on and around its periphery any desired number of times, with reference to the making of an armature of any desired size; but at each side of those places or points at which wires are to be wound around the armature-ring to form bobbins, I introduce between the successive folds or plications of the band a thin metallic strip or plate, *s*, which lies crosswise of the band, and with its ends projecting a distance equal or about equal to the thickness of the coil of wire which is to form the bobbins. Each series or pile R of transverse plates *s* is built up on a line parallel to the radial line passing through the middle of the adjacent space B, as shown, but with one or more folds or plications of the band between each two in succession, and, where the bobbins are to be arranged, as close together as possible. The piles R which come between two adjacent bobbins will branch in a **V** form from a single base-pile, R', and such base pile may be made of strips which gradually increase in width, or of edgewise overlapping strips, or of two series of narrow but gradually widening strips, as may be preferred. The armature shown in the drawings is spaced or divided up by the piles or series R so as to give eight intermediate spaces, B, as bobbin spaces or recesses in which to wind the bobbin-wires; but the spacing may be varied at pleasure, so as to give fewer or smaller bobbin spaces or recesses. Plates and bands may be painted or otherwise coated or covered with insulating material, if so desired, though for most purposes the oxide ordinarily present will suffice for purposes of insulation. When

the armature has thus been built up to the desired size or extent, the outer end of the band is secured to the outer fold by riveting or otherwise, and rivets or bolts *e* are passed radially through each pile or series of plates, and through the interlying band-folds, so as to secure all firmly in place. The bobbins are then wound and connections made in the manner described in said recited patents, or otherwise, as may be preferred. As plates and bands are thus entirely disconnected with each other, except over the comparatively small area where the former cross the latter, and as practically they are insulated from each other over these areas, and as open air-spaces exist between them at all other points, I thus secure greater exemption from the evils of heating, induction, &c., and lessen the first cost, and also secure in the completed machine a considerable and material increase of electric generating capacity.

It will be but a slight modification, instead of making the band *c* continuous, as above described, to divide it up into a series of bands or rings, each outer one exceeding the diameter of the next inner one by twice the thickness of one of the plates, and in the following claims I will use the term "band-formed armature-ring" as including the construction described, whether the band that forms the ring be coiled continuously or be subdivided into separate ring-shaped bands, as above described. Of course the edges of the bands may be notched at or along the spaces B; or each two adjacent plates *s*, which are interposed between two band-rings or band-folds, may be connected by cross-bar *s'*, Fig. 4, so as to form a compound or H-shaped plate; or other modification in the form of the plates or bands may be made; and while I prefer the use of the inner or base ring, A, on which to coil or wind, one or more central or inside coils of the band may be used as a base by which or from which to make the necessary connections with the hub, and on which to coil and build, as above described.

I claim herein as my invention—

1. The plates *s*, in combination with a band-formed armature-ring, substantially as described.

2. A band-formed armature-ring having separate plates interposed at suitable intervals between the folds, layers, or plications of the ring, substantially as set forth.

In testimony whereof I sign this specification, in the presence of two witnesses, this 17th day of July, 1883.

     CHARLES F. BRUSH.

Witnesses:
 ALBERT E. LYNCH,
 GEO. W. KING.

Assigned to Brush Electric Co. JAN. 8 187_

UNITED STATES OF AMERICA

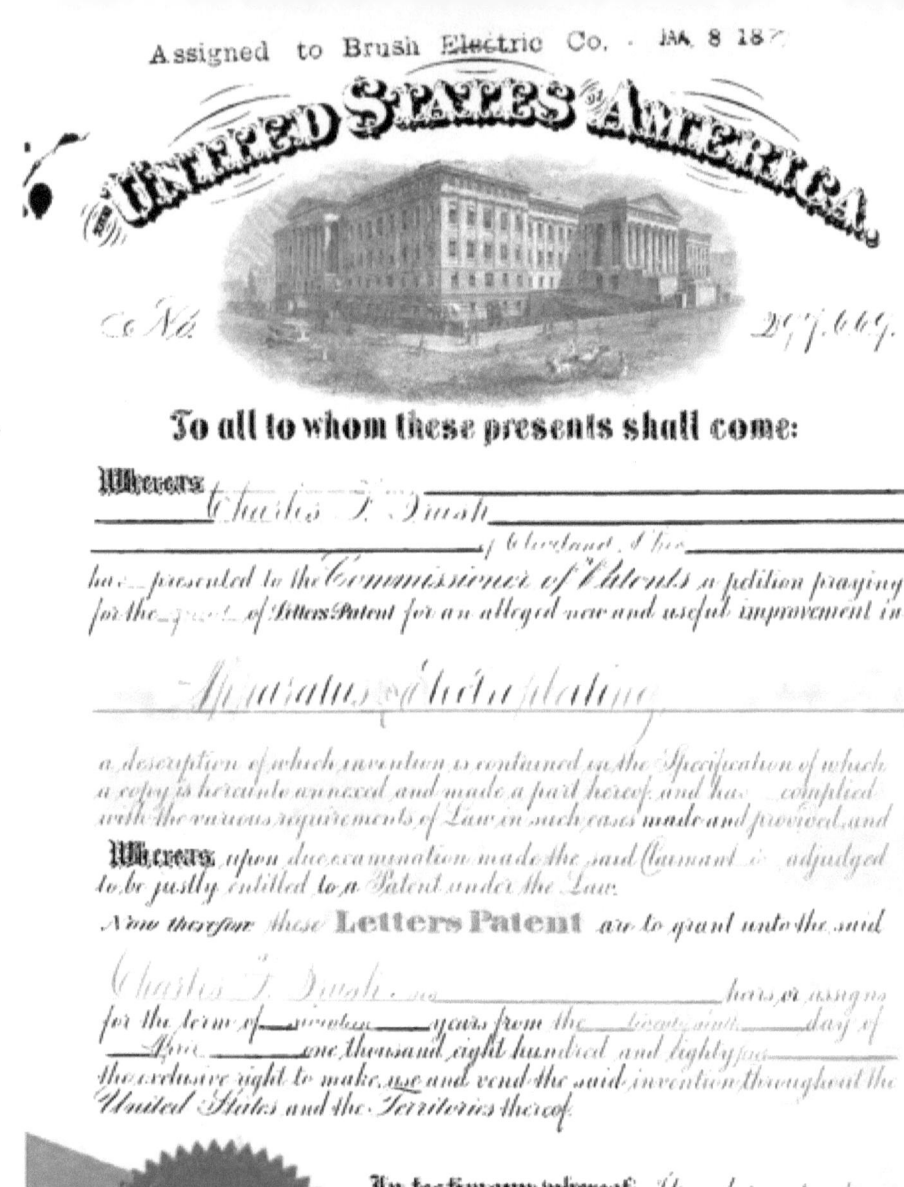

No. 257,669

To all to whom these presents shall come:

Whereas Charles F. Brush _____ of Cleveland, Ohio _____ has presented to the Commissioner of Patents a petition praying for the grant of Letters Patent for an alleged new and useful improvement in

Apparatus of Electroplating

a description of which invention is contained in the Specification of which a copy is hereunto annexed and made a part hereof, and has complied with the various requirements of Law in such cases made and provided, and

Whereas, upon due examination made the said Claimant is adjudged to be justly entitled to a Patent under the Law.

Now therefore these **Letters Patent** are to grant unto the said Charles F. Brush _____ his heirs or assigns for the term of seventeen years from the twenty-ninth day of April one thousand eight hundred and eighty-two the exclusive right to make, use and vend the said invention throughout the United States and the Territories thereof.

In testimony whereof I have hereunto set my hand and caused the seal of the **Patent Office** to be affixed at the City of Washington this twenty-ninth day of April in the year of our Lord, one thousand eight hundred and eighty-two and of the Independence of the United States of America the one hundred and eighth.

Countersigned: _____ Acting Secretary of the Interior
Commissioner of Patents.

(No Model.) 2 Sheets—Sheet 2.

C. F. BRUSH.
APPARATUS FOR ELECTROPLATING.

No. 297,669. Patented Apr. 29, 1884.

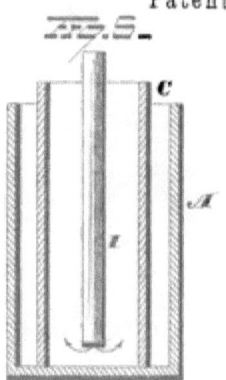

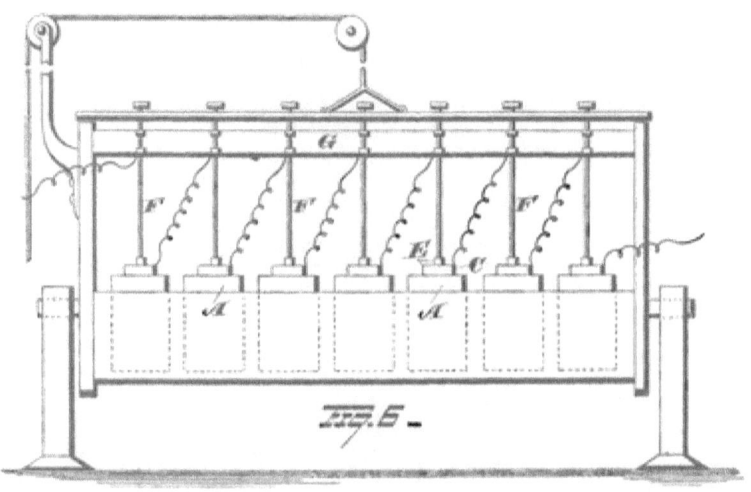

WITNESSES
S. G. Nottingham
Geo. H. Downing

INVENTOR
Chas. F. Brush.
By Leggett & Leggett
Attorney

(No Model.) 2 Sheets—Sheet 1.
C. F. BRUSH.
APPARATUS FOR ELECTROPLATING.
No. 297,669. Patented Apr. 29, 1884.

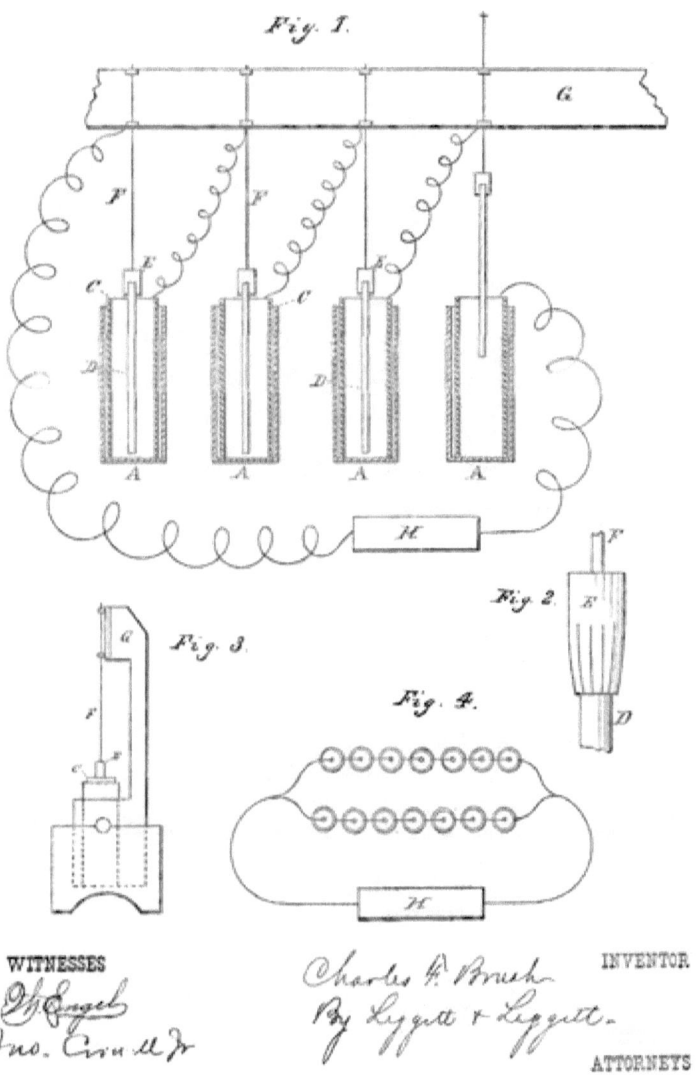

UNITED STATES PATENT OFFICE.

CHARLES F. BRUSH, OF CLEVELAND, OHIO.

APPARATUS FOR ELECTROPLATING.

SPECIFICATION forming part of Letters Patent No. 297,669, dated April 29, 1884.

Application filed May 27, 1881. (No model.)

To all whom it may concern:

Be it known that I, CHARLES F. BRUSH, of Cleveland, in the county of Cuyahoga and State of Ohio, have invented certain new and useful Improvements in Apparatus for Electroplating; and I do hereby declare the following to be a full, clear, and exact description of the invention, such as will enable others skilled in the art to which it pertains to make and use it, reference being had to the accompanying drawings, which form a part of this specification.

My invention relates to the electroplating of the "carbons" used in the production of electric light; and its object is to provide convenient appliances for carrying on the process rapidly and economically, and to secure an equal deposit of metal on all the carbons plated simultaneously.

In Letters Patent No. 196,425, granted to me October 23, 1877, I have pointed out some of the advantages and functions of an electro-deposit of copper or other suitable metal when applied to the rods or sticks of carbon used in electric lighting, and therefore will not recount them here. In the following description of my invention I will assume that copper is the metal to be applied to the carbons, although I do not in any manner limit myself to this metal, as any other suitable metal may be applied in the same manner by correspondingly changing the solution and anodes employed. When several sticks of carbon are attached, by clamps or wires, in the usual manner, to one conductor and subjected to the action of an electric current in a copper bath, the metal is liable to be deposited very unequally on the several carbons. If the carbons were precisely alike in texture and conductivity, and were equally well connected with the source of current, this unequal action would not occur; but these favorable conditions cannot be attained with any degree of certainty in practice. When unequal action has once commenced, its cause becomes aggravated as the process proceeds, because those carbons which, owing to superior conductivity or connection, first receive a covering of metal are relatively to the others still more favorably circumstanced to receive a further deposit, owing to their increased conductivity, due to the metal covering them. Since it is essential that the metal coating of carbons to be used for electric lighting should be of a certain thickness, depending on the size of the carbons and the strength of the current employed in order to secure the best results, the evil I have pointed out becomes a serious obstacle to their manufacture. I overcome the above-described difficulty entirely by employing a separate anode and bath for each carbon to be plated, arranging the several baths, to the number of many hundreds, if desired, in series, like the cells of a battery arranged for "tension," and passing a current of suitably small volume and sufficiently high electro-motive force through the series. Since the passing current is the same in all the cells or baths, the amount of metal deposited thereby is necessarily the same in all.

In the drawings, Figure 1 represents, partly in section, one view of an apparatus embodying my invention. Fig. 2 shows in detail the clamp E. Fig. 3 shows an end view of the apparatus illustrated in Fig. 1. Fig. 4 shows the multiple series modification of my invention. Fig. 5 is a vertical section of a cell with a tube inserted therein for furnishing a blast of air to the solution for stirring its contents. Fig. 6 is a view in side elevation of the pivoted frame adapted to be tilted for emptying the jars, and also provided with a bar for simultaneously raising and lowering a series of the carbons.

In Fig. 1, A A are glass jars arranged side by side in a suitable frame or rack. (Not shown.) C C are copper cylinders placed inside the jars. D D are the carbons to be plated, supported inside the copper cylinders by means of clamps E E, attached to rods F F. These rods slide vertically through metallic eyes attached to the frame G, so as to allow the insertion of the carbons. The carbon of the first cell is attached to the negative pole of the current-generator H, while the copper cylinder of the same cell is connected electrically with the carbon of the second cell, and so on through the series, until finally the copper cylinder of the last cell is connected with the positive pole of the generator H. The jars A A are filled with a suitable copper solution and current applied from the source H.

The action of the apparatus is obvious without further explanation.

Fig. 2 is an enlarged view of the clamp E. It consists of a metal tube slightly larger in-

ternally than the carbon D, having its lower portion split into several sections, as shown. These are then bent inward, so as to grasp the carbon D tightly, and make sufficiently good electrical connection therewith when one end (preferably the pointed end) of the latter is thrust into the tube. A screw-clamp may also be used, but is not so convenient.

The frame G, Fig. 1, may be arranged so as to admit of being raised or lowered, thus simultaneously immersing or lifting from the jars A all the carbons D; or a bar, U, may be employed, as shown in Fig. 6, for this purpose when the jars are mounted in a swinging frame.

Any suitable means may be employed for stirring the solution in the several jars from time to time to keep it sufficiently homogeneous. A small jet of air forced through a tube, T, to the bottom of each cell, by means of the mouth or otherwise, so as to rise in bubbles through the liquid, is a convenient method. Small tubes of metal or rubber may be placed permanently in all the cells, if desired, and supplied with a blast of air from time to time, as required, by means of a bellows or otherwise.

The rack supporting the jars A A and frame G may be hung on trunnions at its ends, as shown in end elevation in Fig. 3. This arrangement admits of readily emptying all the jars A A by dumping their solution into a suitable receptacle, and of quickly washing them out by directing a jet of water into them successively while in the horizontal position.

In practice I find it convenient to employ several sets of apparatus such as I have described, the plated carbons being removed from and fresh ones supplied to each set successively while the plating process is going on in the other sets.

Fig. 4 illustrates diagrammatically how two or more sets or series of apparatus such as I have described may be arranged in "multiple arc" and operated simultaneously by one current, which thus divides itself between them. In this case the total electrical resistance of the several cells is liable to be very nearly the same in each of the different series, since it is the average cell multiplied by the number, so that the same advantage of uniformity of product is obtained in this series multiple arrangement, if properly proportioned, as in the simple series arrangement first described.

What I claim is—

1. The combination, with a number of electroplating-baths, each provided with an anode adapted to surround an electric-light carbon, of devices for supporting an electric-light carbon centrally (or approximately so) within each anode, and electric conductors for connecting the electroplating-baths in series, so as to be traversed by the same current, substantially as set forth.

2. The combination, with a number of electroplating-baths, each provided with an anode adapted to surround an electric-light carbon, and electric conductors for connecting the baths in series, of devices for supporting an electric-light carbon centrally (or approximately so) within each anode, and for raising and lowering said carbons, substantially as set forth.

3. The combination, with a number of electroplating-baths, each containing an anode adapted to surround an electric-light carbon, of a series of clamps, each adapted to support an electric-light carbon centrally (or approximately so) within each anode, and means for raising and lowering the clamps simultaneously, substantially as set forth.

4. The combination, with a tilting frame having a series of jars or receptacles supported therein, each jar or receptacle being provided with an anode and suitable bath, of devices for supporting an electric-light carbon in each bath, electric conductors for connecting the baths in series, and devices for raising and lowering the carbons simultaneously, substantially as set forth.

In testimony whereof I have signed my name to this specification in the presence of two subscribing witnesses.

CHARLES F. BRUSH.

Witnesses:
JNO. CROWELL, Jr.,
HERMAN MORAN.

Assigned to Brush Electric Co. -- JAN 8 18__

THE UNITED STATES OF AMERICA

No. 311,576

To all to whom these presents shall come:

Whereas Charles F. Brush of Cleveland, Ohio has presented to the Commissioner of Patents a petition praying for the grant of Letters Patent for an alleged new and useful improvement in Armatures of Dynamo Electric Machines, a description of which invention is contained in the Specification of which a copy is hereunto annexed and made a part hereof, and has complied with the various requirements of Law in such cases made and provided, and

Whereas, upon due examination made, the said Claimant is adjudged to be justly entitled to a Patent under the Law.

Now therefore these **Letters Patent** are to grant unto the said Charles F. Brush, his heirs or assigns for the term of seventeen years from the twentieth day of January, one thousand eight hundred and eighty-five the exclusive right to make, use and vend the said invention throughout the United States and the Territories thereof.

In testimony whereof I have hereunto set my hand and caused the seal of the Patent Office to be affixed at the City of Washington this twentieth day of January in the year of our Lord one thousand eight hundred and eighty-five and of the Independence of the United States of America the one hundred and ninth.

Countersigned: Benj. Butterworth
Commissioner of Patents

Secretary of the Interior

(No Model.)

C. F. BRUSH.
ARMATURE FOR DYNAMO ELECTRIC MACHINES.

No. 310,876. Patented Jan. 20, 1885.

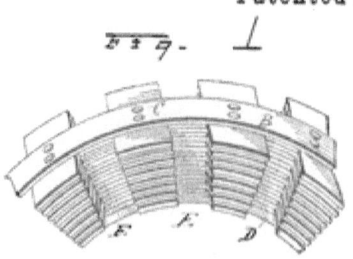

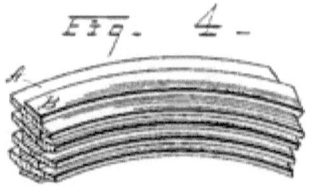

WITNESSES

INVENTOR

Attorneys

UNITED STATES PATENT OFFICE.

CHARLES F. BRUSH, OF CLEVELAND, OHIO.

ARMATURE FOR DYNAMO-ELECTRIC MACHINES.

SPECIFICATION forming part of Letters Patent No. 310,876, dated January 20, 1885.

Application filed May 13, 1884. (No model.)

To all whom it may concern:

Be it known that I, CHARLES F. BRUSH, of Cleveland, in the county of Cuyahoga and State of Ohio, have invented certain new and useful Improvements in Armatures for Dynamo-Electric Machines; and I do hereby declare the following to be a full, clear, and exact description of the invention, such as will enable others skilled in the art to which it pertains to make and use the same.

Figure 1 is a perspective view of a part of the completed armature-ring without the bobbins. Figs. 2 and 3 show the strips used in forming the ring, and Fig. 4 is a perspective view similar to Fig. 1, showing the ring as it appears before the bobbin-spaces are cut out.

The present invention relates to that kind of armature-ring for dynamo-electric or electro-dynamic machines for which Patent No. 285,457 was granted to me September 25, 1883; and it consists in building up the armature-ring of alternating narrow and wide bands of iron, the wide bands being subsequently cut away to the width of the narrow band in the places where the bobbins are to be wound. The ring may be built up in several ways; but I prefer to form it by winding together into the form of a roll a wide and a narrow band until sufficient convolutions have been formed to make up the desired thickness of the ring. It is evident, however, that the ring may be built up of short pieces held between the superposed convolutions of a longer band wound into the form of a roll; or the layers may be distinct concentric pieces held in place by rivets or the like. In any case a ring is formed of alternately wide and narrow layers, and the wide layers are afterward cut away to form the bobbin-spaces, as described above.

In the drawings, A is a band of soft iron, of the full width of the armature, and B is a narrower band of the same material, preferably of about the width of that part of the ring upon which the wire is wound. These two bands are built up or wound together so as to alternate one with another, as shown in Fig. 4, and the layers are then firmly secured together by rivets or bolts passing radially through the same, as indicated at C, Fig. 1. The bands may be built upon a base-ring, D, to give greater rigidity to the ring and afford a means of attaching the hub. The ring having been formed in this way, the wider bands, and, if necessary, part of the narrower ones, are cut away at E to form the radial slots, into which the insulated wire is wound to form the bobbins. The cutting away may be done by any suitable slotting or milling machine, or in any other way known to the trade.

One or both of the bands may be covered with insulation—such as Japan varnish or paper—or a strip of paper or other insulator may be interposed between the layers during the building up of the ring.

I claim herein as my invention—

1. An armature-ring formed of bands or strips of iron of different widths, the bands or strips being cut away to form bobbin-spaces, substantially as set forth.

2. An armature-ring formed of alternate layers of wide and narrow band-iron, the wide bands being cut away at the bobbin-spaces to the width of the narrow bands.

In testimony whereof I sign this specification, in the presence of two witnesses, this 23d day of April, 1884.

CHARLES F. BRUSH.

Witnesses:
E. B. PHILLIPS,
ALBERT E. LYNCH.

Assigned to Brush Electric Co. Jan 8 18

UNITED STATES OF AMERICA

No. 312,184

To all to whom these presents shall come:

Whereas _Charles F. Brush_ of _Cleveland_ _Ohio_ has presented to the Commissioner of Patents a petition praying for the grant of Letters Patent for an alleged new and useful improvement in

Electric Arc Lamps

a description of which invention is contained in the Specification of which a copy is hereunto annexed and made a part hereof, and has complied with the various requirements of Law in such cases made and provided, and Whereas, upon due examination made the said Claimant is adjudged to be justly entitled to a Patent under the Law.

Now therefore these **Letters Patent** are to grant unto the said _Charles F. Brush_ _his_ heirs or assigns for the term of _seventeen_ years from the _sixth_ day of _January_ one thousand eight hundred and eighty _five_ the exclusive right to make, use and vend the said invention throughout the United States and the Territories thereof.

In testimony whereof, I have hereunto set my hand and caused the seal of the **Patent Office** to be affixed at the City of Washington this _____ day of _____ in the year of our Lord one thousand eight hundred and eighty _____ and of the Independence of the United States of America the one hundred and ninth.

Countersigned: _Benj. Butterworth_
Commissioner of Patents

(No Model.)

C. F. BRUSH.
ELECTRIC ARC LAMP.

No. 312,184.   Patented Feb. 10, 1885.

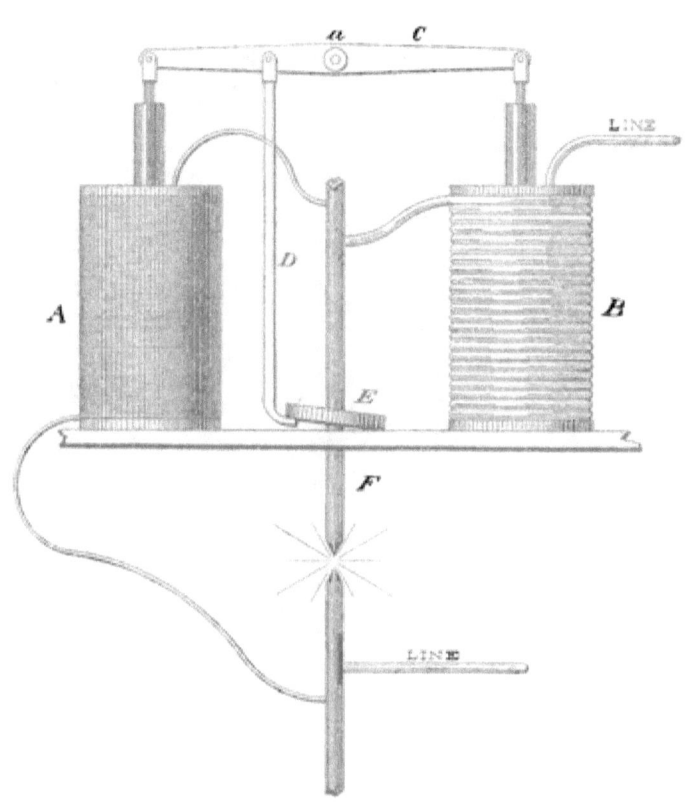

WITNESSES

INVENTOR
Chas. F. Brush
By Leggett & Leggett ATTORNEYS

UNITED STATES PATENT OFFICE.

CHARLES F. BRUSH, OF CLEVELAND, OHIO.

ELECTRIC-ARC LAMP.

SPECIFICATION forming part of Letters Patent No. 312,184, dated February 10, 1885.

Application filed August 7, 1880. (No model.)

To all whom it may concern:

Be it known that I, CHARLES F. BRUSH, of Cleveland, in the county of Cuyahoga and State of Ohio, have invented certain new and useful Improvements in Electric Lamps; and I do hereby declare the following to be a full, clear, and exact description of the invention, such as will enable others skilled in the art to which it pertains to make and use it, reference being had to the accompanying drawings, which form part of this specification.

My invention relates to electric-light regulators, and has for its object the automatic control of the arc length, not necessarily depending on variation in the strength of the working-current.

I accomplish my object by employing two axial magnets—one of low resistance located in the working-circuit, and the other of high resistance located in a shunt around the arc between the carbons. These magnets are so arranged that they constantly tend to impel the carbon-moving mechanism in opposite directions, the main-circuit magnet tending to separate the carbons, and the shunt-circuit magnet tending to bring the carbons together, but with an inferior force.

In the drawings, A is a hollow helix or "axial magnet" of high resistance, having its ends connected with the upper and lower carbons, respectively. B is a similar helix, but of comparatively very low resistance, located in the main-line circuit including the carbons. These helices are provided with movable iron cores pivoted to opposite ends of a lever, C, which in turn is pivoted to a fixed support at *a*. D is a lifting and feeding arm, through the agency of which, together with the ring-clamp E, the upper carbon, F, is primarily lifted and afterward allowed to feed. The number of convolutions of the helix B is such that when the arc between the carbons is of normal length, and the helix A consequently excited to its normal strength, the attraction of the former helix for its core shall be just sufficient to sustain the carbon F, notwithstanding the counter attraction of the helix A. Any increase in the length of the arc between the carbons will shunt more current through the helix A, increasing its attraction for its movable core and allowing the clamp E, through the lever D, to ease its grip on the carbon or carbon-holder F, so that the latter moves downward by gravitation. If the arc becomes too short, the magnetism of the helix A is weakened. This is evidently equivalent to an increase of magnetism in the helix B, and the carbon F is raised as at first. Thus it will be seen that, although the magnetism of the helix B may remain perfectly constant, its available carbon lifting and sustaining force varies in an inverse sense with the length of the arc between the carbons through the agency of the variable current hereby produced in the helix A; consequently two or more regulators controlled by this device may be operated in a single electric circuit, each regulator performing its functions independently.

The axial magnets A and B may each consist of a pair of helices with corresponding cores connected together by a heel-piece in the manner customary with double axial magnets. They may also be arranged in various positions and with or without a lever, C, provided always that they tend to actuate the carbon F in opposite directions.

A regulator provided with common magnets—that is, magnets with fixed cores and armatures arranged to approach and recede from the ends of the cores—when combined with the main shunt-circuits in the manner above described is objectionable in practice on account of certain inherent disadvantages from which the solenoid or axial magnets are free.

With the common magnets the available range of motion is very small on account of their rapidly varying attraction for their armatures as the distances of the latter vary. This necessitates powerful magnets and a nice adjustment of armature distances, which adjustment is difficult to maintain.

The evil of the rapidly varying attraction with slight changes of armature distance is aggravated by the circumstance that one armature is farthest from its magnet while the other is nearest, and the contrary when the other limit of motion is reached.

With magnets and armatures arranged with relation to each other so that the moving part or parts may travel through a considerable distance with a substantial uniformity of pulling force, thus acting as in axial magnets, a

comparatively wide range of motion is attainable with very little change of power.

In this application I do not broadly claim the combination, with either of the carbons of an electric lamp, of two electro-magnets irrespective of their type, one being located in the main circuit and the other in a constantly closed shunt-circuit of high resistance, and devices actuated by the electro-magnets for establishing and regulating the arc, as such subject-matter and such others as are not herein claimed are reserved for another application and for a division of this application.

Having fully described my invention, what I claim as new, and desire to secure by Letters Patent, is—

1. In an electric lamp, the combination of solenoid or axial magnet helices or equivalent magnets, one helix located in the main circuit and the other helix located in a constantly closed shunt-circuit of comparatively high resistance, with the feeding-carbon of an electric lamp, and devices operated by the simultaneous coaction of said magnet-helices to move the feeding-carbon to establish the arc and regulate the length of the arc, substantially as set forth.

2. In an electric lamp, the combination, with the feeding-carbon, of solenoid or axial magnet helices or equivalent magnets, one helix located in the main circuit and the other helix located in a constantly closed shunt-circuit of comparatively high resistance, and devices operated by the simultaneous coaction of said magnet-helices to move the feeding-carbon to establish the arc, regulate the length of the arc, and feed of the carbon, substantially as set forth.

3. In an electric lamp, the combination, with the feeding-carbon, of solenoid or axial magnet helices or equivalent magnets, one helix located in the main circuit and the other helix located in a constantly closed shunt-circuit of comparatively high resistance, and devices actuated by the simultaneous coaction of said magnet-helices and adapted to grip and move the carbon-holder of the feeding-carbon to establish the arc and regulate the length of the arc, substantially as set forth.

4. In an electric lamp, the combination, with the feeding-carbon, of solenoid or axial magnet helices or equivalent magnets, one helix located in the main circuit and the other helix located in a constantly closed shunt-circuit of comparatively high resistance, and devices actuated by the simultaneous coaction of said magnet-helices and adapted to grip and move the carbon-holder of the feeding-carbon to establish the arc, regulate the length of the arc, and feed of the carbon, substantially as set forth.

In testimony whereof I have signed my name to this specification in the presence of two subscribing witnesses.

CHARLES F. BRUSH.

Witnesses:
LEVERETT L. LEGGETT,
JNO. CROWELL, Jr.

Assigned to Brush Electric Co. — JAN 8 18

The United States of America

To all to whom these presents shall come:

Whereas Charles F. Brush of Cleveland, Ohio has presented to the Commissioner of Patents a petition praying for the grant of Letters Patent for an alleged new and useful improvement in

Armatures of Dynamo Electric Machines

a description of which invention is contained in the Specification of which a copy is hereunto annexed and made a part hereof, and has complied with the various requirements of Law in such cases made and provided, and Whereas upon due examination made the said Claimant is adjudged to be justly entitled to a Patent under the Law.

Now therefore these **Letters Patent** are to grant unto the said Charles F. Brush his heirs or assigns for the term of seventeen years from the twenty-fourth day of February one thousand eight hundred and eighty-five the exclusive right to make, use and vend the said invention throughout the United States and the Territories thereof.

In testimony whereof I have hereunto set my hand and caused the seal of the **Patent Office** to be affixed at the City of Washington this twenty-fourth day of February in the year of our Lord one thousand eight hundred and eighty-five and of the Independence of the United States of America the one hundred and ninth.

Countersigned: Ben Butterworth
Commissioner of Patents

M. S. Joslyn
Acting Secretary of the Interior

(No Model.)

C. F. BRUSH.
ARMATURE FOR DYNAMO ELECTRIC MACHINES.

No. 312,807. Patented Feb. 24, 1885.

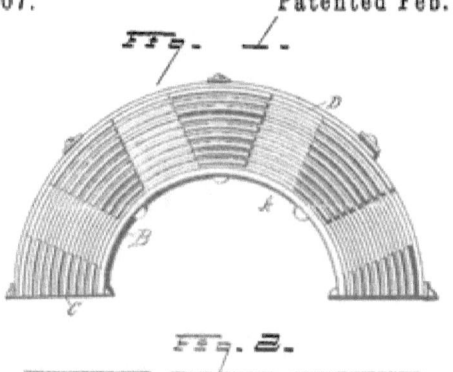

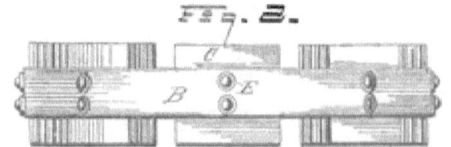

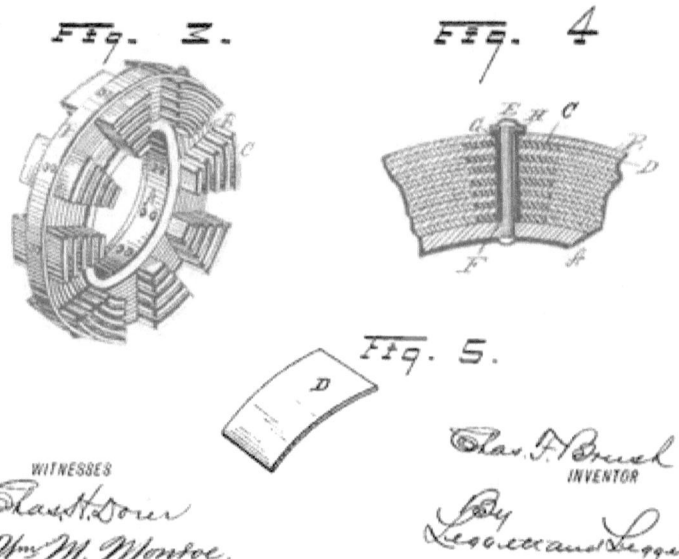

UNITED STATES PATENT OFFICE.

CHARLES F. BRUSH, OF CLEVELAND, OHIO.

ARMATURE FOR DYNAMO-ELECTRIC MACHINES.

SPECIFICATION forming part of Letters Patent No. 312,807, dated February 24, 1885.

Application filed May 13, 1884. (No model.)

To all whom it may concern:

Be it known that I, CHARLES F. BRUSH, of Cleveland, in the county of Cuyahoga and State of Ohio, have invented certain new and useful Improvements in Armatures for Dynamo-Electric Machines; and I do hereby declare the following to be a full, clear, and exact description of the invention, such as will enable others skilled in the art to which it pertains to make and use the same.

Figure 1 is a side view of half of the armature-ring as it appears before the wire is wound on. Fig. 2 is a top view of the same. Fig. 3 is a perspective view of the complete ring; and Fig. 4 is a section through the armature, showing one of the rivets. Fig. 5 shows a filling-in strip.

The invention relates to certain improvements upon the armature described in Patent No. 285,457, granted to me September 25, 1883. In the said patent I described an armature-core built up of superposed bands or layers of soft iron, between which were interposed suitable cross-pieces, which extended laterally to the full width of the armature, so as to form the projections between which the bobbins are wound. When so constructed, the armature-core is left with air-spaces extending from one cross-piece to another between the layers, and it is the purpose of my present invention to fill up this space with a separate strip of iron, so as to still further add to the capacity of the machine by increasing the amount of magnetic material in the armature-core. In the aforesaid patent I showed how this space might be filled with a strip connecting the two cross-pieces on either side of each bobbin-space, the strip and cross-pieces being stamped or cut out of a piece of sheet-iron in the form of the letter H. In the present construction, however, this cutting is saved, as the filling-in strip is made separate from the cross-pieces, and may be cut from ordinary band-iron.

My present improvement also relates to the rivets or bolts by means of which the layers or bands and the cross-pieces are held together; and it consists in insulating the rivets or bolts, in whole or in part, from the other metallic parts, so as to prevent the same from forming a path for the Foucault currents from one band to another, thereby diminishing the heating and increasing in a corresponding degree the efficiency of the machine.

In the drawings, A represents the base-ring upon which the band-iron is wound.

B indicates the layers of band-iron, and C the interposed cross-pieces. The band-iron may be either wound as a continuous spiral, in the manner of a roll of ribbon, the cross-pieces being interposed during the winding, or the layers may be built up in concentric rings, there being one or more separate pieces of band-iron to each ring. The cross-pieces gradually increase in width from the base-ring outward, so as to render the sides of the bobbin-spaces parallel.

D indicates the filling-in pieces, which are cut from ordinary band-iron, and after being bent, like the cross-pieces C, to correspond with the circular form of the armature, they are interposed, with the cross-pieces, in the winding or building up of the armature, so as to fill the spaces between the bands from one cross-piece to another. The filling-in strips D may be omitted during the winding or building up of the core, and afterward driven into the openings left between the bands. I prefer to coat the cross-pieces C and filling-in strips D with Japan or other insulating varnish before they are put into the armature, for the better security against Foucault currents. The same pieces may be also wrapped with paper, cloth, or other insulating envelope to further secure this object. The bands are secured to each other and to the base-ring by rivets or bolts E. F is an insulating sheath or bushing surrounding the shank of the rivet, and G is an insulating-washer under the outer head of the same. A metallic washer, H, is interposed between the rivet-head and the insulating-washer to give sufficient bearing-surface. One end of the rivet may be left uninsulated, as shown, and, if desired, one rivet only of each pair may be insulated. A suitable insulating material may be made from superposed layers of shellacked paper, the paper being rolled into the shape of a tube of a size to fit closely the rivet and the hole drilled therefor.

It will be noticed that the cross-pieces C

all extend the full distance between the bobbins, this being in some cases preferable.

I claim herein as my invention—

1. An armature formed of superposed layers of band-iron having interposed between them laterally-projecting cross-pieces that form the side walls of the bobbin-spaces, and separable filling-in strips interposed between the cross-pieces, substantially as set forth.

2. An armature-ring formed of superposed layers or convolutions of band-iron, with laterally-projecting cross-pieces interposed between the same, said cross-pieces forming the side walls of the bobbin-spaces, and rivets or bolts extending through both bands and cross-pieces, and insulated in whole or in part therefrom, substantially as set forth.

3. An armature-ring having its central part made up of superposed layers of band-iron, and having lateral extensions forming the bobbin-spaces, said extensions consisting of interposed cross-pieces extending from bobbin to bobbin the full thickness of the ring, substantially as set forth.

In testimony whereof I sign this specification, in the presence of two witnesses, this 23d day of April, 1884.

CHARLES F. BRUSH.

Witnesses:
 E. R. PHILLIPS,
 ALBERT E. LYNCH.

Assigned to Brush Electric Co. Jan 8 15

UNITED STATES OF AMERICA

No. _____

To all to whom these presents shall come:

Whereas Charles F. Brush of Cleveland Ohio
has presented to the Commissioner of Patents a petition praying for the grant of Letters Patent for an alleged new and useful improvement in

Method of Preparing Glass for Ornamentation

a description of which invention is contained in the Specification of which a copy is hereunto annexed and made a part hereof, and has complied with the various requirements of Law in such cases made and provided; and

Whereas upon due examination made the said Claimant is adjudged to be justly entitled to a Patent under the Law.

Now therefore these **Letters Patent** are to grant unto the said Charles F. Brush _____ his heirs or assigns for the term of seventeen years from the _____ day of _____ one thousand eight hundred and eighty _____ the exclusive right to make use and vend the said invention throughout the United States and the Territories thereof.

In testimony whereof I have hereunto set my hand and caused the seal of the Patent Office to be affixed at the City of Washington this _____ day of December in the year of our Lord one thousand eight hundred and eighty _____ and of the Independence of the United States of America the one hundred and tenth.

Countersigned:
_____
Commissioner of Patents

_____
Secretary of the Interior

(No Model.)

C. F. BRUSH.
METHOD OF PREPARING GLASS FOR CEMENTATION.

No. 331,764. Patented Dec. 8, 1885.

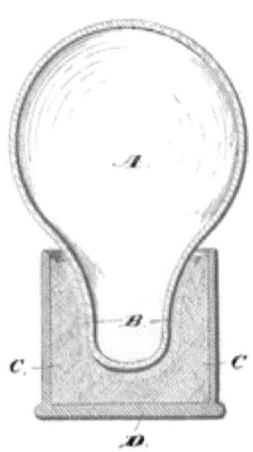

WITNESSES
Jas. E. Hutchinson
S. G. Nottingham

INVENTOR
Chas. F. Brush
By H. A. Seymour Attorney

UNITED STATES PATENT OFFICE.

CHARLES F. BRUSH, OF CLEVELAND, OHIO.

METHOD OF PREPARING GLASS FOR CEMENTATION.

SPECIFICATION forming part of Letters Patent No. 331,764, dated December 8, 1885.

Application filed August 21, 1885. Serial No. 175,011. (No specimens.)

To all whom it may concern:

Be it known that I, CHARLES F. BRUSH, of Cleveland, in the county of Cuyahoga and State of Ohio, have invented certain new and useful Improvements in Methods of Preparing Glass for Cementation; and I do hereby declare the following to be a full, clear, and exact description of the invention, such as will enable others skilled in the art to which it appertains to make and use the same.

My invention relates to an improvement in the method of preparing glass for cementation.

Hitherto it has been customary to fix incandescent-lamp bulbs and other similar articles into sockets by means of a cement composed of plaster-of-paris or analogous substance. It has been found difficult, however, to obtain a perfect and permanent junction between the glass and the cement, the smooth surface of the glass not affording a hold for the cement. This is especially noticeable where the portion of the glass to be cemented is of a round shape.

The object of my invention is to provide a method of procedure by which the glass may be firmly cemented in position, and held for an indefinite long time without liability of working loose.

With this end in view my method consists in, first, coating the glass with a preparation which will tenaciously adhere thereto; secondly, embedding granulated material in the said coating before it hardens; and, thirdly, applying the cement in the ordinary manner to the roughened surface.

To illustrate the method above briefly outlined, I have shown its application to the bulb of an incandescent lamp, and the further explanation of the method will be made in connection therewith, although I do not wish to be understood as limiting its use to that or any particular form or class of objects.

In the accompanying drawing, A represents the bulb of an incandescent lamp; D, the socket in which it is set; C, the plaster or cement; and B, the coating, which adheres tenaciously to the glass, with the granulated material embedded therein, the whole being shown in vertical section. The preparation B, with which the glass is coated, is of such a nature that when it dries it will be hard, and will cling tenaciously to the glass. An alcoholic solution of shellac varnish forms a very effective preparation for this purpose. Before the varnish hardens the portion of the glass coated therewith may be dipped in dry sand, powdered glass, or similar granulated material; or the sand, powdered glass, &c., may be sprinkled thereon; or the granulated material might be introduced into the varnish coating before it is applied to the glass, and the two applied simultaneously. When the varnish, with the granulated material embedded therein, has become thoroughly dry, the exterior surface of the coating B will be rough, and will afford an excellent retaining-surface for the plaster or other form of cement. The portion of bulb A provided with the roughened surface, is placed within the socket D, and the plaster or other form of cement C is placed around it in the ordinary manner.

Having fully described my invention, what I claim as new, and desire to secure by Letters Patent, is—

1. The method of preparing glass for cementation, consisting, essentially, in coating the glass with a preparation which will cling tenaciously thereto, and providing the said coating preparation with granulated material, substantially as set forth.

2. The method of preparing glass for cementation, consisting, essentially, in first coating the glass with a preparation which will adhere tenaciously thereto, and, secondly, embedding hard granulated material in the coating before it hardens, substantially as set forth.

3. The method of setting a glass bulb in a socket, consisting, essentially, in coating the glass with a varnish or other preparation, which will cling tenaciously thereto, embedding hard granulated material in the coating, and applying a plaster or other cement to the roughened surface, substantially as set forth.

In testimony whereof I have signed this specification in the presence of two subscribing witnesses.

CHARLES F. BRUSH.

Witnesses:
J. POTTER,
ALBERT E. LYNCH.

UNITED STATES OF AMERICA

No. 335,269

To all to whom these presents shall come:

Whereas Charles F. Brush, of Cleveland, Ohio, has presented to the Commissioner of Patents a petition praying for the grant of Letters Patent for an alleged new and useful improvement in

Electrical Switches

a description of which invention is contained in the Specification of which a copy is hereunto annexed and made a part hereof, and has complied with the various requirements of Law in such cases made and provided, and

Whereas upon due examination made the said Claimant is adjudged to be justly entitled to a Patent under the Law.

Now therefore these **Letters Patent** are to grant unto the said Charles F. Brush, his heirs or assigns for the term of seventeen years from the second day of February one thousand eight hundred and eighty-six the exclusive right to make, use and vend the said invention throughout the United States and the Territories thereof.

In testimony whereof I have hereunto set my hand and caused the seal of the Patent Office to be affixed at the City of Washington this second day of February in the year of our Lord one thousand eight hundred and eighty-six and of the Independence of the United States of America the one hundred and tenth.

Countersigned:

Acting Secretary of the Interior.

(No Model.)

C. F. BRUSH.
ELECTRICAL SWITCH.

No. 335,269. Patented Feb. 2, 1886.

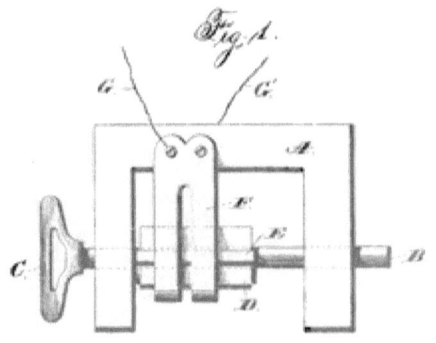

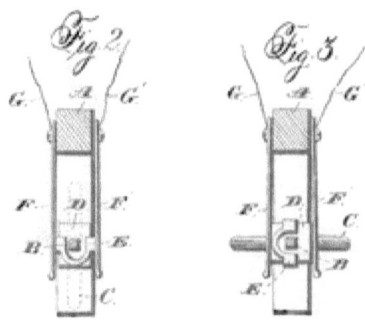

WITNESSES
Jas E. Hutchinson
S. G. Nottingham

INVENTOR
Chas. F. Brush
By H. A. Seymour Attorney

UNITED STATES PATENT OFFICE.

CHARLES F. BRUSH, OF CLEVELAND, OHIO.

ELECTRICAL SWITCH.

SPECIFICATION forming part of Letters Patent No. 335,269, dated February 2, 1886.

Application filed August 26, 1885. Serial No. 175,368. (No model.)

To all whom it may concern:

Be it known that I, CHARLES F. BRUSH, of Cleveland, in the county of Cuyahoga and State of Ohio, have invented certain new and useful Improvements in Electrical Switches; and I do hereby declare the following to be a full, clear, and exact description of the invention, such as will enable others skilled in the art to which it appertains to make and use the same.

My invention relates to an improvement in electrical switches.

The object is to provide an electrical switch which shall operate to simultaneously open or close a circuit at two points, which shall be quick, positive, and partially self-acting in its operation, and which shall automatically preserve the integrity of the contacts when closed and prevent accidental displacement when open.

With these ends in view my invention consists in certain features of construction and combinations of parts, as will be hereinafter described, and pointed out in the claims.

In the accompanying drawings, Figure 1 is a view of one form of the switch complete; and Figs. 2 and 3 represent cross-sections of the same, showing it in a closed and open adjustment, respectively.

A is a frame of insulating material, in opposite sides or ends of which is journaled a shaft, B, having on one end the operating-handle C. Upon that portion of the shaft which crosses the interior space of the frame is rigidly attached a block of insulating material, D, having an approximately square cross-section, Figs. 2 and 3. Upon two opposite faces of D, parallel to the shaft, are attached contact-pieces of metal E, which are metallically connected together by a strip passing across on end of D, and curved so as to avoid contact with the shaft. These contact-pieces and the connecting-strip are usually made in one piece and bent to shape, and are preferably fastened to the insulating material by being partially embedded, dovetail fashion, in its surface. They present a raised metallic surface above the face of the insulated block; but the metallic surface so formed should not be as wide as is the face of the block in the direction of its rotation.

Two flat contact-springs, F F', insulated from each other, are attached at one end to opposite sides of the frame, their free ends resting with a spring-pressure upon opposite faces of the block D. To these springs are respectively connected the two ends G G', of the circuit to be controlled by the switch.

By turning the handle C to one position, Fig. 2, the contact-springs F F' will rest upon the contact-strip E, and the current can pass from one spring to the other by means of E, thus closing the circuit. By now turning the handle C to a position at right angles to the former one, (see Fig. 3,) the circuit will be broken, the springs then resting on the plain faces of D.

It will be seen that there are several advantages secured by this construction: First, when the switch is closed, the handle may be turned slightly either way without breaking contact. This secures a rubbing action on the contact-surfaces. Secondly, when a further turning of the handle causes the corners of the block to strike the contact-springs, the latter are raised suddenly and quickly out of contact, breaking the circuit at both sides of the block at once, thus distributing the sparking over two points. Thirdly, until the block is turned so far as to secure an ample separation of the contact-surfaces, the pressure of the springs acts to force it back and re-establish contact, thus preventing the chance of the switch being left in a position where a permanent arc could be formed between the contacts; also, when the switch is open, as shown in Fig. 3, the springs hold the block firmly in position and prevent accidental closing of the circuit.

It is evident that the switch here shown and described might be changed in form and arrangement of parts without departing from the spirit and scope of my invention; hence I do not wish to limit myself strictly to the construction herein set forth; but,

Having fully described my invention, what I claim as new, and desire to secure by Letters Patent, is—

1. In an electrical switch or current-breaker, an insulating-block made angular in cross-section, and an electric conductor projecting outwardly from the two opposite plane surfaces of the block, said conductor being of less width than said plane surfaces to insure

plane surfaces of insulating material adjacent to and on opposite sides of each end of the conductor, in combination with a pair of spring contact-arms arranged to press on opposite sides of the insulating block or conductor, whereby imperfect contacts are avoided and the switch positively retained in its open or closed position, substantially as set forth.

2. In an electric switch or circuit breaker, the combination, with a block of insulating material secured to a rotary shaft, and an electric conductor insulated from the shaft and projecting outwardly from opposite sides of the block, of a pair of spring-arms arranged to press on opposite sides of the block or conductor, substantially as set forth.

In testimony whereof I have signed this specification in the presence of two subscribing witnesses.

CHARLES F. BRUSH.

Witnesses:
J. POTTER,
ALBERT E. LYNCH.

UNITED STATES OF AMERICA

No. 336,___

To all to whom these presents shall come:

Whereas _____ Charles F. Brush, _____ of _____ Cleveland, _____ Ohio _____ has presented to the Commissioner of Patents a petition praying for the grant of Letters Patent for an alleged new and useful improvement in _____ Armatures for Dynamo-Electric Machines _____ a description of which invention is contained in the Specification of which a copy is hereunto annexed and made a part hereof, and has complied with the various requirements of Law in such cases made and provided, and Whereas upon due examination made the said Claimant is adjudged to be justly entitled to a Patent under the Law.

Now therefore these **Letters Patent** are to grant unto the said Charles F. Brush, his _____ heirs or assigns for the term of seventeen years from the _____ day of _____ one thousand eight hundred and eighty _____ the exclusive right to make, use and vend the said invention throughout the United States and the Territories thereof.

In testimony whereof I have hereunto set my hand and caused the seal of the Patent Office to be affixed at the City of Washington this _____ day of _____ in the year of our Lord one thousand eight hundred and eighty _____ and of the Independence of the United States of America the one hundred and tenth.

Countersigned: _____

_____ Acting Secretary of the Interior

_____ Commissioner of Patents

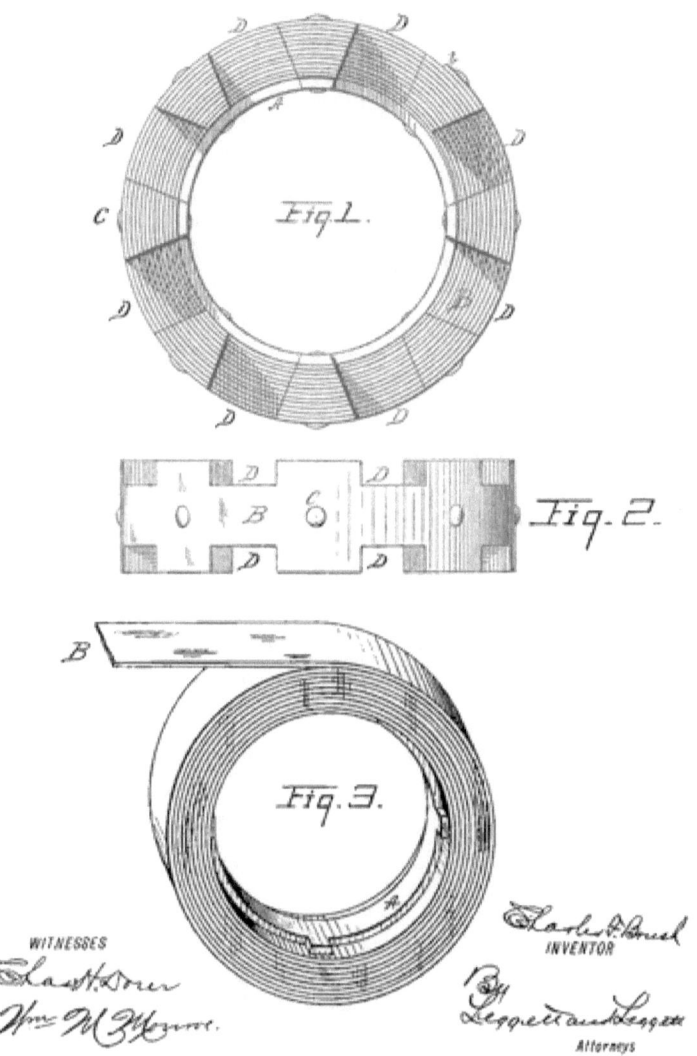

United States Patent Office.

CHARLES F. BRUSH, OF CLEVELAND, OHIO.

ARMATURE FOR DYNAMO-ELECTRIC MACHINES.

SPECIFICATION forming part of Letters Patent No. 336,087, dated February 16, 1886.

Application filed May 13, 1884. Serial No. 131,325. (No model.)

To all whom it may concern:

Be it known that I, CHARLES F. BRUSH, of Cleveland, in the county of Cuyahoga and State of Ohio, have invented certain new and useful Improvements in Armatures for Dynamo-Electric Machines; and I do hereby declare the following to be a full, clear, and exact description of the invention, such as will enable others skilled in the art to which it pertains to make and use the same.

Figure 1 is a side view of my improved armature-ring without the bobbins. Fig. 2 is a top view of the same. Fig. 3 shows the ring partially formed and before the bobbin-spaces have been cut out.

The present invention relates to armature-rings for dynamo-electric machines of the kind shown in Patent No. 285,457, granted to me September 25, 1883.

According to the present invention a band-formed armature-ring is constructed by winding or building up a series of superposed layers of band-iron of the full width of the armature and then cutting away portions to form the bobbin-spaces. I prefer to form the ring by winding the band-iron upon a suitable base-ring, and in order to insulate the layers one from another I may cover the band with suitable varnish or paint, or wind in with the iron an interposed ribbon of paper or other suitable insulating web. It is evident that the ring may also be formed by winding two or more bands together, or by building up the ring with separate concentric layers, or by winding one or more long bands with interposed short pieces of the same width.

In the drawings, A is the base-ring, to which the hub is secured, and upon which the band-iron is wound or built up. One end of the band-iron B is secured by rivets or otherwise to the base-ring, and the band is then wound tightly around the base-ring and upon itself in the manner shown in Fig. 3 until the desired thickness of ring is obtained, when the end of the band is secured, as at b, Fig. 1. Suitable bolts or rivets, C, are then passed through the ring radially to secure the layers together, after which the bobbin-spaces are formed by cutting away at the places indicated at D in Figs. 1 and 2. This may be done by the ordinary milling, planing, or slotting machines. The ring thus completed may be wound with wire in the ordinary manner, and will form an armature of exceptional solidity and efficiency.

I claim herein as my invention—

An armature composed of superposed layers of band-iron wound one upon another, the opposite faces of which are provided with radial grooves situated directly opposite one another and extending the entire width of the ring, the side walls of the grooves being made integral with the layers of the band, substantially as set forth.

In testimony whereof I sign this specification, in the presence of two witnesses, this 23d day of April, 1884.

CHARLES F. BRUSH.

Witnesses:
E. B. PHILLIPS,
ALBERT E. LYNCH.

Assigned to Brush Electric Co. — Jan 8 1887

UNITED STATES AMERICA

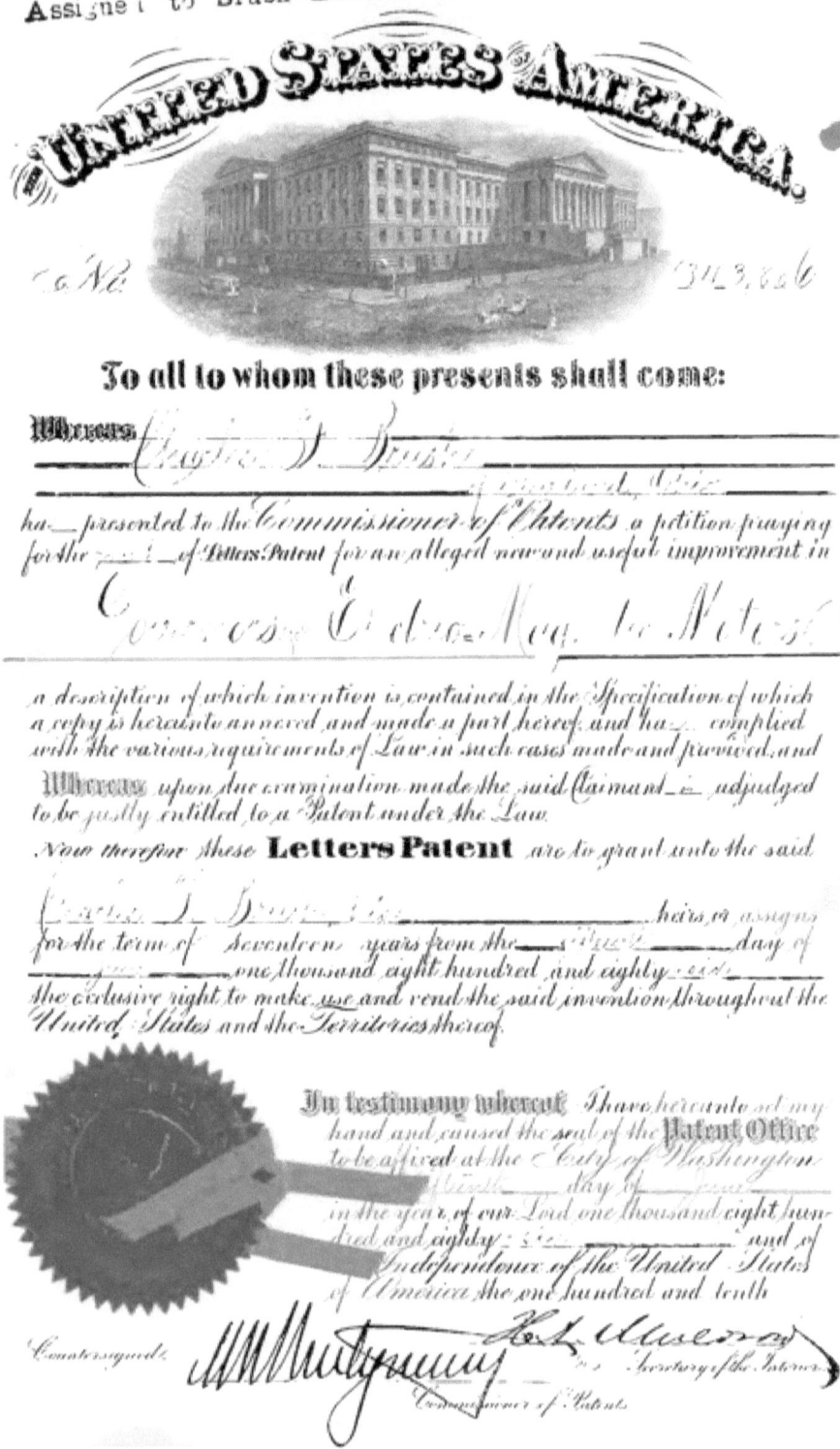

Nº 343,856

To all to whom these presents shall come:

Whereas Charles F. Brush of Cleveland, Ohio ha_ presented to the Commissioner of Patents a petition praying for the grant of Letters Patent for an alleged new and useful improvement in

Generators Electro-Mag. to Motors &c

a description of which invention is contained in the Specification of which a copy is hereunto annexed, and made a part hereof, and ha_ complied with the various requirements of Law in such cases made and provided, and

Whereas upon due examination made the said Claimant is adjudged to be justly entitled to a Patent under the Law.

Now therefore these **Letters Patent** are to grant unto the said

Charles F. Brush &c _____ heirs or assigns for the term of seventeen years from the _____ day of _____ one thousand eight hundred and eighty ___ the exclusive right to make, use and vend the said invention throughout the United States and the Territories thereof.

In testimony whereof, I have hereunto set my hand and caused the seal of the **Patent Office** to be affixed at the City of Washington this _____ day of _____ in the year of our Lord one thousand eight hundred and eighty ___ and of Independence of the United States of America the one hundred and tenth.

Countersigned:
_____ _____
Commissioner of Patents   Secretary of the Interior

(No Model.) 2 Sheets—Sheet 2.

C. F. BRUSH.
GOVERNOR FOR ELECTRO MAGNETIC MOTORS.

No. 343,886. Patented June 15, 1886.

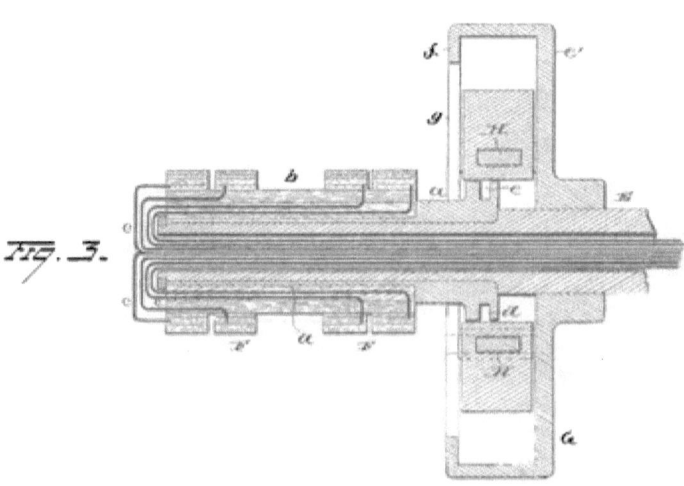

Fig. 3.

WITNESSES

INVENTOR
Chas F Brush

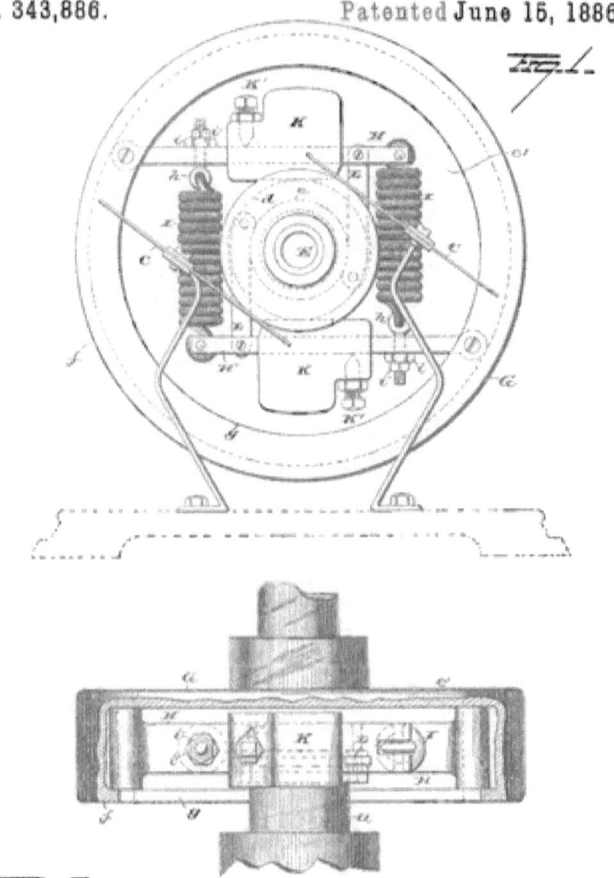

United States Patent Office.

CHARLES F. BRUSH, OF CLEVELAND, OHIO.

GOVERNOR FOR ELECTRO-MAGNETIC MOTORS.

SPECIFICATION forming part of Letters Patent No. 343,886, dated June 15, 1886.

Application filed December 28, 1885. Serial No. 186,921. (No model.)

To all whom it may concern:

Be it known that I, CHARLES F. BRUSH, of Cleveland, in the county of Cuyahoga and State of Ohio, have invented certain new and useful Improvements in Governors for Electro-Magnetic Motors; and I do hereby declare the following to be a full, clear, and exact description of the invention, such as will enable others skilled in the art to which it appertains to make and use the same.

My invention relates to an improvement in governors for electro-magnetic motors.

The variations or fluctuations of current-strength in the circuit of a dynamo or magneto electric machine due to the varying resistance interposed therein in the form of motors, lamps, &c., and to other causes may be regulated and controlled and the current-strength rendered practically uniform by means of a current-regulator connected with the generator. My preferred form of regulator for this purpose being of the type shown and described in Letters Patent No. 224,511, granted to me February 17, 1880.

In the employment of a motor in a circuit in which the current-strength is or is not governed and controlled and rendered practically uniform some means must be provided for automatically controlling the speed of the motor, because with the parts of the motor adjusted to insure a predetermined speed of the motor when subjected to a certain load, the speed will vary, either being increased or decreased whenever the load or current is varied; and my invention has for its object the automatic regulation of the speed of electro-magnetic motors under the varying loads and currents to which they may be subjected.

With this end in view my invention consists in the combination, with adjustable commutator segments or strips or commutator-sleeve, of a centrifugal governor for automatically adjusting the commutator segments or sleeve to regulate the speed of the motor.

My invention further consists in certain features of construction and combinations of parts as will hereinafter be described, and pointed out in the claims.

In the accompanying drawings, Figure 1 is a side view of one form of my improved governor. Fig. 2 is a plan view, and Fig. 3 is a longitudinal section.

C represents the commutator-brushes of an electric motor.

E is the armature-shaft, on which is loosely mounted the commutator-sleeve a, to enable the latter to be freely turned on the shaft.

F represents the commutator sections or segments, which are insulated from the sleeve a by means of the insulating sleeve or cylinder b. Commutator-sections F are electrically connected with the armature-bobbins by flexible conductors c, to allow of the rotary adjustment of the commutator without impairing the electrical connections of the armature and commutator-sections. Sleeve a is provided at one end with an enlarged disk, d, provided with grooves e for the attachment of the governor-connections, as will be explained.

To the armature-shaft E is secured the shell G by set-screw, bolts, or in any other desired manner. The outer end or head, e, of the shell is closed, while its inner end or head, f, is open, as shown at g, to allow of ready access to the parts of the governor located within the shell for the purpose of inspection, adjustment, or oiling. To the inner periphery of the shell are pivoted on opposite sides of its center the governor-arms H H, the inner and free ends of which are connected to the opposite arms by means of the spiral springs I I, the latter being adjustably secured to the arms by the eyebolts h and nuts $i\ i'$.

On each one of the arms H H is placed a weight, K, which may be longitudinally adjusted and secured to the arm in any desired position by the set-screw K'.

To the arms H H, near their outer or free ends, are pivoted the links L L, the opposite ends of which are pivoted to the enlarged disk or flange d and on opposite sides thereof. As the governor-shell rotates with the armature-shaft, carrying with it the parts described, it will be readily understood that the weights K K will at a certain speed be moved by centrifugal action toward the periphery of the shell and away from the armature-shaft, and, through the medium of the connecting-links L L, impart a rotary adjustment to the commutator, varying its position on the armature-shaft.

When the motor is at rest, the spiral springs will firmly retain the weights in close proximity to the shaft and the commutator at the extreme limit of its rotary adjustment in one direction, and in this adjustment of parts the commutator-brushes C will bear on the maximum points of the commutator-sections. Current now being switched into the motor through the commutator-brushes, (and this may be done through a graduated resistance connected with the switch, if desired,) rotary motion is imparted to the armature and its shaft, the speed of which gradually increases until the motor has attained its predetermined or normal rate of speed. At this point the governor-weights will begin to recede from each other and move outwardly toward the periphery of the shell and rotate the commutator on the shaft, carrying the maximum points of the commutator away from the contact-points of the brushes and in the direction of rotation of the armature of the motor. This action decreases the effect of the driving-current until a point is reached where the effect of the current is balanced by the load on the motor, and the speed of the latter remains constant. Now, should the speed of the motor be retarded by a decrease of current-strength with no corresponding diminution of load or by an increase of load with no increase of current-strength, the governor-balls will be retracted and drawn toward each other by the spiral springs, and thereby rotate the commutator in a direction opposite to the motion of the armature-shaft, the effect of which is to move the maximum points on the commutator nearer to the brushes, and thereby increase the speed of the motor. On the other hand, should the speed of the motor be increased above the normal rate, owing to an increase of current-strength or to a decrease of load, the governor-balls will be caused to recede from each other and rotate the commutator in the same direction as that of the armature-shaft, and cause the maximum points on the commutator-sections to be moved away from the brushes, and thereby decrease the speed of the motor; hence it will be observed that by my improvement I am enabled to insure a practically uniform rate of speed under varying loads and varying current-strengths.

By the terms "maximum points," as used in this specification, I mean those points on the commutator where the contact of the brushes will allow the production of maximum effect.

While the construction and arrangement of the parts of the governor may be widely varied without departing from the spirit and scope of my invention, yet the type of governor shown and described has many important advantages in actual practice. The parts composing the governor are few in number, are simple and durable in construction, may be readily adjusted, and are not liable to get out of adjustment or order, and may be manufactured at a small initial cost. The direct connection of the governor with the commutator insures the prompt adjustment of the latter without lost motion and at a minimum expenditure of power, so that the governor is exceedingly sensitive in its action under all circumstances. By locating the parts of the governor in compact form within a rotary shell on the armature-shaft I insure a compact form of machine for shipment, and one requiring but small space for its operation; and, further, such construction and arrangement of parts will offer but little resistance to the rapid rotation of the motor.

While the type of governor shown and described has, when applied to a motor, certain advantages, some of which have been specified, yet I would have it understood that I do not restrict myself to the particular type of governor or to the particular construction and arrangement of parts shown and described.

I am informed that a centrifugal governor has been applied to a dynamo-electric machine for automatically adjusting the commutator segments or sleeve for the purpose of regulating the strength of the current generated by the machine. I am also informed that a centrifugal governor has been applied to an electro-magnetic motor for automatically adjusting the commutator-brushes for the purpose of regulating and controlling the speed of the motor; and hence I would have it understood that I make no claim to such improvements or combinations of parts.

Having fully described my invention, what I claim as new, and desire to secure by Letters Patent, is—

1. In an electric motor, the combination, with a commutator, of a centrifugal governor for automatically adjusting the commutator segments or sleeve for regulating the speed of the motor, substantially as set forth.

2. In an electric motor, the combination, with a commutator, of a centrifugal governor for automatically imparting rotary adjustment to the commutator segments or sleeve for regulating the speed of the motor, substantially as set forth.

3. In an electric motor, the combination, with a commutator-sleeve loosely mounted on the armature-shaft, of a centrifugal governor for automatically adjusting the commutator segments or sleeve for regulating the speed of the motor, substantially as set forth.

4. In an electric motor, the combination, with an adjustable commutator, of a centrifugal governor mounted on the armature-shaft, and adapted to regulate the speed of the motor by its automatic adjustment of the position of the commutator segments or sleeve, substantially as set forth.

5. In an electric motor, the combination, with an adjustable commutator-sleeve or commutator-segments, of a centrifugal governor

connected with the commutator-sleeve, and constructed and arranged to automatically impart rotary adjustment to the commutator-sleeve in the direction opposite to that of the rotation of the armature-shaft when the speed of the motor falls below a predetermined rate, and to move the commutator-sleeve in the same direction as the rotation of the armature-shaft when the speed of the motor exceeds a predetermined rate, substantially as set forth.

In testimony whereof I have signed this specification in the presence of two subscribing witnesses.

     CHARLES F. BRUSH.

Witnesses:
 ALBERT E. LYNCH,
 CHAS. H. DORER.

UNITED STATES OF AMERICA

No. 347,155

To all to whom these presents shall come:

Whereas Charles F. Brush _____ of Cleveland, Ohio _____ has presented to the Commissioner of Patents a petition praying for the grant of Letters Patent for an alleged new and useful improvement in

Multiple Series Arc Cuts,

a description of which invention is contained in the Specification of which a copy is hereunto annexed and made a part hereof, and has complied with the various requirements of Law in such cases made and provided, and Whereas upon due examination made the said Claimant is adjudged to be justly entitled to a Patent under the Law

Now therefore these **Letters Patent** are to grant unto the said Charles F. Brush his _____ heirs or assigns for the term of seventeen years from the _____ day of _____ one thousand eight hundred and eighty _____ the exclusive right to make, use, and vend the said invention throughout the United States and the Territories thereof.

In testimony whereof I have hereunto set my hand and caused the seal of the **Patent Office** to be affixed at the City of Washington this _____ day of _____ in the year of our Lord one thousand eight hundred and eighty _____ and of the Independence of the United States of America the one hundred and eleventh.

H. L. Muldrow
Secretary of the Interior

Countersigned:
R. B. Vance
Commissioner of Patents

(No Model.)

C. F. BRUSH.
MULTIPLE SERIES CUT-OUT.

No. 347,025. Patented Aug. 10, 1886.

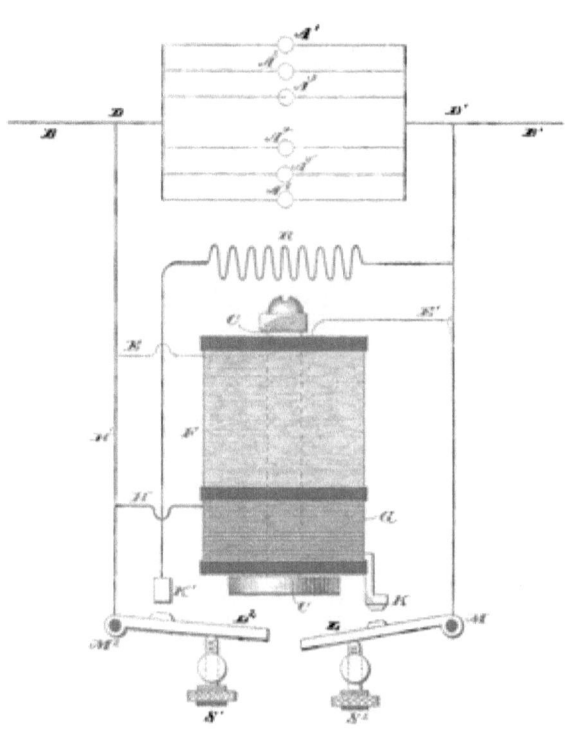

WITNESSES
INVENTOR

United States Patent Office.

CHARLES F. BRUSH, OF CLEVELAND, OHIO.

MULTIPLE-SERIES CUT-OUT.

SPECIFICATION forming part of **Letters Patent No. 347,025, dated August 10, 1886.**

Application filed December 19, 1885. Serial No. 126,157. (No model.)

To all whom it may concern:

Be it known that I, CHARLES F. BRUSH, of Cleveland, in the county of Cuyahoga and State of Ohio, have invented certain new and useful Improvements in Multiple-Series Cut-Outs; and I do hereby declare the following to be a full, clear, and exact description of the invention, such as will enable others skilled in the art to which it appertains to make and use the same.

My invention relates to improvements in automatic cut-outs or shunting devices for multiple-series systems of electrical distribution, and more particularly to that one in which, in combination with each of the groups of electro-receptive devices arranged in multiple series is employed a shunting device for automatically reducing the normal flow of current through the remaining electro-receptive devices of a group upon the failure of one or more of them to operate. The objection to this system is, that it does not provide a complete and safe short circuit for the main current, should all the electro-receptive devices be inoperative, or such a number of them as would result in the destruction of the remaining ones or of the apparatus.

My invention overcomes this difficulty by means of mechanism similar to that shown in the accompanying drawing, which embodies one form of such mechanism and illustrates diagrammatically my invention as applied to one of a series of groups of electro-receptive devices.

In the drawing, A' A² A³ A⁴ A' A⁵ represent the group of electro-receptive devices, which may be, and for the purpose of this illustration I will assume to be, incandescent lamps, each located in a branch circuit from the main conductor B B'.

C is an electro-magnet wound with two coils. One of these, F, is of high resistance and forms a constantly-closed shunt-circuit, D E E' D', around the group of lamps A' A², &c. The other coil, G, is of coarse wire, and has one of its terminals attached at H to a wire, H', leading to D on one side of the group of lamps, the other terminal forming the contact K. An armature-lever, L, is pivoted at M in electrical contact with the wire M D'. When the armature is sufficiently attracted by the magnet, it rises and strikes the contact K.

A second armature, L', also in the field of attraction of the magnet, is pivoted at M' in electrical contact with the wire M² H' D. When this armature is sufficiently attracted by the magnet, it rises and strikes the contact K', closing the shunt-circuit D H' M² L' K' R D' around the group of lamps. In this shunt-circuit is located the resistance R, which has a somewhat higher conductivity than the working conductivity of any one of the lamps. Set-screws S' S' serve to regulate the distance of the armatures from the magnet.

The armatures having been suitably adjusted, and so that L requires a greater attractive force to raise it than L', the operation of the device is as follows: With all the lamps A' A², &c., in operative condition, the normal current in the line B B' will divide itself between the lamps, except a small percentage which will pass around the group by the shunt-circuit, comprising the fine-wire coil F. This percentage of current magnetizes the core of the electro-magnet, but not sufficiently to raise the armature L', owing to the distance at which it is adjusted. Now, if one (or any predetermined number) of the lamps fail to operate, and if, as is presupposed, the current in the main circuit remains constant, the difference of potential at the terminals of the fine-wire coil will increase, magnetizing the core more strongly, and raising the armature L' until it strikes the contact K' and closes the shunt-circuit which includes the resistance-lamps, but not dimming them entirely. The effect of throwing in the resistance R parallel with the lamps and fine coil will be to reduce somewhat the difference of potential at the terminals of the fine coil, which would consequently reduce the strength of the magnet; but as the armature L' has advanced so much farther into the field of attraction it is still held up in contact with K'. Now, if the defective lamp or lamps be replaced and the shunt-circuit including the resistance R be opened by pulling down the armature L', the normal current will flow through the lamps and fine coil, as before; but if the defective lamp or lamps be not replaced, and if others of the group should by inadvertence or malice be allowed to become successively inoperative, it is evident that an increasing current will be forced through the fine coil F, the resistance

R, and such lamps as may remain operative, or if there be no lamps left in operation all the current will be forced through the fine-coil circuit and the resistance-circuit, in either case to the possible and probable injury of the apparatus. Similar difficulty will occur if when the main current is started there should be few or no lamps on any group. Now, the function of the second armature becomes apparent, for with the increased current flowing through the fine coil F, due to the causes I have just indicated, an increased strength of magnetism will result, raising the armature L, which will strike the contact K and close what is practically a short circuit around the group of lamps and around the resistance R and fine coil F, the course of the current in the short circuit being as follows: D H' H, through the coarse coil G to terminal K, then through lever L and wire M D'.

The effect of making the coarse coil G a portion of the short circuit is to retain the armature L in contact with K, notwithstanding that the magnetizing effect of the fine coil F is practically destroyed by the great decrease in difference of potential at its terminals. This form of short-circuiting magnet has been previously patented to me, (Patent No. 234,456,) and such especial construction does not form part of my present invention; nor do I limit myself to the particular construction or arrangement of parts shown in the drawings, as various modifications will readily suggest themselves, and any form of automatic shunting device may be used.

Having fully described my invention, what I claim as new, and desire to secure by Letters Patent, is—

1. In a multiple-series system of electrical distribution, in combination with a group of electro-receptive devices and mechanism operated by the current for automatically reducing the normal flow of current through the remaining electro-receptive devices upon the failure of one or any predetermined number of them to operate, mechanism, also controlled by the current, to automatically short-circuit the current around said group upon the inoperation from any cause of more than said predetermined number of electro-receptive devices, substantially as set forth.

2. In a multiple-series system of electrical distribution, the combination, with a group of electro-receptive devices, of a normally-open shunt-circuit having a resistance less than any one or of any predetermined number of the electro-receptive devices of the group, and mechanism actuated by the current for automatically closing said shunt-circuit and diverting a sufficient amount of current through the same to reduce the normal flow of current through the remaining electro-receptive devices of the group upon the failure of any one or any predetermined number of them to operate, and a supplemental normally-open shunt-circuit of comparatively low resistance, and mechanism actuated by the current for automatically shunting the current around the group and high-resistance shunt whenever the latter is incapable of shunting a sufficient amount of current around the group to preserve intact the remaining operative electro-receptive devices included therein, substantially as set forth.

3. In a multiple-series system of electrical distribution, the combination, with a group of electro-receptive devices, of a constantly-closed shunt having an electro-magnet included therein and two normally-open shunt-circuits of different resistances, the circuit of lowest resistance being included in the helix of an electro-magnet, and devices actuated and controlled by the current for closing the circuit of high resistance and reducing the normal flow of current through the remaining electro-receptive devices of the group upon the failure of one or of any one predetermined number to operate, and for closing the circuit of low resistance and short-circuiting the group, substantially as set forth.

4. In a multiple-series system of electrical distribution, the combination, with a group of electro-receptive devices, of a constantly-closed shunt-circuit of high resistance included in the helix of an electro-magnet, and a normally-open shunt of comparatively low resistance included in the helix of an electro-magnet, and an armature for opening and closing said shunt-circuit, substantially as set forth.

5. In a multiple-series system of electrical distribution, the combination, with a group of electro-receptive devices, of a constantly-closed shunt of high resistance and two normally-open shunt-circuits—one of comparatively high and one of comparatively low resistance—and an electro-magnet included in the constantly-closed shunt and the normally-open shunt of comparatively low resistance, substantially as set forth.

In testimony whereof I have signed this specification in the presence of two subscribing witnesses.

CHARLES F. BRUSH.

Witnesses:
ALBERT E. LYNCH,
L. B. LE VAKE.

Assigned to Brush Electric Co   JAN 8 1887

UNITED STATES OF AMERICA

No. 353,101

To all to whom these presents shall come:

Whereas __Charles F. Brush__ of __Cleveland__, __Ohio__ has presented to the Commissioner of Patents a petition praying for the grant of Letters Patent for an alleged new and useful improvement in __Dynamo Electric Current Regulator__

a description of which invention is contained in the Specification of which a copy is hereunto annexed and made a part hereof, and has complied with the various requirements of Law in such cases made and provided, and Whereas upon due examination made the said Claimant is adjudged to be justly entitled to a Patent under the Law.

Now therefore these **Letters Patent** are to grant unto the said __Charles F. Brush, his__ heirs or assigns for the term of seventeen years from the __second__ day of __November__ one thousand eight hundred and eighty __six__ the exclusive right to make, use and vend the said invention throughout the United States and the Territories thereof.

In testimony whereof, I have hereunto set my hand and caused the seal of the Patent Office to be affixed at the City of Washington this __second__ day of __November__ in the year of our Lord one thousand eight hundred and eighty __six__ and of the Independence of the United States of America the one hundred and eleventh.

D. L. Hawkins
Secretary of the Interior

Countersigned:
Commissioner of Patents

(No Model.) 4 Sheets—Sheet 4.
C. F. BRUSH.
AUTOMATIC ELECTRIC CURRENT REGULATOR.
No. 351,961. Patented Nov. 2, 1886.

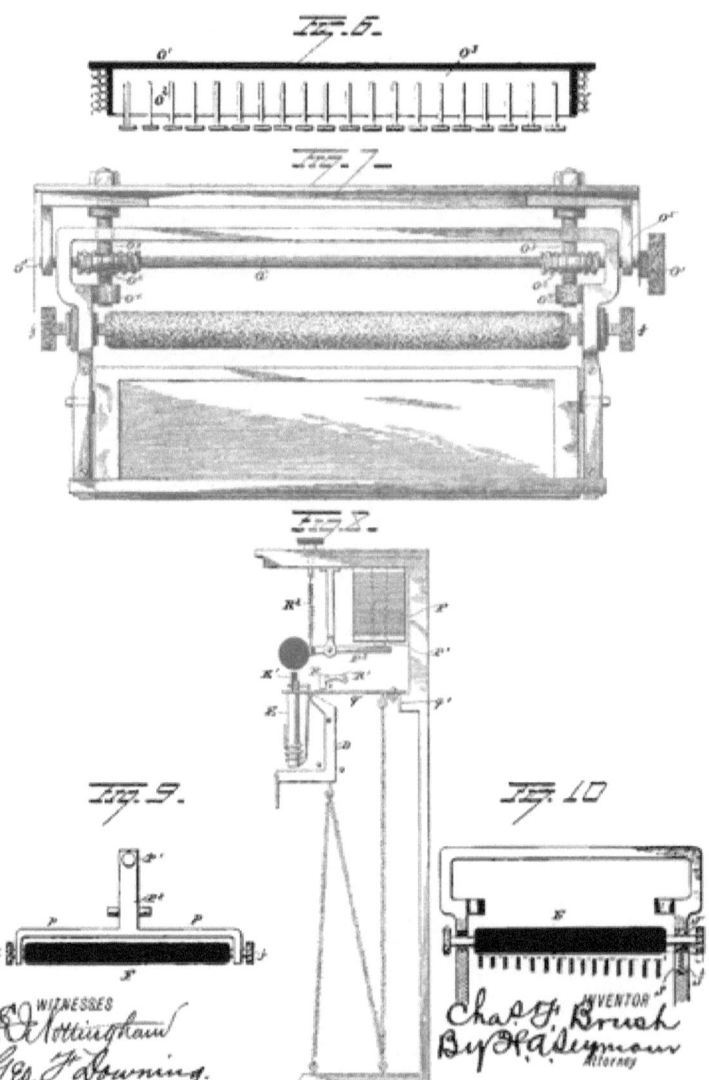

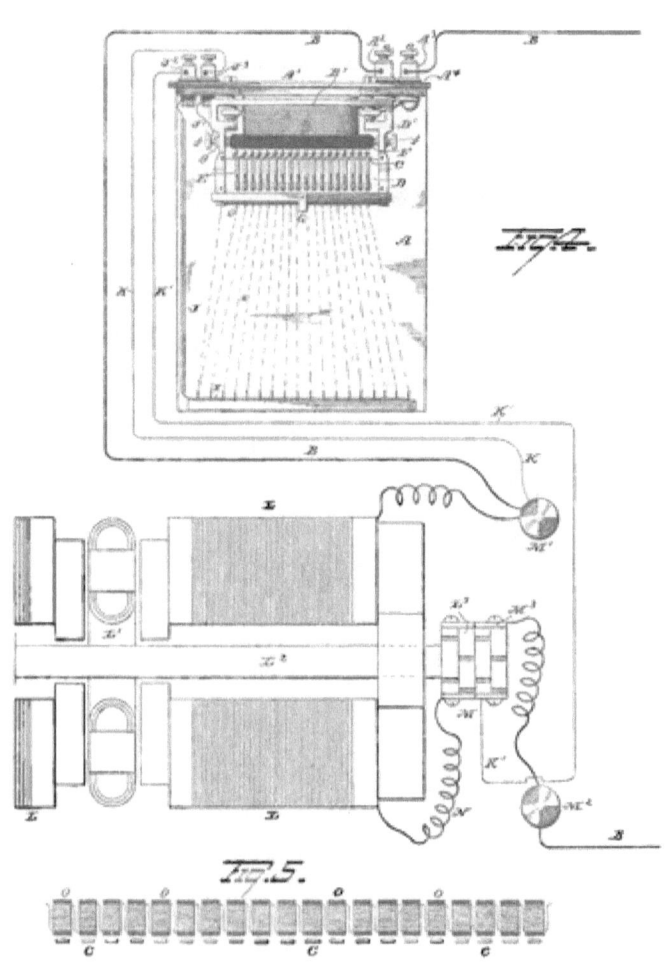

(No Model.) 4 Sheets—Sheet 2.

C. F. BRUSH.
AUTOMATIC ELECTRIC CURRENT REGULATOR.

No. 351,961. Patented Nov. 2, 1886.

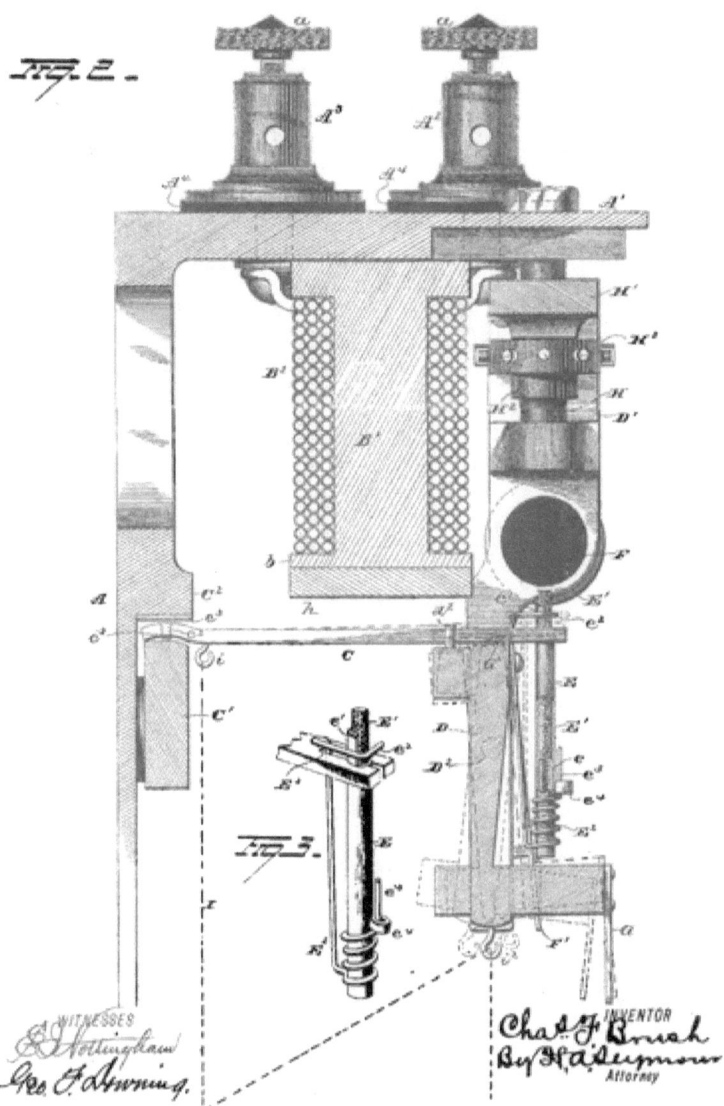

(No Model.) 4 Sheets—Sheet 1.

C. F. BRUSH.
AUTOMATIC ELECTRIC CURRENT REGULATOR.

No. 351,961. Patented Nov. 2, 1886.

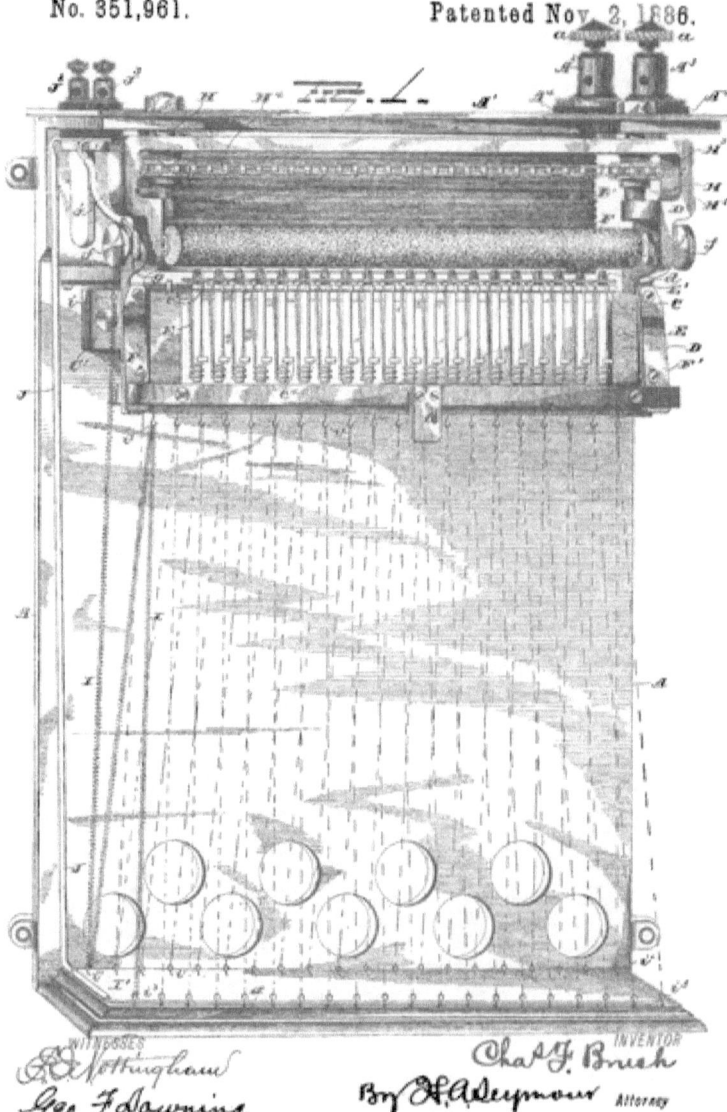

UNITED STATES PATENT OFFICE.

CHARLES F. BRUSH, OF CLEVELAND, OHIO.

AUTOMATIC ELECTRIC-CURRENT REGULATOR.

SPECIFICATION forming part of Letters Patent No. 351,961, dated November 2, 1886.

Application filed June 9, 1886. Serial No. 204,634. (No model.)

To all whom it may concern:

Be it known that I, CHARLES F. BRUSH, of Cleveland, in the county of Cuyahoga and State of Ohio, have invented certain new and useful Improvements in Automatic Electric-Current Governors or Regulators; and I do hereby declare the following to be a full, clear, and exact description of the invention, such as will enable others skilled in the art to which it appertains to make and use the same.

My invention relates to an improvement in automatic electric-current governors or regulators, and has for its object the automatic control and regulation of the strength of the current in an electric circuit in which the current strength is subject to variations due to variations in the speed of the armature of the dynamo-electric machines, or to varying resistance in the circuit owing to an increase or decrease of work or of the number of translating devices included therein, or to other or both of the causes specified.

The invention consists in the combination, with an electric circuit, of a series of resistances and means actuated by the varying current strength in the circuit for automatically switching into an electric circuit the series of resistances (some or all of them) in multiple arc with each other.

The invention further consists in combinations of parts and features of construction, as will be hereinafter described, and pointed out in the claims.

In the accompanying drawings, Figure 1 is a view in side elevation of one form of electric-current governor embodying the invention, only one of the wire resistances being shown in detail, the remaining resistances being illustrated in dotted lines. Fig. 2 is a detached view, partly in section and partly in end elevation, illustrating by dotted lines the position assumed by the parts in the simultaneous adjustment of the series of contact-rods. Fig. 3 is a detached view in perspective of one of the tubular holders, contact-rod, and a portion of the armature. Fig. 4 illustrates the governor applied to the circuit of a dynamo-electric machine for automatically controlling the magnetic field of the machine to govern and control the current in the working-circuit; and Figs. 5, 6, 7, 8, 9, and 10 illustrate modifications.

A represents a frame, which may be made of cast-iron, wood, or other material, and of any desired shape and form. It is provided at its upper end with the top portion or forwardly-projecting flange, A', from which are suspended the operating parts of the governor.

A² A³ are binding-posts secured to the top of the frame, and insulated therefrom by insulating-washers A⁴. To the binding-posts are detachably connected, by the screws a, the ends of the circuit B, which, for convenience of reference, I will designate as the "main" circuit.

B' represents a long electro-magnet, the opposite ends of the conductor, composing its helix B², being permanently secured to the binding-posts A² A³, whereby the electromagnet B' is included in the main circuit and energized by the current flowing therein.

C represents a series of armatures located at a considerable distance below the broad pole-piece b of electro-magnet B', in order to insure a practically uniform pull of the magnet on the armatures throughout their entire range of movement, and thereby cause a slight increase or correspondingly slight decrease in the strength of the magnet to attract or release the armatures. The armatures are each supported, as represented in Fig. 2, on a strip, C', of wood or other insulating material fastened to the frame underneath the ledge C², which latter is formed on the frame itself, the strip C' and the ledge C² being located at such distance apart as to form a groove within which the ends of the armatures are inserted. The insulating-strip C', fastened to the under side of the ledge C², operates to insulate the armatures from the frame. The inner end of each armature is provided with a hole or depression, c', in which is received a pin or stud, c^2, fastened to the strip C', which serves to retain the inner end of the armature against lateral or endwise displacement, and allow the armature to be supported on the edge of its downwardly-curved rear end and rock thereon, and thus be subjected to only the minimum amount of friction in its operation. The outer

or free ends of the **series of armatures** rest on **a bar or strip, D,** **of wood** or other insulating material, and hence are retained at an equal distance from the pole of the magnet B', and are retained against lateral displacement by the guide-pins d'. The **bar** or **strip D** is journaled **between the depending arms** d of the **bracket D'** **by the pivotal bearing D',** **to allow the strip to be slightly rotated on its axis for a purpose which will be hereinafter explained.** To the free end of each armature is fastened a depending **tubular holder, E,** **which is closed** at its lower end, and **contains in its lower portion** **a** spiral spring, e. Within the holder is inserted a **contact-piece** or **rod, E',** **which is preferably made** of carbon, but **may be made of any other suitable material.** Contact-piece E' is a straight rod, preferably cylindrical in cross-section, **and** loosely fits within the tubular holder and rests upon the spiral spring e, contained therein. That portion of the tubular holder extending above the armature is cut away so as to form a semicircular bearing e', against which rests one side of the projecting end of the contact piece or rod E'. **To the** lower portion **of the tubular** holder **is secured** one end of a wire spring, E², which extends upwardly **and passes through an** elongated slot, E³, in the **armature, the upper** end of the spring **being bent laterally and then** forwardly and around **in front of the contact-rod, the straight end** e⁴ **bearing against the contact-rod and forcing it into contact** **with its semicircular seat or bearing** e'. The spring E² **is sufficiently strong to force the** contact-rod **against its seat or bearing** e' with sufficient **force to securely clamp the contact-rod and retain it in its proper adjustment.** On each tubular holder is fastened a **hook,** e⁵, **on which is suspended a weight,** e⁶, **for the purpose of adjusting the armature, so that it will respond to a predetermined pull of the magnet. Instead of a weight, an adjustable spring might be connected with the holder for this purpose.** Above **the series of contact-rods is located a rod, bar, or cylinder, F, which is preferably made of carbon,** although **any other suitable electric conductor might** **be used for this purpose. Carbon is the** preferred **material for the series of contact-rods and the main contact bar or rod F, because of** **its well-known great refractory qualities, good conductivity, and the fact of its cheapness enabling the parts to be renewed or replaced at a small expense.**

The **rod or cylinder F is journaled at its opposite ends** **on adjustable screw-points** f, **so that it may be easily removed when necessary, and may be readily rotated so as to present a fresh surface for the series of contact-rods to engage with whenever any portion of the surface of the cylinder F becomes uneven or unduly worn or burned away.**

As hereinbefore stated, the bar or strip D, **on which rest the free ends of the series of armatures, is journaled between the brackets** d. The object of **this** is to provide for the simultaneous adjustment of all the contact-rods of the series, which result is effected as follows: By pressing on the thumb-piece G, attached to the lower edge of the strip or bar D, and moving its lower edge rearwardly, its upper and forward edge, G', will be moved forwardly and engage each one of the spring-arms E², and simultaneously retract the entire series, and thus operate to release the clamping arms or fingers e⁴ from their contact-rods, as shown by dotted lines is Fig. 2, and allow the contact-rods to be forced upwardly by their spiral-spring supports within the holders into contact with the main contact bar or cylinder F. This operation is quickly performed and simultaneously adjusts the contact-rods so that their outer ends will be in alignment with each other; or, in other words, the main contact-bar F forms a straight and an even gage against which the ends of the several contact-rods are forced simultaneously, and thus brought into perfect alignment with each other. The position of the parts in effecting this operation is illustrated in Fig. 2. The next operation is to simultaneously separate the contact-rods a very slight but a uniform distance from the main contact rod or cylinder F, which is effected as follows, reference being had to Fig. 2: After the spring-clamps have been retracted and the contact-rod clamp disengaged by the action of the edge G' of the oscillating bar or strip D, the lower edge of the latter is pulled outwardly, as shown by the dotted lines in Fig. 2, which operates to move the upper edge rearwardly, and cause the forward edge, G', to engage the under side of all the armatures and lift them a slight distance, as represented by dotted lines in Fig. 2, the effect of which is to slightly raise each one of the tubular holders and contact-clamps carried thereon, and, as the ends of the contact-rods rest against the cylinder F, they will be held stationary while the tubular holders are raised, and hence the several clamps or arms e⁴ will each be moved upwardly on its contact-rod and form a new point of engagement therewith. This having been done, the edge G' of the bar or strip D is moved outwardly again, allowing the armatures to descend and carry with them their contact-rods, and thus separate the ends of the latter a very slight distance from the surface of the main contact bar or cylinder F. As all the armatures are moved exactly the same distance in effecting the adjustment of the contact-rods, the ends of the latter will all be equally distant from the main contact-cylinder. Springs F', attached to the bracket-arms, engage the adjustable strip or bar D and prevent it being accidentally displaced. I have already called attention to the fact that the armatures are located at quite a distance from the pole-piece of the long electro-magnet, in order to insure a uniformity of pulling action of the magnet on the armature. This distance of separation may be varied as occasion may require by the following means: The electro-magnet is preferably secured in a permanent manner to the top A' of the frame. The bar

as a support for the matures, is journaled at D', which latter is le in the following he frame are secured at each end, which form guides for the :et, thereby enabling moved thereon. On s is placed a nut, H', onstitutes a sprocket-hain, H', engages the By moving the chain D' is raised and the d toward the pole of by moving the chain the bracket is lowered away from the nce all of the arma-e simultaneously ad-be pole-piece of the djustment is conven-tus to the automatic f electric currents of the pole-piece of the), h, of wood or other ial, which serves as a op for the armatures. ces, only one being others of the series ted lines. Each one iferably composed of small gage, which is and then stretched, g attached to a hook, end of the armature, e is carried down and tened to the insulated and from thence the y and attached to a strip or bar D, and downwardly, and its to a hook, i', secured f the frame. All of to or otherwise elec-the copper wire J or conductor. nce in the spiral form is, and then fastening wn and described, I ntages: When the re-l and expanded, the il conductors operates ite for the slack in the om sagging and mak-ime or any other one e series. Again, by : form of a spiral, and cribed, a great length hin a comparatively il is subjected to the ir, and thus the heat ice by the current is zigzag arrangement of vs the apparatus to be ively small compass, lespace for its accom-modation in use. The **conductor J, with** which is connected one end of each resistance of the entire series, is electrically connected with the conductor J, which leads and is permanently secured to the binding-post J², while a conductor, J', is connected at one end to the other binding-post, J², and its other end is connected to the pivotal screw f. Both of the pivotal screws f, which support the main contact cylinder or rod F, are insulated from the bracket by the insulating-washers g. Thus it will be observed the conductor J is electrically connected with one end of each resistance of the entire series, while the conductor J' is electrically connected with the main contact bar or cylinder F.

Having described the construction and arrangement of the several parts of one form of electric-current governor embodying my invention, I will now describe its operation when used for controlling the volume of current in the external or working circuit of a dynamo-electric machine by automatically varying the intensity of the magnetic field in which the armature rotates to compensate for varying resistance in the external or working circuits of the dynamo.

The broad principle of automatically regulating the strength of the current in the main circuit of a dynamo by automatically controlling and varying the intensity of the magnetic field of the dynamo-machine is fully set forth and illustrated by other forms of current governors in Letters Patent granted to me as follows: No. 224,551, February 17, 1880, and No. 239,313, dated March 29, 1881, and hence need not be elaborated here.

In Fig. 4 I have represented the improved current-governor included in the circuit of a dynamo-electric machine. L represents the field-of-force magnets of the dynamo; L', the armature; L', the armature-shaft; L², the commutator. The helices of the field-magnets are connected in series, one end of the conductor N being connected with the commutator-brush M, and the other end to the binding-post M', which forms one terminal of the machine. The other binding-post or terminal, M², is connected with the other commutator-brush, M². To the binding-posts or terminals M' M² are connected the two ends of the external or working circuit, B. In the working-circuit is included the current-governor, the circuit being severed and the ends secured to the binding-posts A¹ A². As the ends of the helix of the electro-magnet B' are connected to the binding-posts A¹ A², the electro-magnet B' will thus be included in the main circuit and energized by the current flowing therein. The binding-post J² is connected with the binding-post or terminal M' by the conductor K, and the binding-post J³ is connected with the commutator-brush M, or a binding-post electrically connected with the commutator-brush M by the conductor K'. Thus there is provided a normally-open shunt-circuit around the field-of-force magnets, **one** end of the shunt-circuit

commencing with the binding-post M', and leading by the conductor K to the binding-post J², and from thence by the conductor J' to the main contact rod or bar F. The other end, K', of the shunt is connected to the commutator-brush M, or a binding-post electrically connected therewith, and the binding-post J² of the current-governor, and by the conductor J' is connected with one end of each one of the series of resistances, the latter being electrically connected with the series of independent contact-rods by the series of armatures. The shunt-circuit is thus open between the main contact-rod F and the series of small contact rods E', the space between the main and independent contacts being very slight, as illustrated in the drawings.

Now, so long as the shunt-circuit remains open, all of the current generated by the machine will circulate in the external circuit and in the field-of-force magnets of the machine; but in the event that the resistance in the working-circuit is diminished for any reason—as, for instance, by the switching out of electric lamps, motors, or other translating devices therefrom—the current in the main circuit becomes abnormally strong, and operates to correspondingly augment the strength and pull of the electro-magnet B', which in turn attracts the series of armatures. As it is a mechanical impossibility to construct and arrange a series of armatures so that all will respond to exactly the same pull of the magnet, or so that all will be exactly equal in sensitiveness, it follows that when the electro-magnet B' is energized it will cause the most sensitive armature of the series to respond and be raised, and thereby cause its contact-rod E' to engage the main contact-bar F, the effect of which is to close the shunt-circuit around the field-of-force magnets through one of the resistances I, and thus divert a portion of the current developed by the dynamo from the field-magnets, the amount thus diverted or shunted away from the field-magnets being proportioned to the relative resistance of the shunt and the main circuit. Should the amount of current thus shunted be insufficient to weaken the field-magnets enough to decrease the current strength in the main circuit to correspond to the decrease in the resistance interposed therein, the electro-magnet B' will attract another one of the series of armatures, and thus automatically throw into the shunt-circuit another resistance I in multiple arc with the resistance first switched in. In the same manner will the electro-magnet B' continue to successively throw into the shunt-circuit a sufficient number of the resistances in multiple arc with each other to such an amount or proportion of the current generated by the machine as will operate to weaken the field-magnets to a point corresponding with the decreased resistance in the working-circuit. On the other hand, any increase of resistance in the working-circuit will operate to decrease the strength of the electro-magnet B' and cause the armatures of the series to successively drop and open circuit the resistances I, and thereby increase the resistance of the shunt-circuit and divert more current through the field-magnets, augmenting their strength until the strength of the current developed by the machine shall correspond to the increased work or resistance interposed in the main or working circuit. In view of the fact that each one of the resistances of the series may be of any fixed or predetermined electrical resistance, and that any number of such separate resistances may be arranged to be thrown into the shunt-circuit around the field-magnets in multiple arc with each other, and, further, that the armatures and contacts for automatically switching the resistances into and out of the shunt-circuit are constructed and arranged to be actuated by slight fluctuations in the strength of the current in the main or working circuit, I am enabled to maintain a practically uniform volume of current in the main circuit, although the resistance therein is greatly varied, either by an increase or a decrease of work interposed therein.

By manipulating the governor in the manner hereinbefore described all of the series of contact points or rods may be simultaneously and uniformly adjusted with respect to the main contact-bar, and when the surface of the latter becomes worn unevenly by the continued contact and engagement of the small contact points or rods therewith, a fresh and even surface may be readily presented by slightly rotating the main carbon rod or bar on its journals.

While I have shown and described one form and construction of current-governor embodying my invention and one of its different applications, I do not restrict myself to the particular use set forth nor to the particular construction and arrangement of parts shown and described.

The main electro-magnet, instead of being constructed as a single magnet, as shown, may consist of a number of separate and independent magnets, O, included in series with each other, as illustrated in Fig. 5; or a solenoid, O', may be employed and each armature be provided with a core, O², entering the space O³ in the solenoid, as illustrated in Fig. 6.

Again, instead of using an endless chain and sprocket-wheels for adjusting the armature with respect to the pole of the magnet, I may use, and preferably shall use, adjusting devices of the character illustrated in Fig. 7, in which o is a worm-rod journaled in bearings o² on the main frame, one end of the rod having a hand-wheel, o', attached thereto for rotating it. Worm o engages the worm-gears o² o². By rotating the hand-wheel and worm the bracket may be readily raised or lowered and retained in any desired adjustment.

Again, instead of employing a series of armatures, I may dispense with the armatures and use a solenoid and adjust the main contact bar or rod as illustrated in Figs. 8 and 9. In this

modified form of construction P represents a solenoid included in the main circuit, and P' its core, the lower end of which is secured to one end of a lever, P², the outer end of which is constructed with lateral arms p, between which is journaled the main contact bar or rod F. Beneath the contact-bar F are located the series of tubular holders E, each supporting its contact-rod E'. Each holder E is supported in position by an elastic strip, q, of conducting material, one end of which is attached to a flange or strip, q', fastened to the frame and insulated therefrom, while the outer end of each strip is fastened to one of the tubular holders. A spring-clamp is attached to each holder for the purpose of clamping the small contact-rods, and an oscillating strip or bar, D, is situated below the strip for simultaneously adjusting all the contact-rods by first releasing all of the clamps and allowing all of the contact-rods to be forced upwardly against the main contact bar or rod F, and then raising all of the tubular holders and afterward lowering them to adjust all of the contact-rods E' evenly and uniformly, as has been fully set forth. A bar, R, of non-conducting material, attached to a pivoted arm, R', rests upon the entire series of strips q, and serves as a stop for each one and retains them in a uniform adjustment. When the current in the main circuit is abnormally strong, the core of the solenoid will be raised and operate to depress the main contact-bar F, and cause it to engage one or more of the contact-points E' and automatically switch into the shunt-circuit around the field-magnets some or all of the resistances in multiple arc with each other, and thus weaken the magnetic field of the machine to correspond with the decrease of resistance in the working-circuit, while an increase of resistance in the main circuit will operate to weaken the strength of the solenoid and allow the spring R' to raise the main contact-bar, and thereby switch out of the shunt-circuit some or all of the resistances of the series and divert more current through the field-magnets of the machine to cause the latter to produce an increased amount of current proportioned to the increased amount of resistance interposed in the working-circuit.

The main contact-bar may be cylindrical, or it may be square, octagonal, or of any other form in cross-section. Instead of wire resistance I may use a series of carbon resistances, and each may be made so that its resistance may be varied.

Again, instead of employing the series of contact-rods, tubular holders, and spring-clamps, I may use carbon disks journaled in the free ends of the armature or elastic strips, and provide means for imparting a slight rotary movement to each disk every time it is raised or lowered, and thus insure a uniform wear of its periphery.

Again, the main contact-bar may be journaled on adjustable screw-pivots, and one of them be supported in a vertical slot, S, in the bracket, as illustrated in Fig. 10, the bearing S' being supported by a spring, S². When all of the contact-rods have been released and forced upwardly by their springs against the main contact-bar, one end of the latter may be depressed slightly and then released and allowed to be raised by the spring S². This operation will adjust the contact-rods so that the space between the series of contact-rods and the main contact-bar will gradually increase from one end of the series to the other, and thus cause the contacts to be successively actuated from one end of the series to the other.

Having fully described my invention, what I claim as new, and desire to secure by Letters Patent, is—

1. The combination, with a series of resistances and a series of contacts connected therewith, of a translating device constructed and arranged to actuate said contacts and automatically and independently switch some or all of the resistances into an electrical circuit in multiple arc with each other, substantially as set forth.

2. The combination, with a series of resistances and a series of independently-movable contacts connected therewith, of a translating device for automatically and independently switching some or all of the resistances into an electrical circuit in multiple arc with each other, substantially as set forth.

3. The combination, with a series of resistances and a series of armatures connected therewith, of a translating device for automatically and independently actuating said armatures and switching some or all of the resistances into an electrical circuit in multiple arc with each other, substantially as set forth.

4. The combination, with a system or series of resistances and a system or series of armatures, each provided with a contact electrically connected with one of the resistances, of a main contact, and a translating device for automatically and independently actuating said armatures and switching some or all of the resistances into an electrical circuit in multiple arc with each other, substantially as set forth.

5. The combination, with an electro-magnet and a series of resistances, of a series of armatures adapted to be actuated by the electro-magnet and automatically switch some or all of the resistances into an electrical circuit in multiple arc with each other.

6. The combination, with a conductor forming a contact, of a series of independently-adjustable contacts and means for simultaneously adjusting the series, substantially as set forth.

7. The combination, with a series of armatures, each provided with a contact adapted to be fed to compensate for wear, of means for simultaneously adjusting the series of contacts, substantially as set forth.

8. The combination, with a series of resistances and a series of independently-movable carbon contacts electrically connected therewith, of a translating device for automatically and independently actuating said contacts and

switching some or all of the resistances into an electrical circuit in multiple arc with each other, substantially as set forth.

9. The combination, with a series of resistances and a series of independently-movable carbon contacts electrically connected therewith, of a main carbon contact and a translating device for automatically and independently actuating the contacts of the series and switching some or all of the resistances into an electrical circuit in multiple arc with each other, substantially as set forth.

10. The combination, with a series of resistances and a series of independently-movable contacts electrically connected therewith, of an adjustable conductor forming a contact common to the series of contacts, substantially as set forth.

11. The combination, with an electro-magnet, (one or more,) of a series of armatures for actuating a series of contacts and means for simultaneously and equally varying the distance between the armatures and the electro-magnet, (one or more,) substantially as set forth.

12. The combination, with a series of contacts and devices for gripping or clamping each contact, of means for simultaneously releasing all of the contacts from their gripping or clamping mechanism, substantially as set forth.

13. The combination, with a series of contacts, of means for simultaneously adjusting and clamping all the contacts of the series.

14. The combination, with a series of contacts, of means for releasing all the contacts, means for imparting equal and simultaneous adjustment to all the contacts, and means for simultaneously clamping all the contacts, substantially as set forth.

15. The combination, with a series of independently-movable contacts, of a contact common to the series, constructed and adapted to be adjusted so as to present different surfaces to the action of the different contacts of the series.

16. The combination, with a series of resistances and contacts electrically connected therewith, of a translating device, and devices combined therewith, all the resistances for automatically and independently switching some or all of the resistances into an electrical circuit in multiple arc with each other on the increase of current strength in the circuit, including said translating device, substantially as set forth.

17. The combination, with a contact and an electro-magnet, of an armature and a contact supported thereby and means for feeding the movable contact to compensate for wear, said parts being constructed and arranged to either close the circuit by the direct engagement of the contacts or open the circuit by their separation, substantially as set forth.

18. The combination, with a carbon contact and an electro-magnet, of a series of armatures and a series of carbon contacts, and means for feeding the contacts of the series to compensate for wear, substantially as set forth.

19. The combination, with a main contact and an electro-magnet, of a series of contacts adapted to engage the main contact and devices for clamping, feeding, and releasing the movable contacts, substantially as set forth.

20. The combination, with an armature, of a contact-holder connected with the armature, a spring for feeding the contact, and a clamping device for retaining the contact in any desired adjustment, substantially as set forth.

21. The combination, with an electro-magnet included in the circuit of an electric generator and a series of resistances, of devices actuated by the electro-magnet for automatically and independently switching one or more of the resistances into a shunt-circuit in multiple arc with each other on the increase of strength of the current in the circuit including the electro-magnet, substantially as set forth.

22. The combination, with an electro-magnet included in the circuit of an electric generator and a series of resistances, of a series of armatures adapted to be actuated by the electro-magnet and automatically switch some or all of the resistances into a shunt-circuit in multiple arc with each other on the increase of the strength of the current in the circuit including the electro-magnet, substantially as set forth.

23. The combination, with an electro-magnet included in the main or working circuit of a dynamo-electric machine, of a series of resistances and means actuated by the electro-magnet for automatically and independently switching some or all of the resistances in multiple arc with each other into a shunt-circuit around the field-magnets of the dynamo-electric machine on an increase of current strength in the main or working circuit, substantially as set forth.

24. The combination, with a holder or support, of a contact bar or rod detachably secured in said holder and a spring for forcing the contact bar or rod outwardly from its holder, and a spring-actuated clamp connected with the holder and adapted to engage the contact bar or rod and secure it in any desired adjustment, substantially as set forth.

25. The combination, with an electro-magnet or solenoid and a series of armatures, of a main contact and a series of contacts, and means for simultaneously adjusting the series of armatures with relation to the electro-magnet, substantially as set forth.

26. The combination, with a rotary adjustable conductor constituting a main contact, and a series of independently-movable contact bars or rods, of a translating device included in an electrical circuit and means combined therewith for automatically and independently actuating some or all of said movable contacts, substantially as set forth.

27. The combination, with a rotary adjustable carbon bar or cylinder constituting a main contact and a series of independently-movable carbon rods constituting contacts, of a translating device and means combined therewith for automatically and independently actuating some or all of said movable contacts, substantially as set forth.

In testimony whereof I have signed this specification in the presence of two subscribing witnesses.

CHARLES F. BRUSH.

Witnesses:
J. POTTER,
L. B. LE VAKE.

UNITED STATES OF AMERICA

No. 376,630

To all to whom these presents shall come:

Whereas Charles F. Brush of Cleveland, Ohio, has presented to the Commissioner of Patents a petition praying for the grant of Letters Patent for an alleged new and useful improvement in

Electro Magnetic Device

a description of which invention is contained in the Specification of which a copy is hereunto annexed and made a part hereof, and has complied with the various requirements of Law in such cases made and provided, and

Whereas upon due examination made the said Claimant is adjudged to be justly entitled to a Patent under the Law.

Now therefore these **Letters Patent** are to grant unto the said Charles F. Brush, his heirs, or assigns, for the term of Seventeen years from the seventeenth day of January one thousand eight hundred and eighty-eight the exclusive right to make, use, and vend the said invention throughout the United States and the Territories thereof.

In testimony whereof I have hereunto set my hand, and caused the seal of the Patent Office to be affixed at the City of Washington this seventeenth day of January in the year of our Lord one thousand eight hundred and eighty-eight and of the Independence of the United States of America the one hundred and twelfth.

Secretary of the Interior

Countersigned:

Commissioner of Patents

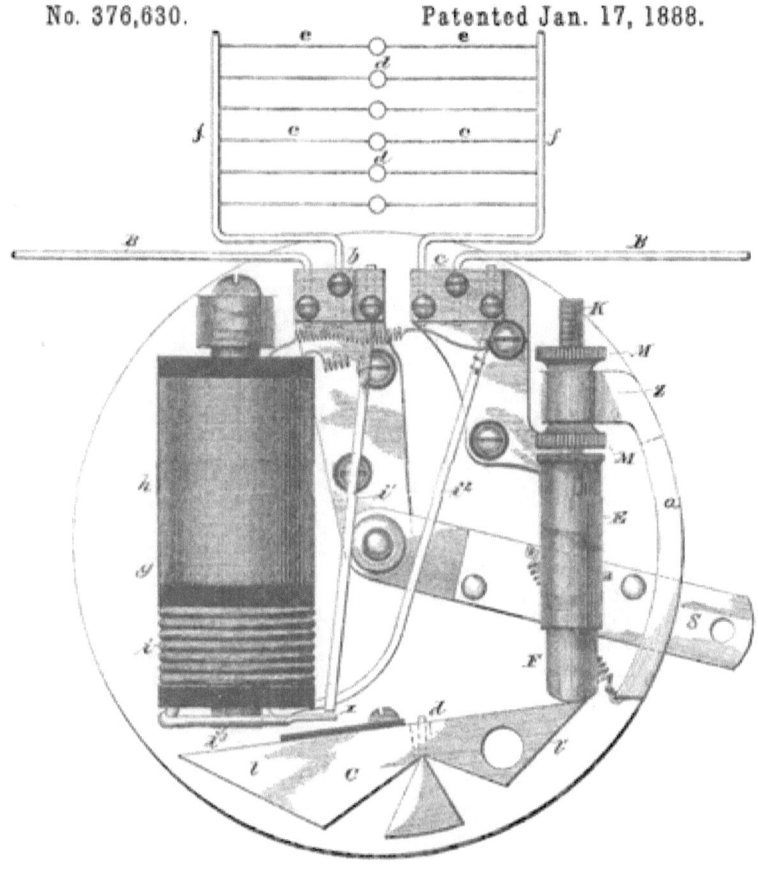

(No Model.) 2 Sheets—Sheet 1.

C. F. BRUSH.
ELECTRO MAGNETIC DEVICE.

No. 376,630. Patented Jan. 17, 1888.

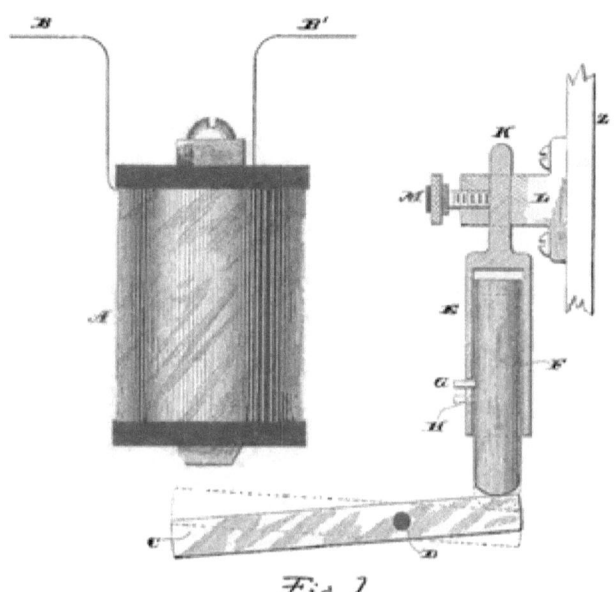

Fig. 1.

WITNESSES

INVENTOR
Charles F. Brush.
Attorney

UNITED STATES PATENT OFFICE.

CHARLES F. BRUSH, OF CLEVELAND, OHIO.

ELECTRO-MAGNETIC DEVICE.

SPECIFICATION forming part of Letters Patent No. 376,630, dated January 17, 1888.

Application filed December 19, 1885. Serial No. 186,182. (No model.)

To all whom it may concern:

Be it known that I, CHARLES F. BRUSH, of Cleveland, in the county of Cuyahoga and State of Ohio, have invented certain new and useful Improvements in Electro-Magnetic Devices; and I do hereby declare the following to be a full, clear, and exact description of the invention, such as will enable others skilled in the art to which it appertains to make and use the same.

My invention relates to an improvement in electro-magnetic devices.

Under certain circumstances it is desirable to arrange an electro-magnetic device in such manner that a temporarily abnormal current will not cause the device to respond, even though such temporary increase may be beyond a predetermined point, where a continuous abnormal current will result in the functional action of the device. This I believe has not hitherto been accomplished. For instance, if there be included in a circuit of arc lamps electro-magnets whose armatures are adjusted to respond to a certain strength of current, and if the supplying current be started suddenly, an abnormal flow of current will result, owing to the fact that the carbons of the lamps are in contact and the resistance of the external circuit therefore low. This abnormal current, though temporary, may be of a strength sufficient to cause the electro-magnets to attract their armatures, which, in the cases under consideration, is not desirable.

The object of my invention is to overcome the above difficulty, however caused, and I accomplish it by mechanism shown in the accompanying drawings, Figure 1 of which shows, partly in section, one form of my invention. Fig. 2 illustrates the invention as embodied in a multiple-series cut-out.

A is an electro-magnet whose coil forms part of a circuit, B B'.

C is an armature pivoted at D in such a manner that the end of the armature toward the electro-magnet and directly under its influence will be considerably heavier than the other end.

E is a cylinder closed at its upper end and open at the lower. A plunger, F, fits nearly air-tight in the cylinder and projects from the lower end. The bottom of the plunger is rounded and rests normally on the remote end of the armature. The weight of the plunger is such that while, when resting on the armature, it assists to overcome the preponderance of the heavier end, it does not do so entirely. A pin, G, fastened to the plunger F projects through the side of the cylinder, and working in a vertical slot, H, limits the vertical motion of the plunger. The cylinder at its upper end is attached rigidly to the rod K, which passes through a hole in the lug L, which is securely fastened to the frame-work (a portion of which is shown at Z) of the apparatus. The cylinder is adjustably supported by means of a set-screw, M, passing through the lug and impinging on the rod K. This adjustment, it will be seen, serves to determine the position of the armature.

The action is as follows: I will assume, for the purpose of illustration, that the electro-magnet is in a circuit of arc lamps fed by a dynamo-electric machine, and that the distance of the armature from the magnet has been suitably adjusted. If no current be flowing, the parts will be in the position shown by the continuous lines in the drawings, the plunger F being at its highest position from the preponderance of the magnet end of the armature. If, now, the normal current be sent through the circuit B B', the magnet will attract the armature, and the latter will move up toward the magnet, but at a rate limited to the motion of the plunger, which, being nearly air-tight, drops slowly, dash-pot fashion, and if the armature attempt to move faster than the plunger drops the magnet is then deprived of the assistance of the weight of the plunger, and as the relations of the weights and distances are suitably proportioned the magnet is unable to raise the dead-weight of the armature alone. Consequently when the plunger has descended to its lowest point, as shown by the dotted lines, the weight of the plunger is borne by the pin G, resting on the bottom of the slot H in the cylinder, and the armature will make no further movement except under the influence of an increased current to which it is set to respond. If, now, the current be temporarily stopped, as by the "flashing" of the machine,

the carbons in the arc lamps will all in a few seconds have come together and again complete the circuit, causing an abnormal flow of current until the arcs have been re-established.

The action of my improved apparatus, under these and the similar circumstances above indicated as due to the sudden starting of the machine at full speed, will be as follows: When the current is stopped, the electromagnet will become inoperative and the armature will fall back, raising the plunger to its highest point. This will occur in the case of flashing while the carbons of the lamps are feeding into contact. Then upon the re-establishment and consequent abnormal flow of current the armature will be attracted and the plunger commence to descend; but owing to the slow movement of the plunger, as above explained, before the armature can get to a position where it would be raised completely by the magnet, under the influence of the increased current, the abnormal flow of current will have ceased, the normal arcs in the lamps having become established.

It will of course be understood that the movement of the armature when fully attracted by the magnet may be utilized to perform any desired function.

The magnet A may be located in a shunt to some electro-receptive device or devices operated by a main current.

In Fig. 2 I have shown the invention as applied to a multiple series cut-out, in which a is the supporting-frame having two insulated binding-posts, b c, fastened thereto. One end of the main circuit B is secured in the post c. Incandescent lamps or other electro-receptive devices, d, are included in the branch circuits e, which latter are connected at their opposite ends to the conductor f, the opposite ends of which are connected, respectively, to the binding-posts b c. Electro-magnet g is wound with two coils, h and i, the coil h being of high resistance and forming a constantly-closed shunt-circuit around the group of incandescent lamps or other electro-receptive devices, d. The other coil, i, is of coarse wire, and has one of its terminals attached to a conductor, f', which is connected to the binding-post c, and its other terminal, i', forming a contact, I, which is located in close proximity to the lower end of the conductor i', attached to the binding-post b. The terminal i² serves as a spring-contact, and is normally out of contact with the end of conductor f'. An armature, C, is pivoted at d, the end l, located beneath the electro-magnet, being considerably heavier than the opposite end, l'. The plunger F rests upon the end l' of the armature and operates in the manner hereinbefore described.

The operation of the multiple series cut-out is as follows: When the lamps d d, &c., are in operative condition, the normal current on the line B B will divide itself between the lamps d, excepting the small percentage of current which will pass around the group by the shunt-circuit, including the fine-wire coil h. Should a number of the lamps d become inoperative from any cause, the increased current diverted through the fine-wire coil h will energize the magnet g sufficiently to raise the armature C and cause the latter to force the contact I into engagement with the lower end of the conductor f', and thus form a shunt-circuit of low resistance around the group of lamps, through which low-resistance shunt the current will be diverted. As this low-resistance circuit has the coarse-wire coil of the magnet included therein, the current flowing through it, when the circuit is closed, will augment the strength of the magnet g, and thus hold the armature firmly in its raised position. In order to prevent the armature C from responding to an abnormal flow of current of short duration, due to the causes specified, or to any other, and which would operate to cut out the group of lamps d, I provide the cut-out with the plunger attachment, which causes the armature to rise so slowly that the abnormal flow of current will have ceased before the armature can rise to a position where it could be completely raised by the lifting power of the magnet. Thus the cut-out will automatically switch out of circuit the group of lamps d whenever a predetermined number of them should fail to operate, but will not respond to an abnormal flow of current of short duration, and thereby accidentally switch the group of lamps out of circuit. The cut-out is provided with a switch-lever, S, for manually switching out of circuit the group of lamps d.

Fig. 2, and the descriptive matter relating thereto, is incorporated herein simply to make compliance with the request of the Patent Office that some practical embodiment of the invention should be disclosed; but by this disclosure I do not relinquish any right to claim any subject-matter of invention that may exist in the device illustrated in Fig. 2, and reserve such right for a separate application.

I do not limit myself to the special construction or arrangement of parts shown.

Having fully described my invention, what I claim as new, and desire to secure by Letters Patent, is—

1. The combination, with a helix included in an electric circuit and an armature, of a supplemental actuating device constructed and arranged to operate slowly through a predetermined distance and assist the helix in moving the armature gradually to a predetermined distance from the helix and then to release the armature to the sole action of the helix, substantially as set forth.

2. In an electro-magnetic device consisting primarily of an electro-magnet and an armature controlled thereby, a dash-pot, the moving portion of which, without being connected, except by simple contact, with the armature or moving parts attached thereto, assists the

armature, during a portion of its movement, to respond to the attractive influence of the magnet, but at a limited rate of motion, the position of said movable portion of the dash-pot being controlled by said armature when not under the influence of the magnet, substantially as set forth.

In testimony whereof I have signed this specification in the presence of two subscribing witnesses.

CHARLES F. BRUSH.

Witnesses:
ALBERT E. LYNCH,
L. B. LE VAKE.

Assigned to Brush Electric Co. -- FEB 8 18__

UNITED STATES AMERICA

To all to whom these presents shall come:

Whereas Charles F. Brush of Cleveland, Ohio has presented to the Commissioner of Patents a petition praying for the grant of Letters Patent for an alleged new and useful improvement in Dynamo Electric Machines

a description of which invention is contained in the Specification of which a copy is hereunto annexed and made a part hereof, and has complied with the various requirements of Law in such cases made and provided, and

Whereas upon due examination made the said Claimant is adjudged to be justly entitled to a Patent under the Law.

Now therefore these **Letters Patent** are to grant unto the said Charles F. Brush and __ heirs or assigns for the term of seventeen years from the ____ day of ____ one thousand eight hundred and eighty ____ the exclusive right to make, use and vend the said invention throughout the United States and the Territories thereof.

In testimony whereof I have hereunto set my hand and caused the seal of the Patent Office to be affixed at the City of Washington this ____ day of ____ in the year of our Lord one thousand eight hundred and eighty ____ and of the Independence of the United States of America the one hundred and twelfth.

Countersigned: Benton J. Hall
Commissioner of Patents

Secretary of the Interior

(No Model.) 2 Sheets—Sheet 2.
C. F. BRUSH.
GOVERNOR FOR ELECTRO MAGNETIC MOTORS.

No. 383,857. Patented June 5, 1888.

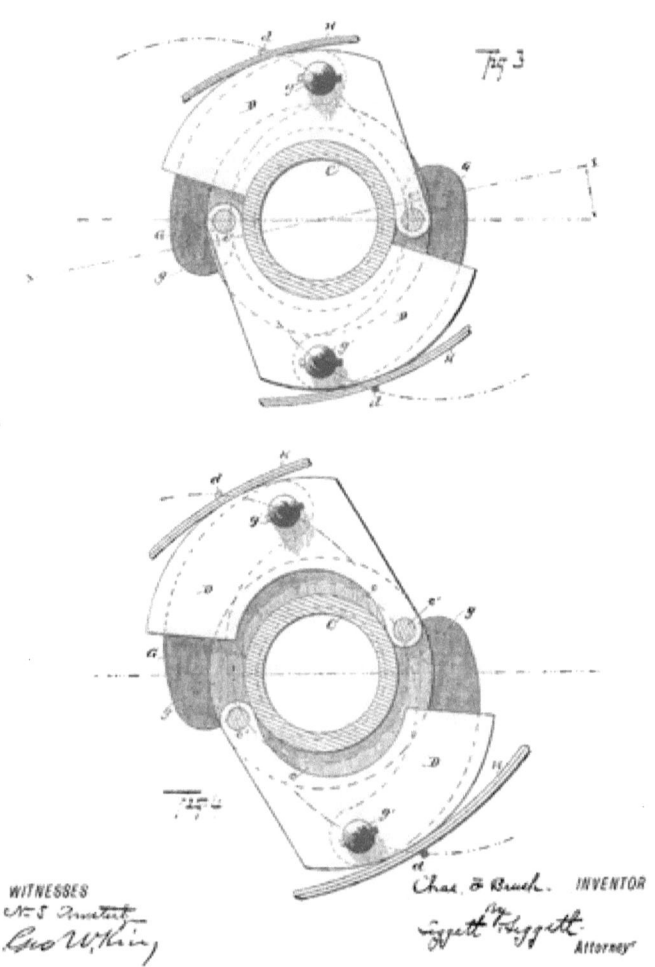

(No Model.) 2 Sheets—Sheet 1.

C. F. BRUSH.
GOVERNOR FOR ELECTRO MAGNETIC MOTORS.

No. 383,857. Patented June 5, 1888.

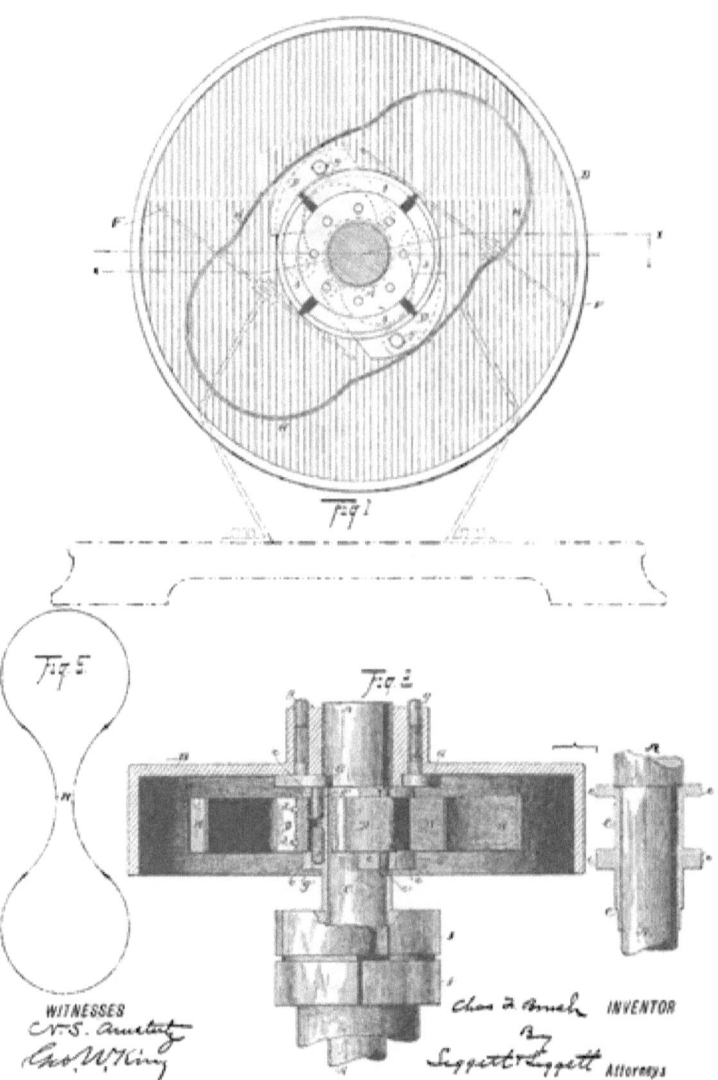

United States Patent Office.

CHARLES F. BRUSH, OF CLEVELAND, OHIO.

GOVERNOR FOR ELECTRO-MAGNETIC MOTORS.

SPECIFICATION forming part of Letters Patent No. 383,857, dated June 5, 1888.

Application filed August 1, 1887. Serial No. 245,763. (No model.)

To all whom it may concern:

Be it known that I, CHARLES F. BRUSH, of Cleveland, in the county of Cuyahoga and State of Ohio, have invented certain new and useful Improvements in Governors for Electro-Magnetic Motors; and I do hereby declare the following to be a full, clear, and exact description of the invention, such as will enable others skilled in the art to which it pertains to make and use the same.

My invention relates to improvements in governors for electro-magnetic motors, in which an endless spring is mounted on and made to embrace the governor-weights. The weights are mounted on links of the crank variety, and are pivotally connected with the commutator-sleeve, with the arrangement of parts such that a limited outward movement of the weights is sufficient to rotatively advance the commutator-sections from maximum to minimum points of effectiveness, to the end that prompt action and a wide range of governing capacity are attained.

With these objects in view my invention consists in certain features of construction and in combination of parts, hereinafter described, and pointed out in the claims.

My present invention is designed more especially as an improvement on a governor for which Letters Patent No. 343,886 were granted to me June 15, 1886, and to which reference is hereby made.

In the accompanying drawings, Figure 1 is a side elevation. Fig. 2 is a plan partly in section. Figs. 3 and 4 are enlarged side views in detail, showing, respectively, different positions of the weights and connected parts. Fig. 5 is an edge view of the endless spring employed.

A represents the armature-shaft, on which is mounted and rigidly secured the governor shell or casing B.

F are the commutator-brushes, and f the commutator-sections that are mounted on the sleeve C, the latter being journaled on the shaft A.

The parts mentioned thus far may be substantially the same as those shown and described in the aforesaid Letters Patent, and therefore need not be described in detail here.

The commutator-sleeve C has external annular flanges, c, that are made to embrace with an easy fit the governor-weights D, the latter being preferably of substantially the form shown. The weights at their rear ends, by means of pins d, are pivotally connected to the flanges c, such pivotal connections being made on opposite sides of the commutator-sleeve and as near as practicable to the axis of the sleeve, such radial distance being so short that only a limited movement of the weights is required to rotate the sleeve the number of degrees necessary in shifting the commutator-sections between the points of maximum and minimum effectiveness. The weights are mounted on links G of the crank variety, the axis g of the links being journaled in suitable holes made through the hub of the casing and parallel with the shaft A, the wrists g' of the links operating in holes made laterally through the respective weights. The normal or closed position of the weights and links is shown in Fig. 3, the inner periphery of the weights engaging the sleeve, with the links approximately at a quarter throw from the line $x\,x$, taken through the axles of the links. With such relation of parts, the weights, when thrown outward by centrifugal force, are by the action of the links drawn forward with accelerated movement, a slight outward movement of the weights being sufficient to advance the commutator-sections some degrees. (See Fig. 4.) It is evident that the less radial distance the weights have to move the quicker such movements can be made and the less range of working-tension of the spring will be required and the more prompt will be the action of the governor.

H is an endless spring that is mounted on and made to embrace the weights. The spring acts centripetally on the weights in opposition to the centrifugal force of the latter. The spring, preferably, is of thin flat material, and for convenience in shaping and tempering may be wrought in two or more pieces with overlapping ends riveted or otherwise secured together. A spring of such construction is shown in Fig. 5, where four pieces are riveted together; also, in this figure is shown a preferable form of spring before it is strained, the spring having curved or approximately-semicircular ends with reverse curves along the sides thereof. If a stiffer spring is required, it should be made of two or more thicknesses

of thin material rather than of a single layer of **thicker material, as the** latter is more liable to **break.**

Pins d of **the** weights enter corresponding holes made **in** the spring and hold the latter in position on **the** weights. With the weights in their closed position, the seats **for the** spring are, comparatively speaking, wide apart, and the weights having, as already stated, but little outward movement it follows that the spring, when distended far enough to embrace the weights, will have been strained to within a few degrees of its maximum working-tension, and consequent upon such limited range of working-tension the spring is prompt and effective in action and durable in use.

The construction of the governor is of a simple character, the parts are few in number, and the friction and wear merely nominal.

What I claim is—

1. The combination, **with** the armature-shaft and governor-casing **connected** therewith, of a commutator-sleeve loosely mounted on the armature-shaft, governor-weights pivotally connected with the commutator-sleeves, and links pivoted at **one end to the** weights and at their opposite end **to the** governor-casing, substantially as set **forth.**

2. The combination, with **the armature-shaft** and governor-casing connected therewith, **of** a commutator-sleeve loosely mounted on the armature-shaft, governor-weights pivoted to the commutator-sleeve, **links** pivoted **to** the governor-weights and governor-casing, **and an** endless spring engaging the governor-**weights,** substantially **as set** forth.

3. The combination, **with the** armature-shaft and governor-casing **connected** therewith, of a commutator-sleeve loosely mounted on the **ar**-mature-shaft, governor-weights pivoted at one end to the commutator-sleeve, and links pivoted at one end to the governor-casing and at their opposite ends to the governor-weights at **a** point between its ends, substantially **as** set forth.

4. The combination, with the armature-shaft and governor-casing **connected** therewith, of a commutator-sleeve loosely mounted on the armature-shaft, and governor-weights pivoted at **one** end to the commutator-sleeve **and con**-nected by links to the governor-casing, **said** weights being **formed** to partly encircle **the** commutator-sleeve, substantially **as set** forth.

5. The combination, with the armature-shaft and governor-casing connected therewith, of a commutator-sleeve having external flanges, governor-weights located between the flanges and pivotally connected therewith, and links pivotally connecting the weights **and govern**or-casing, substantially as set **forth.**

6. The combination, with **the armature-shaft and** governor-casing connected **therewith, of** a commutator-sleeve loosely mounted **on the ar**-mature-shaft, governor-weights **pivoted at one** end to the commutator-sleeve, **links** pivoted to the governor-weights and governor-casing, and an **endless spring consisting of two or more pieces riveted together and arranged to embrace the weights, substantially as set forth.**

In testimony whereof I sign this specification, in the presence of two witnesses, this 13th day of July, 1887.

      CHARLES F. BRUSH.

Witnesses:
 CHAS. H. DORER,
 ALBERT E. LYNCH.

UNITED STATES OF AMERICA

No. 391,394

To all to whom these presents shall come:

Whereas _____ Charles F. Brush _____
_____ of _____ Cleveland _____ & _____ Ohio _____
has presented to the Commissioner of Patents a petition praying
for the grant of Letters Patent for an alleged new and useful improvement in

_____ Dynamo Electric Motor _____

a description of which invention is contained in the Specification of which
a copy is hereunto annexed and made a part hereof, and has complied
with the various requirements of Law in such cases made and provided, and

Whereas upon due examination made the said Claimant is adjudged
to be justly entitled to a Patent under the Law.

Now therefore these Letters Patent are to grant unto the said
_____ Charles F. Brush, his _____ heirs or assigns
for the term of Seventeen years from the _____ sixteenth _____ day of
_____ October _____ one thousand eight hundred and eighty eight
the exclusive right to make, use and vend the said invention throughout the
United States, and the Territories thereof.

In testimony whereof I have hereunto set my
hand and caused the seal of the Patent Office
to be affixed at the City of Washington
this _____ day of _____
in the year of our Lord one thousand eight hundred and eighty _____ and of
the Independence of the United States
of America the one hundred and thirteenth.

Countersigned: Benton J. Hall
Commissioner of Patents

D. L. Hawkins
Assistant Secretary of the Interior

(No Model.)

C. F. BRUSH.
SAFETY ATTACHMENT FOR ELECTRIC MOTORS.

No. 391,114.   Patented Oct. 16, 1888.

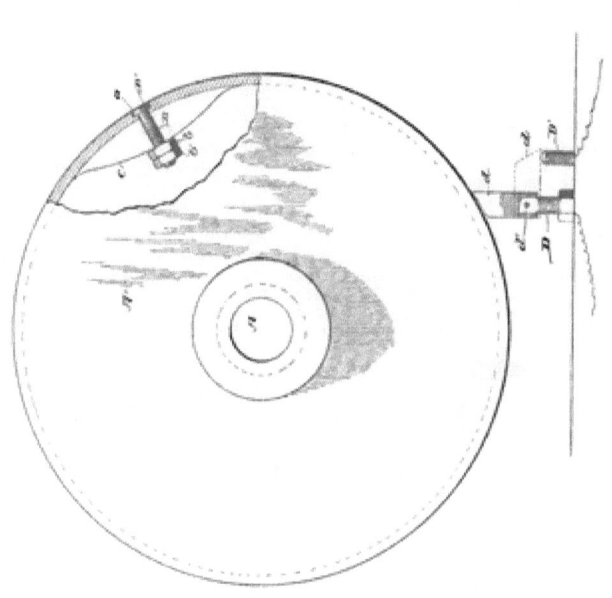

WITNESSES.   Chas. F. Brush. INVENTOR.
                          Liggett & Liggett Attorney.

United States Patent Office.

CHARLES F. BRUSH, OF CLEVELAND, OHIO.

SAFETY ATTACHMENT FOR ELECTRIC MOTORS.

SPECIFICATION forming part of Letters Patent No. 391,114, dated October 16, 1888.

Application filed August 1, 1887. Serial No. 245,862. (No model.)

To all whom it may concern:

Be it known that I, CHARLES F. BRUSH, of Cleveland, in the county of Cuyahoga and State of Ohio, have invented certain new and useful Improvements in Safety Attachments for Electro-Magnetic Motors; and I do hereby declare the following to be a full, clear, and exact description of the invention, such as will enable others skilled in the art to which it pertains to make and use the same.

My invention relates to safety attachments for electro-magnetic motors, and is preferably applied to the governor of such motor, in which, with excessive speed of the motor, a weight is moved outward by centrifugal force against the action of a retaining-spring, the outward movement of the weight being made to close a switch for short-circuiting or cutting out the motor.

In the accompanying drawing is shown a simple and preferable arrangement of mechanism for carrying out my invention.

The figure is a side elevation, a portion of the governor-casing being broken away to show the weight and spring.

A represents the armature-shaft, that may have any variety of electromotor mechanism attached.

A' represents the governor-casing, the rim thereof having a hole, a, for the passage of the centrifugal weight B. The latter is more conveniently made in the form of a bolt, the hole a being countersunk to receive the head B' of the bolt in position flush with the casing.

C is the retaining-spring, made to act centripetally on the weight or bolt, the latter passing through a hole made at the center of the spring, with nuts b and b' for compressing the spring, to give the desired tension to the latter.

A preferable form of circuit-closer or switch is as follows: D and D' are standards or posts set at suitable distance apart in convenient proximity to the casing A', these posts being respectively connected with the positive and negative terminals of the motor in any suitable way. A switch-lever or circuit-closer, d, is pivoted at d' to the post D. The lever in its depressed position (shown in dotted lines) extends from one post to the other and short-circuits or cuts out the motor. The lever d may be tilted to the upright position shown in solid lines, the pivotal joint being such that the lever may be turned back a trifle past the center of gravity, so that when left free the lever will stand erect. In its upright position the lever should come as close as may be to the periphery of the casing A' without actual contact with the latter, the lever being made to move in the same plane with the weight B. The spring having been strained to give the proper tension for holding the weight as against the centrifugal force of the latter up to a given speed of the motor, if such speed is exceeded the weight will move outward, and in so doing will collide with the lever d, a slight touch of the weight moving at its highest speed being sufficient to tilt the lever forward, so that the latter will fall by gravity upon the post D', and thus short-circuit or cut out the motor.

In carrying out my invention the mechanical structure and arrangement of parts may be varied indefinitely—for instance, according to the different variety of governor or electric motor to which the safety attachment may be applied—it not being essential to apply the safety attachment directly to the governor, although it is usually more convenient to do so. Any other wheel, rim, or revolving part connected with the motor and suitable for attaching the weight and spring would answer just as well as the governor-casing; also, the form of switch shown, although preferable, might be changed in a variety of ways, according to circumstances, and still be made to accomplish the purpose, so long as the outward movement of the weight cuts out or short-circuits the motor by its impingement against any suitable switching device when the motor has reached a predetermined speed.

What I claim is—

1. In an electric motor, the combination, with a switch, of a radially-movable pin or weight connected with the governor-casing and adapted to be thrown outward by centrifugal action and engage the switch-lever and close the switch, substantially as set forth.

2. In an electric motor, the combination, with a switch arranged in close proximity to the governor-casing, of a radially-movable pin or weight connected with the governor-casing, and a spring for restraining the outward movement of the pin or weight, said pin or weight and switch being relatively arranged, so that should the motor attain an abnormally-high

rate of speed the switch will be engaged by the pin and shifted to its closed position, and thereby cut the motor out of circuit, substantially as set forth.

3. In an electric motor, the combination, with a switch supported on the frame or stationary portion of the motor, said switch constructed to remain normally open and when closed requiring a manual adjustment to be reopened, of a pin or weight connected to a moving portion of the motor and adapted to be actuated by centrifugal force and engage and close the switch should the motor attain an abnormally high rate of speed, substantially as set forth.

In testimony whereof I sign this specification, in the presence of two witnesses, this 13th day of July, 1887.

CHARLES F. BRUSH.

Witnesses:
CHAS. H. DORER,
ALBERT E. LYNCH.

The United States of America

No. _____

To all to whom these presents shall come:

Whereas *Charles F. Brush* of *Cleveland, Ohio* has presented to the Commissioner of Patents a petition praying for the grant of Letters Patent for an alleged new and useful improvement in _____ *Fuse Block* _____

a description of which invention is contained in the Specification of which a copy is hereunto annexed and made a part hereof, and has complied with the various requirements of Law in such cases made and provided, and

Whereas upon due examination made the said claimant is adjudged to be justly entitled to a Patent under the Law.

Now therefore these **Letters Patent** are to grant unto the said *Charles F. Brush* _____ his heirs or assigns for the term of Seventeen years from the _____ day of _____ one thousand eight hundred and ninety _____ the exclusive right to make, use and vend the said invention throughout the United States and the Territories thereof.

In testimony whereof I have hereunto set my hand and caused the seal of the **Patent Office** to be affixed at the City of Washington this _____ day of _____ in the year of our Lord one thousand eight hundred and ninety _____ and of the Independence of the United States of America the one hundred and fourteenth.

Countersigned:
C. E. Mitchell
Commissioner of Patents

Cyrus Bussey
Assistant Secretary of the Interior

(No Model.)

C. F. BRUSH.
FUSE BLOCK.

No. 427,548. Patented May 13, 1890.

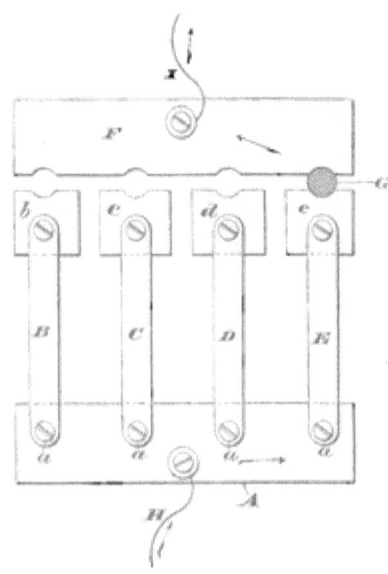

Witnesses
E. T. Nottingham
R. S. Ferguson

Inventor
Charles F. Brush
By his Attorney
H. A. Seymour

UNITED STATES PATENT OFFICE.

CHARLES F. BRUSH, OF CLEVELAND, OHIO.

FUSE-BLOCK.

SPECIFICATION forming part of Letters **Patent No. 427,548, dated May 13, 1890.**

Application filed November 21, 1889. Serial No. 331,121. (No model.)

To all whom it may concern:

Be it known that I, CHARLES F. BRUSH, of Cleveland, in the county of Cuyahoga and State of Ohio, have invented certain new and useful Improvements in Safety-Fuses for Electric Systems of Distribution; and I do hereby declare the following to be a full, clear, and exact description of the invention, such as will enable others skilled in the art to which it appertains to make and use the same.

My invention relates to an improvement in safety-fuses for electric systems of distribution, the improvement being specially applicable to electric-railway systems.

Heretofore it has been customary to interpose a safety-fuse consisting of a readily-fusible strip of metal in the circuit leading from the trolley of a multiple-arc electric-railway system to the motor on the car, so that the circuit will be broken and the current to the motor interrupted or cut off by the fusion of the safety-strip should the current from any cause become sufficiently great in quantity to endanger the motor by overheating or burning out its coils. When the single fuse in the circuit burns out, it is necessary to insert a new one before the car can safely proceed on its journey, and much time is consumed and trouble caused in replacing the burned-out fuse by a new one.

The object of my invention is to obviate the trouble and loss of time due to the employment of a single safety-fuse, and to provide a number of safety-fuses so arranged that while only one of them will be included in the circuit of the motor a fresh fuse may be instantly switched into the circuit in case one should be burned out.

With this object in view my invention consists in certain features of construction and combinations of parts, as will be hereinafter described, and pointed out in the claim.

In the accompanying drawing, which illustrates one embodiment of my invention, A represents a block or plate of metal or other good electric conductor, to which one end of a series of fuses B C D E, &c., are fastened by screws a, or in any other suitable manner.

The opposite ends of the several fuses or safety-strips are connected to the several metal blocks b c d e, &c., which are insulated from each other.

F is a block or plate, of metal or other good conductor, located in close proximity to the insulated blocks or contacts b c d e and adapted to be electrically connected with any one of said blocks by means of a metal plug G. The block A may be electrically connected with the trolley and the plate F with the motor by conductors H and I, or the connections may be reversed. On the passage of a current from the trolley to the motor the current will flow through the fuse E, and should this fuse or strip be burned out by the current fuse D may be quickly switched into the circuit by means of the plug G. It is evident that a switch-lever or other device might be used in lieu of the plug for electrically connecting either one of the insulated blocks with the block or plate F. Again, the parts may be arranged as shown or in the form of a cylinder, or in any other desired manner; hence I do not restrict myself to the particular construction or arrangement of parts shown and described; but,

Having fully described my invention, what I claim as new, and desire to secure by Letters Patent, is—

The combination, with an electric feed-circuit, of a fuse included therein, said fuse consisting of two plates of conducting material, a series of metallic blocks located between and in proximity to one of said plates, a fusible strip connecting each block with the other plate, and a plug for electrically connecting the blocks with the plate in proximity thereto one at a time, whereby when one fusible strip shall have been blown another may be quickly put into circuit, substantially as set forth.

In testimony whereof I have signed this specification in the presence of two subscribing witnesses.

CHARLES F. BRUSH.

Witnesses:
J. FOLLET,
SIDNEY H. SHORT.

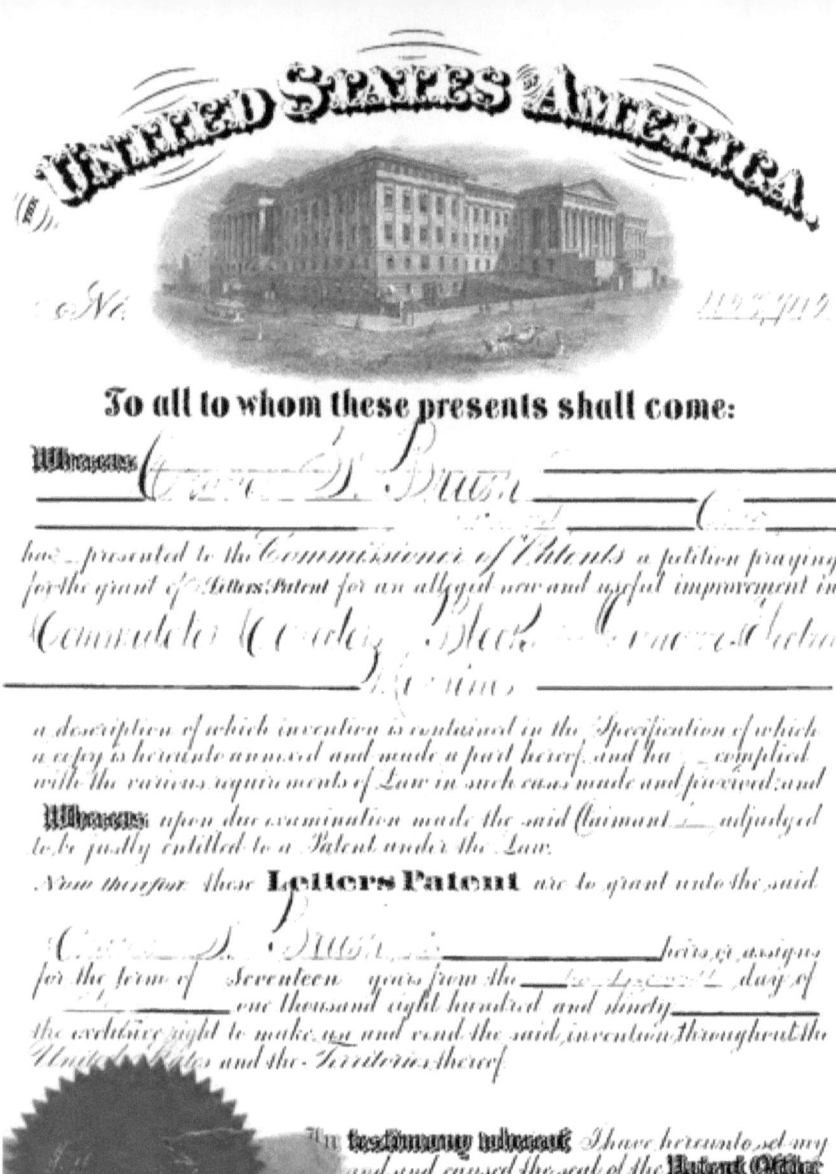

THE UNITED STATES OF AMERICA

No. _____

To all to whom these presents shall come:

Whereas _____

has presented to the Commissioner of Patents a petition praying for the grant of Letters Patent for an alleged new and useful improvement in _____

a description of which invention is contained in the Specification of which a copy is hereunto annexed and made a part hereof, and has complied with the various requirements of Law in such cases made and provided, and

Whereas upon due examination made the said Claimant is adjudged to be justly entitled to a Patent under the Law.

Now therefore these **Letters Patent** are to grant unto the said _____ heirs or assigns for the term of Seventeen years from the _____ day of _____ one thousand eight hundred and ninety _____ the exclusive right to make, use and vend the said invention throughout the United States and the Territories thereof.

In testimony whereof I have hereunto set my hand and caused the seal of the **Patent Office** to be affixed at the City of Washington this _____ day of _____ in the year of our Lord one thousand eight hundred and ninety _____ and of the Independence of the United States of America the one hundred and fourteenth.

Countersigned
C. E. Mitchell
Commissioner of Patents

Cyrus Bussey
Assistant Secretary of the Interior.

(No Model.)

C. F. BRUSH.
COMMUTATOR COLLECTOR OR BLOCK FOR DYNAMO ELECTRIC MACHINES.

No. 428,742. Patented May 27, 1890.

Fig. 1.

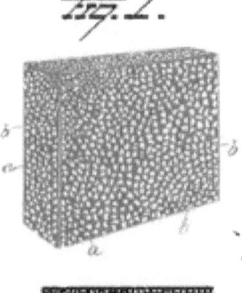

Fig. 2.

Fig. 3.

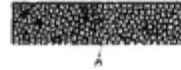

Fig. 4.

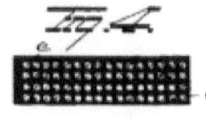

Fig. 5.

Fig. 6.

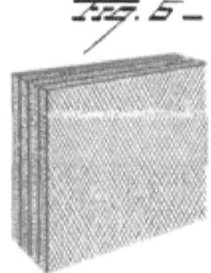

Witnesses
Inventor
Charles F. Brush.
By his Attorneys

UNITED STATES PATENT OFFICE.

CHARLES F. BRUSH, OF CLEVELAND, OHIO.

COMMUTATOR COLLECTOR OR BLOCK FOR DYNAMO-ELECTRIC MACHINES.

SPECIFICATION forming part of Letters Patent No. 428,742, dated May 27, 1890.

Application filed November 22, 1889. Serial No. 331,197. (No model.)

To all whom it may concern:

Be it known that I, CHARLES F. BRUSH, a resident of Cleveland, in the county of Cuyahoga and State of Ohio, have invented certain new and useful Improvements in Commutator-Current Collectors or Blocks for Dynamo-Electric Machines or Electric Motors; and I do hereby declare the following to be a full, clear, and exact description of the invention, such as will enable others skilled in the art to which it appertains to make and use the same.

My invention relates to an improvement in commutator-current collectors or blocks for dynamo-electric machines or motors.

Heretofore attempts have been made to substitute current collectors or blocks made of carbon or carbon and graphite for the copper brushes commonly used; but collectors thus made were found objectionable and defective, owing to their low electrical conductivity and consequent excessive heating when in use.

The object of my invention is to provide a commutator-current collector or block having an electrical conductivity sufficiently high to prevent it from becoming unduly heated when in use and of such form and material as will insure an extended and intimate contact with the commutator and be capable of long continued use without renewal.

With these ends in view my invention consists in a commutator-current collector or block consisting of carbon and metal of good electrical conductivity intimately associated and combined together.

The invention further consists in a commutator-current collector composed of carbon and metal molded into the desired form.

It further consists in a current-collector composed of carbon having finely-divided metal distributed through its mass.

It further consists in a current-collector made of carbon, graphite, and metal.

It further consists in a current-collector made of carbon and metal molded into the desired form and electroplated.

It further consists in certain other features of invention and improvement, as will be hereinafter described, and pointed out in the claims.

In the accompanying drawings, Figure 1 represents a commutator-current collector or block composed of carbon having finely-divided metal distributed throughout its mass. Fig. 2 shows the collector or block provided with an electroplated coating. Figs. 3, 4, 5, and 6 illustrate modifications.

In the manufacture of commutator-current collectors or blocks I take finely divided or pulverized carbon in the form of coke and finely divided or pulverized suboxide of copper, together with a sufficient quantity of pitch or other suitable hydrocarbon, which serves as a binder, and, after thoroughly mixing the mass, mold it in any desired shape or form by placing the mixture in a suitable mold, and subjecting it while in a heated state to great pressure, thereby imparting the desired density and hardness to the completed article and insuring an intimate union of the material of which it is composed. The article after being molded is packed in sand and baked a sufficient length of time to render it hard and suitable for the purpose intended. The operation of baking the collectors or blocks serves to reduce the suboxide of copper to metallic copper, which, being in intimate contact with the carbon and distributed throughout its mass, imparts a sufficiently high electrical conductivity to the article to prevent it from becoming excessively heated when in use. The process of baking renders the block slightly porous, and exposes to the atmosphere the particles of metallic copper located at or near the surface of the block. To solidify the block and protect the particles of metal so exposed, I submerge the block, after baking, in a hot bath of paraffine or equivalent material, which serves to fill the pores, expel the air or any moisture contained therein, and to thoroughly coat and protect the surface of the block.

The relative proportions of the suboxide of copper and carbon which I have found well suited for the purpose are seventy-five per cent. of suboxide of copper, ten per cent. of carbon, and fifteen per cent. of pitch or other equivalent binding material, although these proportions may be widely varied and still insure the production of a greatly-improved article.

Instead of using suboxide of copper, I may use other metallic oxides, or copper or other suitable metals in a finely-divided metallic,

state may be mixed with the carbon and molded into form.

Again, instead of using a mixture consisting of carbon in the form of pulverized coke and metal in a finely-divided state, I also use pulverized coke and graphite mixed with finely-divided metal, and thereby obtain the lubricating qualities of the graphite for lessening the wear of the collector and the commutator segments.

After the collector or block has been molded, as described, it may be electroplated with copper, if desired. Fig. 1 shows a collector or block, in which a represents the carbon—either pulverized coke or coke and graphite—and b the finely-divided copper or other metal distributed throughout its mass. In Fig. 2 the block is provided with an electroplated coating c of copper, which serves to increase the strength and electrical conductivity of the block and insures its good electrical contact with the clamp to which it is secured when in use.

Instead of using finely-divided metal distributed throughout the carbon, I may use fine wires of copper or other metal molded parallel to each other in the block, so that in use the latter may be secured in the clamp in such manner that the wires will form electric conductors between the clamp and commutator. This form of collector is illustrated in Fig. 3, d representing the wires and a the carbon, whether composed of coke or coke and graphite. Again, instead of using fine wires, as illustrated in Fig. 3, I may employ rods e, either round or square, as illustrated in Fig. 4.

Another modification is represented in Fig. 5, in which f represents alternate plates or sheets of copper or other metal, which may be perforated, if desired, and a the layers of carbon.

Fig. 6 shows a block composed of several layers of metal gauze, around and into which the carbon is pressed. The wires composing the gauze are disposed diagonally, as shown, and thus the wearing away of the block continually presents the ends of these wires at new points on the commutator, thus preventing unequal wearing.

It is evident from the foregoing description that the form and construction of my improved commutator-current collector or block may be widely varied, and that the proportions of the mixture of materials and the materials constituting the mixture or combination may also be varied without departing from the invention, and hence I would have it understood that I do not limit the invention to the particular construction of commutator-block shown or described, or to the particular proportions of materials specified; but,

Having fully described my invention, what I claim as new, and desire to secure by Letters Patent, is—

1. A commutator-current collector or block consisting of carbon and interspersed metal, substantially as and for the purpose specified.

2. A commutator-current collector or block consisting of carbon and interspersed metal molded into the desired form, substantially as and for the purpose specified.

3. A commutator-current collector or block consisting of carbon having finely-divided metal distributed throughout its mass, substantially as and for the purpose specified.

4. A commutator-current collector or block consisting of carbon having finely-divided copper distributed throughout its mass, substantially as and for the purpose specified.

5. A commutator-current collector or block consisting of carbon and metal molded together and provided with an electroplated coating, substantially as and for the purpose specified.

6. A commutator-current collector or block consisting of carbon, graphite, and metal molded and compressed into the desired form, substantially as and for the purpose specified.

7. A commutator-current collector or block consisting of a mass of molded and compressed carbon and metal of good electrical conductivity, substantially as and for the purpose specified.

In testimony whereof I have signed this specification in the presence of two subscribing witnesses.

CHARLES F. BRUSH.

Witnesses:
J. POTTER,
SIDNEY H. SHORT.

United States of America

№ _____

To all to whom these presents shall come:

Whereas _____ _____ _____ _____

ha__ presented to the Commissioner of Patents a petition praying for the grant of Letters Patent for an alleged new and useful improvement in _____ _____ _____ _____

a description of which invention is contained in the Specification of which a copy is hereunto annexed and made a part hereof, and ha__ complied with the various requirements of Law in such cases made and provided, and

Whereas upon due examination made the said Claimant _____ adjudged to be justly entitled to a Patent under the Law.

Now therefore these **Letters Patent** are to grant unto the said _____ _____ _____ _____ heirs or assigns for the term of Seventeen years from the _____ day of _____ one thousand eight hundred and ninety _____ the exclusive right to make, use and vend the said invention throughout the United States and the Territories thereof.

In testimony whereof I have hereunto set my hand and caused the seal of the **Patent Office** to be affixed at the City of Washington this _____ day of _____ in the year of our Lord one thousand eight hundred and ninety _____ and of the Independence of the United States of America the one hundred and fourteenth.

Countersigned

C. E. Mitchell

Commissioner of Patents

Assistant Secretary of the Interior

(No Model.)

C. F. BRUSH.
COMMUTATOR COLLECTOR OR BLOCK FOR DYNAMO ELECTRIC MACHINES.

No. 428,743. Patented May 27, 1890.

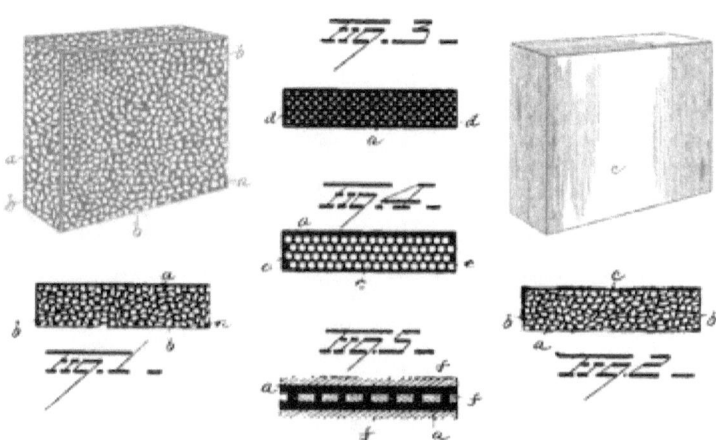

UNITED STATES PATENT OFFICE.

CHARLES F. BRUSH, OF CLEVELAND, OHIO.

COMMUTATOR COLLECTOR OR BLOCK FOR DYNAMO-ELECTRIC MACHINES.

SPECIFICATION forming part of Letters Patent No. 428,743, dated May 27, 1890.

Application filed November 22, 1889. Serial No. 331,198. (No model.)

To all whom it may concern:

Be it known that I, CHARLES F. BRUSH, a resident of Cleveland, in the county of Cuyahoga and State of Ohio, have invented certain new and useful Improvements in Commutator Current Collectors or Blocks for Dynamo-Electric Machines or Electric Motors; and I do hereby declare the following to be a full, clear, and exact description of the invention, such as will enable others skilled in the art to which it appertains to make and use the same.

My invention relates to an improvement in commutator current collectors or blocks for dynamo-electric machines or electric motors.

Attempts have been made to substitute current collectors or blocks made of carbon or carbon and graphite for the copper brushes commonly used; but collectors so made were found objectionable in use owing to the low electrical conductivity of the carbon, the excessive heating of the collectors, and the undue wearing away of the commutator-segments.

The object of my invention is to provide a commutator current collector or block which will be capable of self-lubrication, whereby the wearing of the commutator-segments will be reduced to a minimum; further, to provide a collector or block of such material or materials that it shall possess such a high electrical conductivity and also a capacity for insuring at all times an intimate and extended contact with the commutator that excessive heating of the collector or block shall be obviated.

With these ends in view my invention consists in a commutator current collector or block consisting of graphite or plumbago intimately connected and combined with metal of good electrical conductivity.

The invention further consists in a commutator collector or block composed of graphite and metal molded into the desired form.

The invention further consists in a commutator block or collector made of graphite and finely-divided metal distributed throughout its mass.

It further consists in a commutator current-collector composed of graphite, having finely-divided copper distributed throughout its mass.

It further consists in certain other features of improvement and invention, as will be hereinafter described, and pointed out in the claims.

In the accompanying drawings, Figure 1 represents a commutator current collector or block composed of graphite having finely-divided metal distributed throughout its mass. Fig. 2 shows the collector or block provided with an electroplated coating. Figs. 3, 4, 5, and 6 illustrate modifications.

In the manufacture of commutator current collectors or blocks I take finely-divided or pulverized graphite and finely-divided or pulverized suboxide of copper, together with a sufficient quantity of pitch or other suitable hydrocarbon, which serves as a binder, and, after thoroughly mixing the mass, mold it in any desired shape or form by placing the mixture in a suitable mold and subjecting it while in a heated state to great pressure, so as to impart the desired density and hardness to the completed article and insure an intimate union of the materials of which it is composed. The article after being molded is packed in sand or other suitable material and baked a sufficient length of time to render it hard and suitable for the purpose intended.

The operation of baking the collectors or blocks serves to reduce the suboxide of copper to metallic copper, which, being in intimate contact with the graphite and distributed throughout its mass, forms a good electrical conductor, and thus prevents the block from becoming excessively heated when in use. The process of baking operates to render the block slightly porous and exposes to the action of the atmosphere particles of metal located at or near the surface of the block. To solidify the block and protect the metal particles so exposed, I submerge the block after baking in a hot bath of paraffine or equivalent material, which serves to fill the pores, expel the air or any moisture contained therein, and thoroughly to coat and protect the surface of the block. The relative proportions of the suboxide of copper and graphite which I have found well suited for the purpose are seventy-five per cent. of suboxide of copper, ten per cent. of graphite, and fifteen per cent. of pitch or other equivalent

binding material, although these proportions may be widely varied and still insure the production of a greatly improved article.

Instead of using suboxide of copper I may employ other metallic oxides; or copper or other suitable metals in a finely-divided metallic state may be mixed with the graphite and molded into form. After the collector or block has been molded, as described, it may be electroplated with copper, if desired.

Fig. 1 shows a collector or block in which *a* represents the graphite and *b* the finely-divided copper or other metal distributed throughout its mass. In Fig. 2 the block is provided with an electroplated coating *c* of copper, which serves to increase the strength and electrical conductivity of the block and insures its good electrical contact with the clamp to which it is secured when in use.

Instead of using finely-divided metal distributed throughout the graphite I may use fine wires of copper or other metal molded parallel to each other in the block, so that in use the latter may be secured in the clamp in such manner that these wires will form electrical conductors between the clamp and commutator. This form of collector is illustrated in Fig. 3, the wires being represented by *d*; or instead of using fine wire I may employ rods *e*, either round or square, as illustrated in Fig. 4.

Another modification is shown in Fig. 5, in which *f* represents alternate plates or sheets of copper or other metal, which may be perforated, if desired, and *a* represents layers of graphite.

Fig. 6 shows a block composed of several layers of metal gauze around and into which the carbon is pressed. The wires composing the gauze are disposed diagonally, as shown, and thus the wearing away of the block continually presents the ends of these wires at new points on the commutator, thus preventing unequal wearing.

It is evident from the foregoing description that the form and construction of my improved commutator current collector or block may be widely varied, and that the proportions of the mixture or materials and the materials constituting the mixture or the article may also be varied without departing from the invention, and hence I would have it understood that I do not limit the invention to the particular construction of commutator collector or block shown or described, or to the particular proportions or materials herein specified; but,

Having fully described my invention, what I claim as new, and desire to secure by Letters Patent, is—

1. A commutator current collector or block consisting of graphite combined with interspersed metal of good electrical conductivity, substantially as and for the purpose specified.

2. A commutator current collector or block consisting of graphite and interspersed metal molded into the desired form, substantially as and for the purpose specified.

3. A commutator current collector or block consisting of graphite having metal of good electrical conductivity distributed throughout its mass, substantially as and for the purpose specified.

4. A commutator current collector or block consisting of graphite and finely-divided metal of good electrical conductivity molded into the desired form, substantially as and for the purpose specified.

5. A commutator current collector or block consisting of graphite and finely-divided copper, substantially as and for the purpose specified.

6. A commutator current collector or block consisting of graphite and metal molded into the desired form and provided with an electroplated coating, substantially as and for the purpose specified.

In testimony whereof I have signed this specification in the presence of two subscribing witnesses.

CHARLES F. BRUSH.

Witnesses:
J. POTTER,
SIDNEY H. SHORT.

THE UNITED STATES OF AMERICA

No. _____

To all to whom these presents shall come:

Whereas _____

_____

ha__ presented to the Commissioner of Patents a petition praying for the grant of Letters Patent for an alleged new and useful improvement in

_____

_____

a description of which invention is contained in the Specification of which a copy is hereunto annexed and made a part hereof, and ha__ complied with the various requirements of Law in such cases made and provided, and

Whereas upon due examination made the said Claimant __ adjudged to be justly entitled to a Patent under the Law.

Now therefore these **Letters Patent** are to grant unto the said _____ heirs or assigns for the term of Seventeen years from the _____ day of _____ one thousand eight hundred and ninety ____ the exclusive right to make, use and vend the said invention throughout the United States, and the Territories thereof.

In testimony whereof I have hereunto set my hand and caused the seal of the **Patent Office** to be affixed at the City of Washington this _____ day of October in the year of our Lord one thousand eight hundred and ninety ____ and of the Independence of the United States of America the one hundred and sixteenth.

Countersigned _____   _____
                                    Assistant Secretary of the Interior.
W. E. Simonds
Commissioner of Patents.

(No Model.)

C. F. BRUSH.
SPRING CUSHIONED OR SUSPENDED ARC LAMP.

No. 461,420. Patented Oct. 20, 1891.

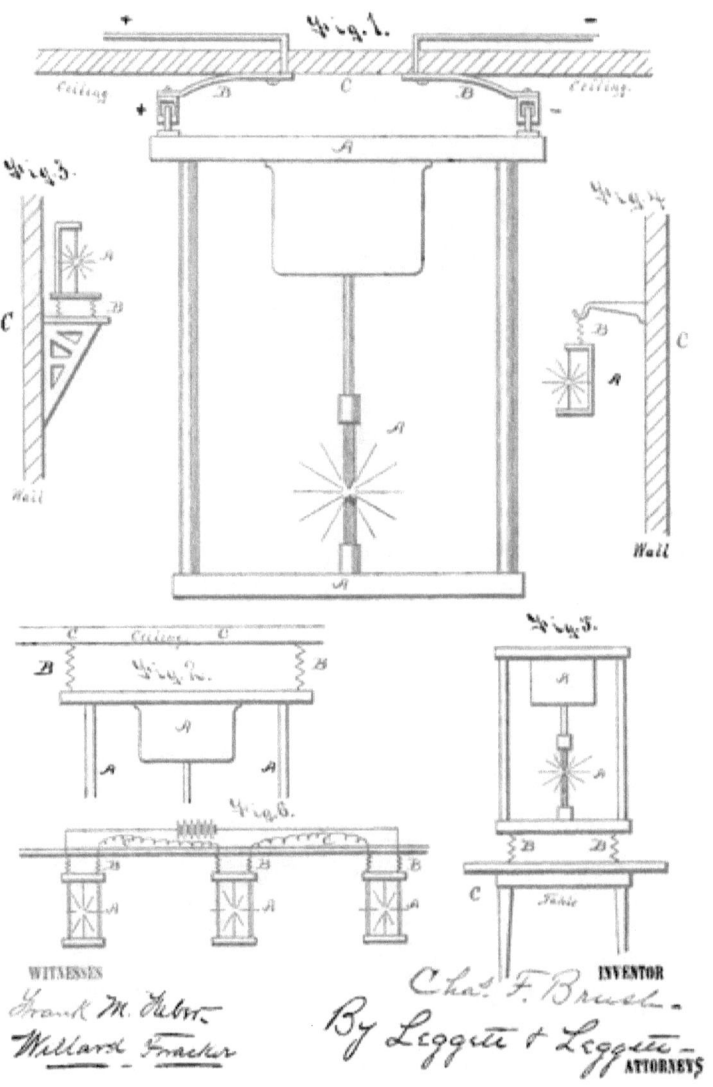

UNITED STATES PATENT OFFICE.

CHARLES F. BRUSH, OF CLEVELAND, OHIO, ASSIGNOR TO THE BRUSH ELECTRIC COMPANY, OF SAME PLACE.

SPRING CUSHIONED OR SUSPENDED ARC LAMP.

SPECIFICATION forming part of Letters Patent No. 461,420, dated October 20, 1891.

Application filed May 28, 1880. Serial No. 10,651. (No model.)

To all whom it may concern:

Be it known that I, CHARLES F. BRUSH, of Cleveland, in the county of Cuyahoga and State of Ohio, have invented certain new and useful Improvements in Spring Cushioned or Suspended Electric Lamps; and I do hereby declare the following to be a full, clear, and exact description of the invention, such as will enable others skilled in the art to which it pertains to make and use it, reference being had to the accompanying drawings, which form part of this specification.

My invention relates to electric lamps, the object being to provide means for preventing the injurious effect to the operation of one or more lamps that are operating in series by reason of jarring or jolting of the lamps support; and with this end in view my invention consists in the combination, with an electric lamp, of a spring or yielding cushion for supporting or suspending the lamp, and thereby preventing the lamp from being disturbed or deranged by the jolting or jarring of its support.

My invention further consists in the combination, with an electric lamp, of suspending or supporting springs formed of electric conducting material and adapted to convey the current to and from the lamp.

In the drawings, Figure 1 is a view in side elevation of an electric lamp suspended from a ceiling or upper support by means of metallic springs electrically connected at one end to the main conductor and at their opposite ends to the terminals of the lamp. Fig. 2 shows spiral springs employed in lieu of the flat springs of Fig. 1. Fig. 3 shows spiral springs inserted beneath the base of the lamp. Fig. 4 represents the lamp suspended from the bracket by means of a spiral spring. Fig. 5 shows a lamp supported upon a table by means of interposed spiral springs which serve as a yielding cushion for the lamp. Fig. 6 illustrates in diagram a series of arc lamps suspended by springs electrically connecting the lamps with the main circuit.

In Fig. 1, A represents an electric-arc lamp of any preferred type of construction, and B B are metallic springs electrically connected at their upper ends with the main conductor, while their lower or free ends are electrically connected with the terminals of the lamp. The springs serve the double function of conveying the current to and from the lamp and also supporting it in a yielding manner, so that any jolting to which its support is subjected will be taken up by the springs and thereby prevent any derangement of the feeding or regulating mechanism of the lamp, and thus avoid any such action of the lamp as would otherwise tend to disturb the regularity of the current in the main or general circuit which would manifestly disturb the operation of the remaining lamps on the circuit.

In the remaining figures of drawings I have represented spiral springs as the supports. In Figs. 2, 4, and 6 the springs are employed to suspend the lamp, while in Figs. 3 and 5 they are arranged beneath the lamp to support it in a yielding manner and do not necessarily serve as electric conductors for conveying the current to and from the lamp.

Where springs or cushions are employed only to support the lamp in a yielding manner the springs or cushions may be constructed from metal, rubber, or any suitable material, or an air-cushion, if found preferable, may be employed.

In practice I have found the employment of a spring or cushion with an arc electric lamp useful in such places as shops, wherein the floor is subject to the jar of heavy machinery, inasmuch as this jar occasionally becomes an element of disturbance to prevent a uniform and steady light.

I am well aware that it is a common expedient to suspend ordinary oil-lamps from springs on account of any jarring of the ceiling or support from which the lamps depend or the surface upon which they are placed. The novel and important feature of this invention is evident when its introduction into a system of two or more arc lamps upon a single circuit is considered. In such a system, with certain types of electric lamps, any derangement of the action of any one lamp will simultaneously derange every other lamp on the circuit. The employment, therefore, of the spring or cushion B, as herein specified, constitutes an operative element of an arc electric-lighting system instead of a mere adjunct to any individual lamp. In a system

such as referred to it may not always be necessary to apply the supporting spring or cushion to every lamp, and my invention therefore comprehends a system wherein one or more or all of the lamps are thus equipped. Only such lamps as are subjected to jolting (be it one or more) require a spring or cushion support.

Having fully described my invention, what I claim as new, and desire to secure by Letters Patent, is—

1. The combination, with an electric circuit and a series of arc lamps included therein, of springs or cushions for supporting one or more of said lamps, substantially as set forth.

2. The combination, with an electric circuit and an electric lamp, of spring-yielding electric conductors connected at one end to the circuit and at their opposite ends with the terminals of said lamp, and serving to suspend the lamp in a spring-yielding manner and also to convey the electric current to and from the lamp, substantially as set forth.

3. The combination, with an electric circuit having two or more translating devices included therein in series, of an electric arc lamp included in said circuit and provided with one or more supporting springs or cushions, substantially as set forth.

In testimony whereof I have signed my name to this specification in the presence of two subscribing witnesses.

     CHARLES F. BRUSH.

Witnesses:
 LEVERETT L. LEGGETT,
 WILLARD FRACKER.

THE UNITED STATES OF AMERICA

№ _____

To all to whom these presents shall come:

Whereas Charles _____ _____ _____

_____ _____ _____ _____

has presented to the Commissioner of Patents a petition praying for the grant of Letters Patent for an alleged new and useful improvement in

_____ _____ _____

a description of which invention is contained in the Specification of which a copy is hereunto annexed and made a part hereof, and ha__ complied with the various requirements of Law in such cases made and provided, and

Whereas upon due examination made the said Claimant __ adjudged to be justly entitled to a Patent under the Law.

Now therefore these **Letters Patent** are to grant unto the said

_____ _____ heirs or assigns for the term of Seventeen years from the _____ day of _____ one thousand eight hundred and ninety ___ the exclusive right to make, use and vend the said invention throughout the United States and the Territories thereof.

In testimony whereof I have hereunto set my hand and caused the seal of the Patent Office to be affixed at the City of Washington this _____ day of _____ in the year of our Lord one thousand eight hundred and ninety-____ and of the Independence of the United States of America the one hundred and sixteenth.

Countersigned: _____

_____
Commissioner of Patents.

_____
Assistant Secretary of the Interior.

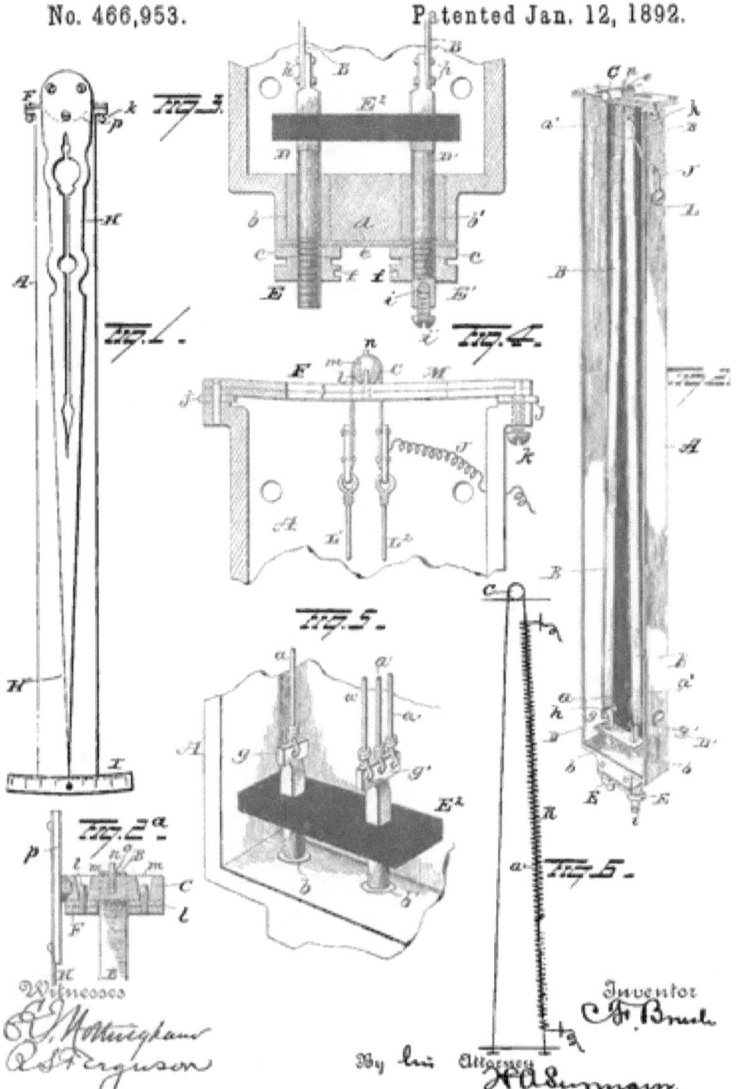

UNITED STATES PATENT OFFICE.

CHARLES F. BRUSH, OF CLEVELAND, OHIO.

AMMETER.

SPECIFICATION forming part of Letters Patent No. 466,953, dated January 12, 1892.

Application filed November 21, 1889. Serial No. 331,120. (No model.)

To all whom it may concern:

Be it known that I, CHARLES F. BRUSH, a resident of Cleveland, in the county of Cuyahoga and State of Ohio, have invented certain new and useful Improvements in Ammeters; and I do hereby declare the following to be a full, clear, and exact description of the invention, such as will enable others skilled in the art to which it appertains to make and use the same.

My invention relates to an improvement in ammeters, the object being to measure and indicate the strength of an electrical current by the differential action of mechanism due to the heat generated by the current to be measured or by a portion of it; and with this end in view the invention consists in certain features of construction and combinations of parts, as will hereinafter be described, and pointed out in the claims.

In the accompanying drawings, Figure 1 is a view of one embodiment of my invention. Fig. 2 is a similar view showing the parts inside the casing. Fig. 2ª is a detached view partly in section, illustrating the rock-shaft and adjacent parts. Fig. 3 is a detached sectional view of the screw-rods, insulating-sleeve, and adjusting-nuts. Figs. 4, 5, and 6 are details and modifications.

A is box or casing, which may be made of cast-iron or other material.

B represents a thin flexible ribbon of German silver or other suitable alloy or metal, which passes around a rock-shaft C. At the lower end of the casing the ends $a\ a'$ of the ribbon are fastened to the screw-rods D D', which extend through insulating-sleeves $b\ b'$, inserted in the lower end of the box. Washers $c\ c'$ surround the screw-rods and are seated upon suitable insulating material, such as asbestus d and mica e, or both, as shown, in order that the washers and screw-rods shall be insulated from the casing and from each other.

E E' are adjusting-nuts, which may be square for the attachment of a wrench or provided with radial holes f for the insertion of a pin to rotate and adjust them to regulate the tension of the ribbons. To connect the ends of the ribbons firmly to the screw-rods, I construct the latter with enlarged flattened ends $g\ g$ and fasten the ends of the ribbon to them by rivets h. Screw-rod D' is provided with a hole i, into which is inserted one end of the circuit in which the instrument is to be included, and with a set-screw i' for clamping the end of the conductor, whereby the screw D' forms a binding-post.

E² is a block of vulcanized fiber or other suitable insulating material, which is perforated at its ends for the reception of the screw-rods and serves as a spacing-block and guide for them.

At the upper and open end of casing A is located a spring F, which may be made of a single steel plate or of two or more, two being shown in the drawings. Spring F is seated upon washers $j\ j$ and a set-screw k, by which it may be adjusted so as to bring the pointer H in proper relation with the scale I. The rock-shaft is constructed and arranged to have a rocking or rolling bearing on the spring, as will be hereinafter explained. To the spring are secured the pins or studs l, which enter the smaller ends of the conical holes m in the rock-shaft, and while serving to retain the latter against displacement permit it to rock backward and forward on the spring. In view of the fact that the rock-shaft presses with great force against the spring F, owing to the high tension to which the ribbon is subjected, it is important that provision be made for decreasing the friction and wear of the bearing-surfaces of the rock-shaft and spring to the minimum to insure a sensitive and reliable operation of the instrument for any considerable period of time. I have found by practical tests that a knife-edge bearing will soon deteriorate to such an extent as to impair the action of the instrument, and hence I have adopted the construction shown in the drawings, by which I secure a rolling contact of the parts and very much lessen their wear and friction. A pin n, fastened to the rock-shaft, passes through a hole o in the ribbon and prevents the latter from slipping on the rock-shaft and causes the latter to rotate in response to the contraction and expansion of the ribbon, as will be hereinafter explained. On one end of the rock-shaft is fastened a disk p, to which is secured the hand or pointer H, the free end of which

moves over an indicating-plate I, which latter may be furnished with a scale such as is ordinarily used in ammeters. The pointer is made quite long and the rock-shaft quite small in its diameter, in order that a slight rocking movement of the latter will move the free end of the pointer through a considerable space to indicate clearly on the plate I such movement, however slight it may be. To the part a' of ribbon B is connected a flexible electric conductor J, which latter is secured at its opposite end to the binding-post L, attached to the casing.

Having described the construction and arrangement of the several parts of the instrument, I will now briefly describe its operation. The adjusting-nuts E E' are first turned down, so as to impart considerable strain upon and tension to the two parts a a' of the ribbon B and spring F. When properly adjusted, the hand H will point to zero on the indicating plate or scale I. When the current to be measured is passed through the instrument, it enters at the binding-post and flows through part a' of the ribbon and escapes through the flexible conductor J and binding-post L. Hence it will be observed that while both parts a a' of the ribbon B and the spring F are under tension such two forces counterbalance each other and the rock-shaft is retained in a state of equilibrium, being always acted upon by these two counterbalancing forces. While varying temperatures will modify the force exerted by spring F upon the rock-shaft, owing to the expansion and contraction of the two parts a a' of the ribbon, due to changes in temperature, still such variations will have no effect upon the pointer, because both parts a a' are acted upon alike, and hence an equilibrium of forces is maintained. However, when the electric current is caused to flow through the instrument the current heats part a' of the ribbon, owing to its resistance to the passage of the current, and the degree of heat to which the part a' is subjected varies with the strength of the current flowing through it. The heating effect of the current operates to expand part a', and as it slackens it relieves spring F of a portion of its restraining force, and thus allows it to retract; but, owing to the fact that the part a of the ribbon is not expanded by the heat generated by the current, it still exerts its normal restraining force on the spring, the result of which is that the latter will partially rotate the rock-shaft and cause the pointer to move over the indicating-plate, the extent of movement being dependent upon the strength of the current flowing through part a' and the consequent degree of heat to which it is subjected thereby. It will thus be observed that the operation of the instrument is not due to the amount of heat to which part a' of the ribbon is subjected, but to the difference in heat to which the two parts a a' of the ribbon are subjected, which difference is due to the passage of the electric current through one of them. The metal is preferably disposed in the form of a ribbon, because in such form it is best exposed to the action of the air and readily expands and contracts, and thus insures a prompt and sensitive action of the instrument.

Instead of employing a ribbon B, I may use two wires L' L², as illustrated in Fig. 4, the wires being connected at their upper ends to the opposite ends of a short strip of metallic ribbon M, which passes around the rock-shaft.

Instead of using one conductor in the form of a ribbon or wire for the passage of the current to be measured, I may use any desired number. In Fig. 5 I have represented three wires a' a' a' for the passage of the current and one wire a as a counter-balance. In this construction two of the wires a' are adjusted so as to be slack, while the tension of one of the wires a' is adjusted so as to equal the tension of the wires a. When the instrument is placed in the circuit of the current to be measured, the current will divide itself equally between the three wires a', and hence in this construction the pointer will be actuated by the heat due to one third of the total strength of the current flowing in the circuit. Again, instead of passing the current through the wire a' the current may be caused to flow through a long helix R, encircling wire a' and transmit heat to the latter, as illustrated in Fig. 6.

As it is evident that many changes in the construction and relative arrangement of the parts of my improvement in ammeters may be made without involving a departure from the principle of the invention, I would have it understood that I do not restrict myself to the particular construction or arrangement of parts shown and described; but,

Having fully described my invention, what I claim as new, and desire to secure by Letters Patent, is—

1. In an ammeter, the combination, with a yielding plate, of a rock-shaft mounted thereon, means for limiting the movements of said rock-shaft in both directions, a pointer or indicator secured to one end of said rock-shaft, a double flexible conductor secured at its ends and connected at a point between its ends with said rock-shaft, and means for causing one part of said conductor to have its temperature altered relatively to the other part of the conductor by the current to be measured and thereby cause a partial rotation of the rock-shaft and with it a movement of the indicator or pointer to indicate the strength of the current on a scale or graduated plate, substantially as set forth.

2. In an ammeter, the combination, with a spring provided with studs, one or more, of a rock-shaft provided with conical holes into which said studs project, and a conductor connected with said rock-shaft and arranged to have the comparative temperatures of the

two parts of said conductor altered by the current to be measured, substantially as and for the purpose specified.

3. In an ammeter, the combination, with a spring and a rock-shaft fulcrumed thereon, of a metallic ribbon passing around the rock-shaft, means whereby the comparative temperatures of the two parts of said ribbon may be altered by the current to be measured, and a pin for retaining the ribbon against displacement, substantially as and for the purpose specified.

In testimony whereof I have signed this specification in the presence of two subscribing witnesses.

CHARLES F. BRUSH.

Witnesses:
J. POTTER,
SIDNEY H. SHORT.

THE UNITED STATES OF AMERICA

No. 514,907

To all to whom these presents shall come:

Whereas **Charles F. Brush**, of Cleveland, Ohio, has presented to the Commissioner of Patents a petition praying for the grant of Letters Patent for an alleged new and useful improvement in **Dynamo-Electric Machines** he having assigned his right, title and interest in said improvement to The Brush Electric Company, of same place, a description of which invention is contained in the Specification of which a copy is hereunto annexed and made a part hereof, and has complied with the various requirements of Law in such cases made and provided, and

Whereas upon due examination made the said Claimant is adjudged to be justly entitled to a Patent under the Law.

Now therefore these **Letters Patent** are to grant unto the said The Brush Electric Company, its successors, heirs or assigns for the term of Seventeen years from the twentieth day of February one thousand eight hundred and ninety-four the exclusive right to make, use and vend the said invention throughout the United States and the Territories thereof.

In testimony whereof I have hereunto set my hand and caused the seal of the Patent Office to be affixed at the City of Washington this twentieth day of February in the year of our Lord one thousand eight hundred and ninety-four and of the Independence of the United States of America the one hundred and eighteenth.

Countersigned:

Commissioner of Patents.

Assistant Secretary of the Interior.

Mr. A. H. Hough,
    Ass't Treasurer,
        Office.

Dear Sir,-

I attach herewith for filing, patent N° 514,907.

                              Yours truly,

                              [signature]
                                        General Manager.

3.   Patent.

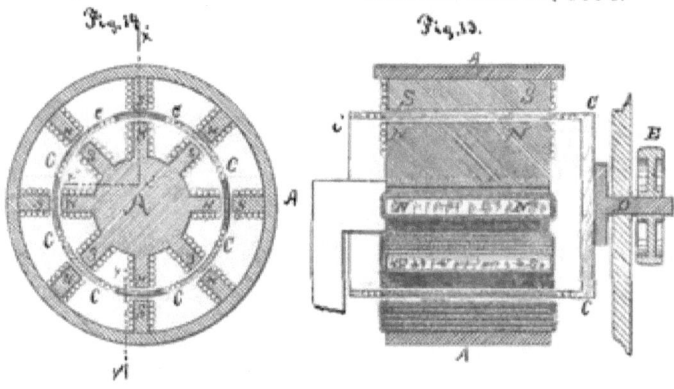
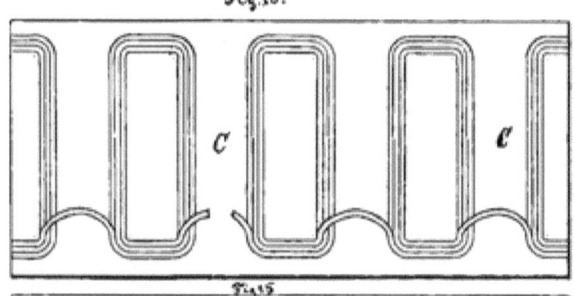
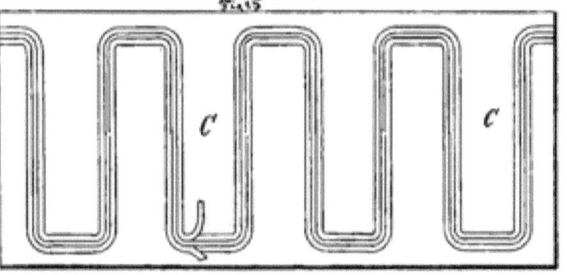

C. F. BRUSH.
DYNAMO ELECTRIC MACHINE.

No. 514,907. Patented Feb. 20, 1894.

4 Sheets—Sheet 3.

Fig. 8.

Fig. 9.
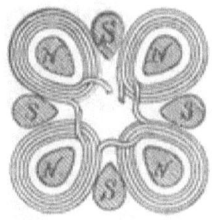

Fig. 10.

Fig. 12.
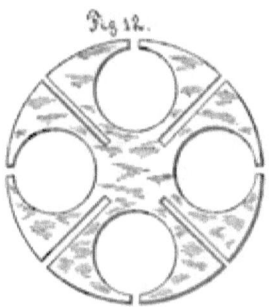

Fig. 11.
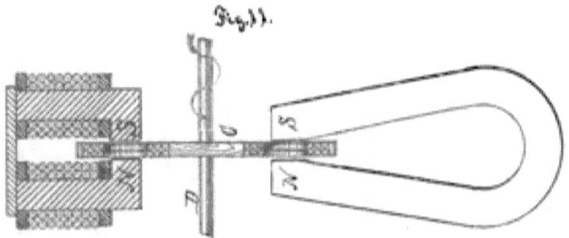

Witnesses Inventor.
Frank M. Faber Charles F. Brush
Livonia L. Lippitt By Leggett & Leggett
  Attys.

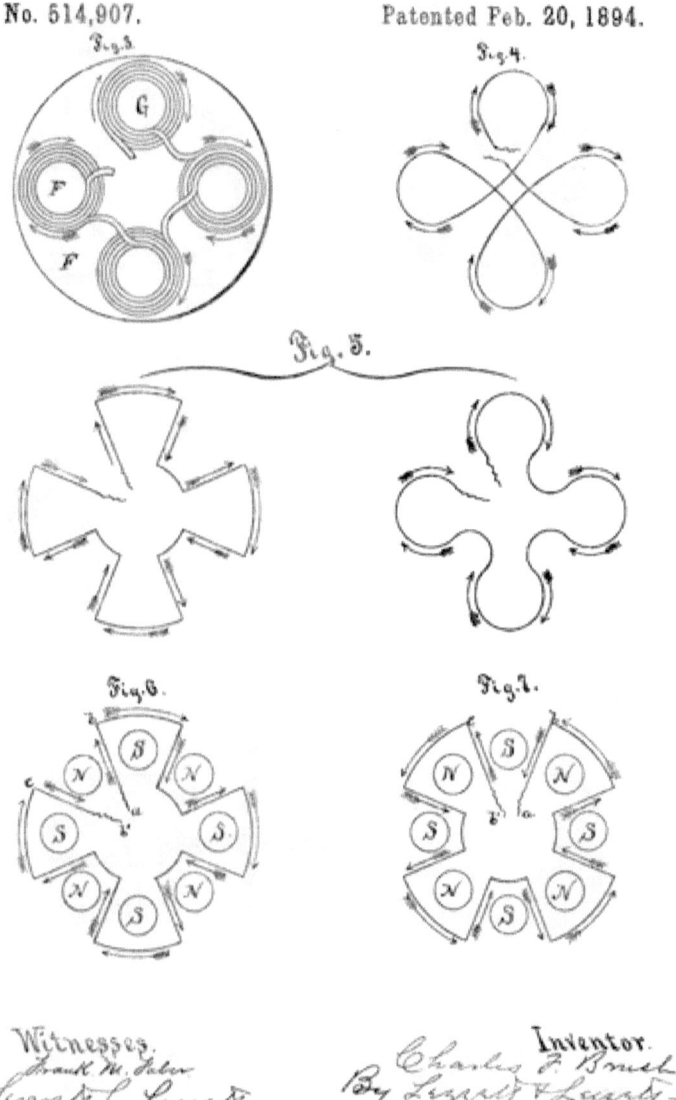

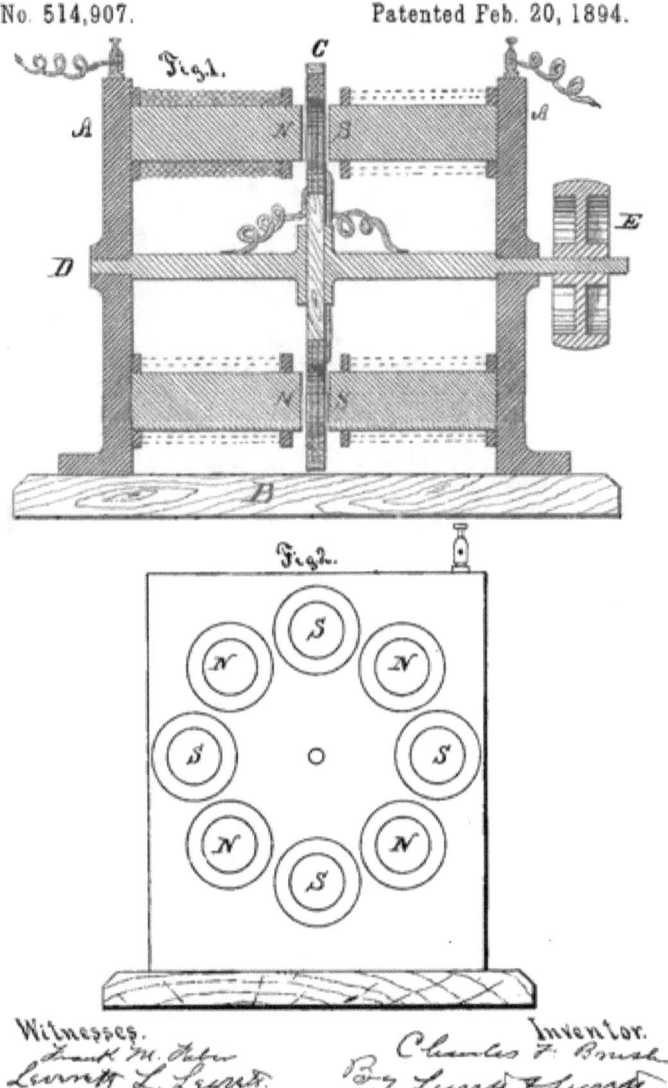

UNITED STATES PATENT OFFICE.

CHARLES F. BRUSH, OF CLEVELAND, OHIO, ASSIGNOR TO THE BRUSH ELECTRIC COMPANY, OF SAME PLACE.

DYNAMO-ELECTRIC MACHINE.

SPECIFICATION forming part of Letters Patent No. 514,907, dated February 20, 1894.

Application filed January 14, 1879.

To all whom it may concern:

Be it known that I, CHARLES F. BRUSH, of Cleveland, in the county of Cuyahoga and State of Ohio, have invented certain new and useful Improvements in Dynamo-Electric Machines; and I do hereby declare the following to be a full, clear, and exact description of the invention, such as will enable others skilled in the art to which it pertains to make and use it, reference being had to the accompanying drawings, which form part of this specification.

My invention relates to dynamo-electric machines, and it consists first, in a peculiar construction of the armature, whereby the full inductive effect of the field-magnets is utilized without the presence of iron or other magnetic substance in the moving armature; second, in an arrangement of field-magnets, whereby the field of force is concentrated into a very small space, in which the armature revolves.

In most dynamo-electric machines before the public, the bobbins of wire on the armature surround one or more cores of soft iron, to the changing magnetism of which the whole (in some) or part (in others) of the effect produced is due. This changing magnetism of the cores, is a source of great loss of driving power, which loss appears as heat in the cores. This is caused not only by the changing magnetism, but by the induction of currents in the iron itself due to its motion in the magnetic field. Thus not only is a large portion of the driving power wasted, but the field of force is largely diverted from its proper function. In other machines, wherein the armature carries no moving iron, the field of force is necessarily so large that much of it cannot be utilized, and the length of moving conductor on the armature is so great as to cause much resistance, and consequent waste of current, attended with heat. If now, a very great concentration of magnetic field can be attained, without diverting any of it from its proper function, then a rapid motion of a short armature conductor may develop a high electromotive force; and there being no changing magnetism or "local" induced currents, very nearly the whole of the driving power may be realized as available current. I have fully accomplished these important results in the apparatus I am about to describe.

Figure 1 of the drawings represents a section through its axis, of a convenient form of dynamo-electric machine embodying my invention.

A A are plates of iron attached to a base of suitable material B. Each of these plates has secured to it, eight magnet cores of iron N. S, arranged as shown in Fig. 2, which is a cross section of Fig. 1. These cores are wound with insulated wire, and are connected in such a manner that when they become magnets by the passage of a current through the wire, unlike poles shall face each other as indicated in Fig. 1, and shall succeed each other in rotation as in Fig. 2.

C, Fig. 1, is the armature carried by the shaft D, which passes through bearings in the upright plates A. Thus by means of the pulley E the armature may be caused to revolve in its own plane between the poles of the magnets N. S.

Fig. 3 shows the armature in plan. It consists of a disk of insulating material F, provided with four openings, in which are placed flat bobbins of insulated copper wire or other suitable conductor G, as shown. These bobbins are connected in such a manner that a current passing through them shall follow the course indicated by the arrows—that is in the same direction in all. They may be connected in a single series, as shown, or so that a current may divide itself between them, still maintaining its proper direction in each.

Fig. 4 shows another method of winding the conductor without altering the direction of the circuit.

Fig. 5 shows still another method of arranging the conductor, which may assist in explaining the induction of currents in it when it is revolved in the magnetic field.

Suppose now, the armature conductor, arranged as in Fig. 5, be placed in front of one of the rows of field magnets, as shown in Fig. 6. Then suppose it to be revolved in the plane of the figure, one-eighth of a revolution to the position shown in Fig. 7. During this movement, the portion $a\ b$ of the conductor pass-

ing in front of the pole S, will have a current induced in it in the direction indicated by the arrow; while the portion b' c passing in front of the pole N, will have a current induced in it in the opposite direction, and so on all around the circle. But since the conductor follows the direction of these currents, all of the eight induced currents combine to produce one current in one direction through the conductor. The other set of field magnets, being of opposite polarity, and facing the conductor on the opposite side, induce a current in the same direction. During the next eighth of a revolution, the current will evidently be reversed. We will then get eight currents alternately in opposite directions during each revolution of the armature.

Instead of employing four bobbins of armature conductor as in Fig. 3, we may employ eight as in Fig. 8, but evidently no increased amount of conductor is permitted by this arrangement, while the use of the insulating disk F for supporting the bobbins is rendered impracticable.

Fig. 9, shows the field-magnet cores N. S, of a different form of cross section or face from those shown in Fig. 2, by which they may be made heavier, and their magnetic power increased, without increasing the general dimensions of the apparatus. The bobbins of armature conductor are also shown of corresponding shape.

It will be evident that any convenient number of magnetic poles may be employed on each side of the armature, as well as the eight shown, provided the armature bobbins are arranged accordingly.

Fig. 10 shows twelve poles, and also the completed arrangement of armature conductor indicated in Fig. 5. In this case the supporting disk of insulating material F, (Fig. 3) is replaced by a plate of the same material provided with radial arms as shown, over which the conductor is laid. The conductor may here be conveniently formed of an insulated copper ribbon of suitable width. It will be noticed that the armature disk is made quite thin in comparison with its other dimensions. This allows the field magnets on its opposite sides to be placed very near each other, thus mutually strengthening each other, and concentrating the entire magnetic field in the small spaces between them, and securing the advantages above enumerated. This great concentration of the field or fields of force, permits of the near approach of the laterally adjoining magnetic poles, without materially diverting the lines of magnetic force from their proper direction, thus permitting the use of a large number of poles on each side of the armature, and a corresponding number of currents to be induced in its conductor during each revolution. We may thus obtain currents of high electro-motive force with an armature conductor of small length, and consequent resistance; and if we give the armature a very rapid rotation, which is quite permissible, there being no iron in it requiring changes of magnetism, we may obtain with a small apparatus an enormous current of electricity, and, for the reason already specified, it will be attended with very little heat in the machine, and very little waste of driving power.

Fig. 11. shows a method by which the proper magnetic poles may be presented on opposite sides of the armature, by means of ordinary electro-magnets, or permanent magnets, placed radially around it.

We have seen that the currents induced in the armature conductor are alternately in opposite directions. These reversals may be corrected by means of a suitable commutator, and the current thus obtained passed around the field-magnets in the usual manner. Or, if the machine is designed to produce an alternating current, for which it is specially adapted, the ends of the armature conductor may be attached to the revolving shaft at each side of the armature, as shown in Fig. 1. Here the shaft is not a continuous piece of metal, but is divided by the insulating armature disk F. If, now, the plates A A are also insulated from each other by means of the wooden base B, they will represent the terminals of the armature conductor; the current being carried to them through the bearings of the shaft. Thus there will be no commutator to be cared for.

Of course the field-magnets cannot be worked by an alternating current. They may be permanent magnets in small apparatus, but must generally be electro-magnets. They may be excited by the current from any suitable apparatus—preferably a small dynamo-electric machine giving a constant current. This may be a separate apparatus, or may have its armature carried by the shaft D, which is the simpler and preferable arrangement.

If, in an armature constructed as indicated in Fig. 8, we insert a short iron core of small diameter in each bobbin of wire, we will not very materially affect the working of the apparatus. But if the core has a considerable diameter, it may seriously affect the functions of the magnets, especially if they are closely associated side by side, by forming an armature between neighboring poles on the same side of the armature, while the core is passing from one to the other. These cores will also become rapidly heated, thus entailing a corresponding waste of driving power. If we lengthen the bobbins in a direction at right angles with the plane of the armature, and introduce longer cores, we must correspondingly separate the two sets of field magnets. We will then have an ordinary form of machine, and will have lost all of the advantages which form the object of my present invention.

Evidently the "insulating armature disk" F may be made of metal, and suitably slotted or divided to prevent the induction of cur-

rents in it, and thus perform the functions of an insulating and supporting material as described; such a disk is shown in Fig. 12.

It is equally evident that two or more currents, either direct or alternating, may be carried from the armature by means of suitable commutators or other conductors, or, that the field magnets may revolve while the armature is stationary; or that the magnets and armature may revolve in opposite directions.

It will be seen that I apply the term "armature" to that part of a dynamo-electric machine in which currents are induced by changing intensity or polarity of magnetic field and without regard to the presence or absence of iron or other magnetic substance in the said armature.

In the drawings Fig. 1 represents a section through its axis of one form of my machine. Fig. 2 is a cross section of the same. Fig. 3 is a plan view of the armature C. Figs. 4 and 5 show modified arrangements of the armature conductor. Fig. 6 shows the same in combination with the field magnets N. S. Fig. 7 shows the armature conductor moved one-eighth of a revolution from its position in Fig. 6. Fig. 8 shows the armature conductor arranged in eight bobbins instead of four. Fig. 9 shows field magnets of other than round cross section, and armature bobbins of corresponding shape. Fig. 10 shows an armature conductor arranged in the manner indicated in Fig. 5, in combination with twelve field magnets. Fig. 11 shows a method of arranging the field magnets radially around the armature. Fig. 12 shows an armature disk of metal, so slotted as to prevent the induction of currents in it.

I have thus far particularly specified the preferred form in which my invention may be embodied. Without a departure however from said invention the device above described may be modified by altering the armature disk to the form of a cylinder and arranging the field magnets accordingly. Such a modification is represented in Figs. 13, 14, and 15 of the drawings. Fig. 13 shows a longitudinal vertical section of this modified form of my invention wherein the disk-shape of armature is replaced by the cylindrical form, the position of the field-magnets being altered to correspond. Here it will be seen that the armature-conductors are located in or upon the cylindrical portion of the revolving armature; and the field-magnets are made to properly face said armature-conductors by being arranged substantially as shown upon the outside and inside of the cylindrical portion of the said revolving armature. Of course either the cylindrical portion referred to, or the field magnets may be made stationary while the other shall revolve, as before stated. Fig. 14 shows a transverse vertical section of the device represented in Fig. 13, and Fig. 15 is a developed view of the revolving armature cylinder of the device shown in Figs. 13 and 14 representing the general plan and arrangement of the armature conductors.

A division of this application was filed June 30, 1882, wherein is claimed certain constructions and arrangements of parts herein shown and described but not claimed.

What I claim is—

1. In a dynamo or magneto electric machine the combination with two series of field magnets, of two or more coils or folds of conductor having their planes substantially in the line of their movement between the poles of the field-magnets, a diamagnetic support or carrier on which said folds or coils are mounted, and a shaft composed of sections separated by insulating material, substantially as set forth.

2. An alternating current generator comprising two series of field magnets, coreless coils or folds mounted on a diamagnetic carrier, and a shaft having insulating material interposed between its sections, substantially as set forth.

In testimony whereof I have signed my name to this specification in the presence of two subscribing witnesses.

CHARLES F. BRUSH.

Witnesses:
JNO. CROWELL, Jr.,
WILLARD FRACKER.

www.ingramcontent.com/pod-product-compliance
Lightning Source LLC
Chambersburg PA
CBHW051232300426
44114CB00011B/709